Islamic Law

of Contracts and Business Transactions

Dr. Muhammad Tahir Mansuri

Contents

PART-I
GENERAL THEORY OF CONTRACTS

v

PREFACE

The injunctions of the Sharī'ah are based upon the interest of man both here and in the hereafter. The aim of the Sharī'ah is to preserve religion, life, intellect, progeny and property. These are the five basic interests of man. They are also known as the maqāṣid al-sharī'ah (objectives of the Sharī'ah)

Preservation of property, being one of the fundamental interests of man and a basic objective of the Sharī'ah occupies a vital and significant place in Islamic legal philosophy. It regards the property of a person as sacred and inviolable as his life and honour. The Qur'ān forbids the unlawful devouring of property by a believer. This includes prohibition against theft, usurpation, embezzlement, bribery and all other unlawful and impermissible means of acquiring wealth. The Qur'ān also prohibits usurious transactions, which bring undue and unjustified enrichment to one party at the cost of the other party. Contracts involving *gharar* and aleatory transactions have also been strictly prohibited in the Qur'ān and the traditions of the Holy Prophet (s.a.w.s.) Aleatory or *gharar* transactions comprise those transactions where both parties or either of the parties to the contract becomes a victim of excessive ignorance with regard to the existence, acquisition, genus, quality, and other necessary attributes of the subject matter. Such ignorance and uncertainty may lead to dispute and litigation among the parties. It also includes uncertainty and lack of knowledge about the material terms of the contract. It is, thus, the requirement of a valid transaction that the object of the obligation be specifically determined so as to avoid exorbitant *gharar*.

The Holy Prophet (s.a.w.s) also forbade certain market practices such as withholding of food items in times of scarcity, collusion to bid up prices, purchase from the farmers at lower prices keeping them ignorant about market prices, sale of something which one does not possess and the sale of food stuff before taking it into possession.

Thus, the Qur'ān and the Sunnah embody some very basic and important rules with regard to transactions. The purpose of all such injunctions is to preserve property and the material wealth of the people.

It is worth mentioning here that the Qur'ān and the Sunnah have not laid down a detailed law of contracts and transactions. They have only provided broad guidelines for economic and commercial activity. It is the *fuqahā'*, who after taking guidance from the principles provided by the Qur'ān and the Sunnah developed a comprehensive system of contracts and transactions. They classified contracts into different categories with regard to their objects and principal features and assigned them different nomenclatures. They discussed the elements and conditions of contracts together with the other necessary characteristics and attributes. They exercised *ijtihād* in the sphere of transactions and framed new rules according to the need of the time.

Modern jurists like Dr. 'Abd al-Razzāq al-Sanhūrī, Muṣtafā Aḥmed al-Zarqā, Shaikh Abū Zahrah, 'Abd al-Salām Madkūr, Dr. 'Abd al-Karīm Zaydān, Dr. Yūsuf Mūsā and many other scholars furthered the process of *ijtihād* in the sphere of business law depending on the principles of public good, custom, original law of permissibility, the redress of harm, and the removal of hardship. They have made valuable contributions to the law of contracts and transactions. The various *fiqh* academies and *Sharī'ah* councils of the Islamic world today are also engaged in further developing and enriching Islamic Law. The Muslim *Ummah*, through this collective and institutionalised effort, has succeeded in finding solutions to a large number of legal problems. It was able through this collective *ijtihād* to develop a viable system of banking and insurance free from elements of *ribā,* hazard and speculation.

The present book aims to highlight the magnificent and valuable work of old jurists as well as modern scholars in the filed of contracts and transactions.

The book has been written to serve as a textbook for the subject of "Islamic Law of Contract" studied by the students of LL.B at International Islamic University as a part of their prescribed scheme of study. It may also prove to be useful for the students of Economics and Business Administration and for all those who are interested in studying Business Law of Islam.

The book is divided into two parts. The first part deals with the general theory of contracts in Islam wherein topics such as general principles of contracts, elements of a contract, delegated authority, division of contracts into valid, voidable and void contracts, *gharar,* · *ribā,* extrinsic conditions, defect of consent, and the classification of contracts with regard to their subject matter have been discussed. The second part deals with specific contracts such as contracts of sale, leasing, partnership, *mudārabah,* suretyship, and assignment of debt. While dealing with these contacts both theory and practice have been emphasised. For example under *murābaḥah* contracts not only have the conditions of *murābaḥah* in *fiqh* been identified, but their applications to banking have also been discussed.

I hope this will prove useful to our students as well as to all those who are interested in studying Islamic Commercial Law.

I would like to acknowledge my debt of gratitude to Professor Dr. Mahmood Ahmad Ghazi for his valuable guidance. I am also thankful to Professor Dr. Amin Muntaṣir and Dr. Jawaid for reviewing the book and

making useful suggestions. My sincere thanks also go to
Professor Imran Ahsan Nyazee for editing the book. May
Allah reward them all for their help and co-operation.

Dr. Mohammad Tahir Mansuri

Islamabad

FOREWORD

Fiqh al-mu'amalat is an important branch of Islamic law which regulates commercial relations among the members of Muslim society. The classical jurists have paid great attention to this field by dealing special chapters in their books on sale, hiring *waqf*, gifts, partnership, surety, assignment of debt, mortgage and many other commercial contracts. They discussed at great length the principles underlying these contracts, and disapproved business practices and modes of acquisition of property and disposition thereof. The aim of all these exercise is to enable a Muslim individual to practise the Islamic teachings in his economic life and observe *Halal* and *Harām* in all his commercial activities.

It is a religious obligation of every Muslim to be conversant with Islamic teachings that regulate his commercial life. Today there is an earnest desire and persistent demand on the past of Muslim *Ummah* for return to Islamic system and Islamic law. In response to this demand many Muslim countries are engaged in bringing their systems in conformity with the ideals and value system of Islam. A number of Muslim countries have adopted provisions of Islamic law in their legal codes.

The Supreme Court of Pakistan has recently declared all forms of interest un-Islamic in the country. It has also declared null and void all these banking laws which are repugnant to the injunctions of Sharī'ah. This judgment is a great steps towards Islamization of commercial laws of the country.

In this background, the importance of producing legal literature and books such as Islamic law of Contracts and Business Transactions increases manifold. The study undertaken by Dr. Tahir Mansoori is a valuable contribution to the process of Islamization of laws and institutions in the Muslim world in general and Islamic Republic of Pakistan in particular.

The study is divided into two parts. The first part is devoted to elaborating theoretical foundations of a contract. In this part the author has provided a general theory of contract wherein he has discussed issues such as meaning of contract. modes of executing a contract. conditions of subject matter. qualification of contracting parties. circumstances that affect legal capacity of a person. classifications of contract with regard to their functions and attributes the extrinsic and intrinsic causes of invalidity of contract. extrinsic conditions and their effect on contract and similar other issues which provide general theory of contract. The second part of study is devoted to description of specific contracts such as contract of sale. hiring. partnership. surety assignment of debt and pledge. The author has not confined himself to outlining rules contained in the classical juristic literature. but has also given modern applications of these contracts and transactions. He has especially highlighted the applications of *murabaha salem. Istisnā'* in the contemporary financial institutions. He has severely criticized *murabaha* practices of the Pakistani banks. He has also raised the issue of indexation of loans. an important contemporary issue. and discussed in detail the arguments of both the proponents and opponents of indexation. He has termed modern insurance contracts as contract of *gharar* and *ribā.* and provided Islamic alternative to the insurance business. In this regard he has especially alluded to the example of Malaysia which has structured its insurance on the basis of *takaful*.

The author has compared many Islamic legal concepts with the modern laws such citations are to be found in the chapters on partnership. *Mudaraba.* surety-ship and assignment of debt.

In short. the book will prove to be of valuable assistance to all those who are engaged in the process of Isamization of commercial system. It will also be a source of guidance for the teachers. students and for all those who are interested in studying Islamic law.

December 19. 2000   Dr. Muhammad Yusuf Faruqi
                                                  Director General

PART-I

GENERAL THEORY OF CONTRACTS

Chapter-1

GENERAL PRINCIPLES OF CONTRACTS IN THE QUR'ĀN ANDTHE SUNNAH

The methodology of the *Sharī'ah* in dealing with *'ibādāt* (devotional acts) and *mu'āmālāt,* i.e., (transactions) is somewhat different in character. A thorough study of the Qur'ān and the Sunnah on this subject reveals that *'ibādāt* have been dealt with in detail, while *mu'āmlāt* have been discussed in general terms. The wisdom appears to be that *'ibādāt* are held to be universal truths that are unaffected by time and space. They are not subject to modification or change by means of *ijtihād* or otherwise. As these fixed commandments were necessary and they have been provided for. The *mu'āmlāt* are matters pertaining to individuals interacting amongst themselves. The variety of this interaction is neither foreseeable nor capable of being complied with by a regime of fixed rules. They are also changeable in different epochs of time within various geographical entities.

Imām ibn Taymiyyah explaining the difference between *'ibādāt* and *mu'āmlāt* writes:

> The acts and deeds of individuals are of two types: *'ibādāt* (devotional acts) whereby their religiousness is improved and *'ādāt* (transactions) which they need in their worldly matters. An inductive survey of sources of the *Sharī'ah* establishes that devotional acts are sanctioned by express injunctions of the *Sharī'ah*. Thus, what is not commanded cannot be made obligatory. As for transactions, the principle governing them would be permissibility and absence of prohibition. So, nothing can be prohibited unless it is proscribed by Allah and His Messenger.[1]

Ibn Taymiyyah , *al -fatāwā al- Kubrā* , Beriut: Dār al-Kutub

al-'Ilmiyyah, 1987,vol.29, pp.16,18.

In view of this, the *Sharī'ah* has laid down rules in connection with *mu'āmlāt* in general terms so that different people at different places and in different times may seek guidance. By giving a general framework, the Lawgiver conceded the right to Muslim jurists to frame specific rules for *mu'āmlāt*, which may be deemed necessary under prevailing circumstances. This methodology envisaged by the *Sharī'ah* provides people a reasonable degree of liberty in their dealings with each other and entering into contracts and transactions.

Keeping such treatment of the *mu'āmlāt* in Islamic law under consideration the broad principles can be elaborated as follows.

1. Free Mutual Consent

Free mutual consent of the contracting parties is a prerequisite for the validity of a contract. This is the cause that brings into being the obligations arising from a contract. The consent that is required for the formation of valid contract is a free consent. A consent that is obtained through coercion, fraud, misrepresentation or some other illegal means renders a contract invalid in the *Sharī'ah*. Similarly a contract made in a state of intoxication or by way of jest or through mistake is also invalid in Islamic Law. This is because the elements of free consent and the intention of the parties to enter into a contract and accept consequential obligations is missing in such cases.

The principle of free mutual consent has been emphasized in a number of verses of the Qur'ān and Aḥādīth of the Holy Prophet (s.a.w.s). A number of verses and traditions can be cited in support.

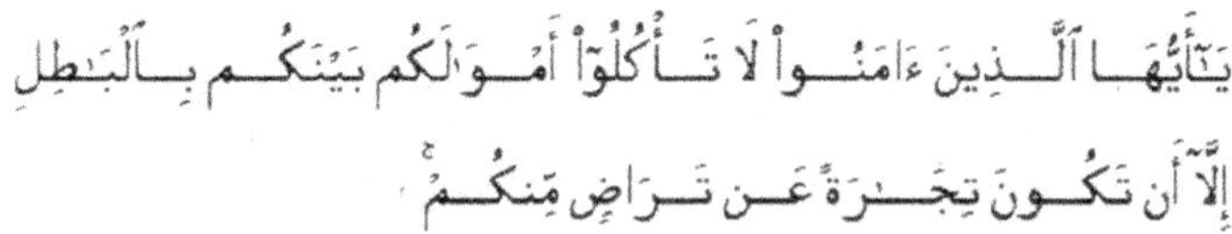

O you who believe, devour not your property among yourselves by unlawful means except that it be trading by your mutual consent.[2]

---

[2] Qur'ān 4:29.

The Holy Prophet (s.a.w.s) said:" The contract of sale is valid only by mutual consent"[3]. In another ḥadīth the Holy Prophet (s.a.w.s) said: "My people are forgiven for that which they have done through mistake, forgetfulness and under coercion"[4]

The principle of free consent requires that the consenting parties have certain and definite knowledge of the subject matter of the contract and the rights and obligations arising from it.

2. Prohibition of Gharar

Prohibition of gharar is another principle that governs all contracts and transactions. The Arabic word *gharar* conveys the meanings of indeterminacy, speculation, hazard and risk. As a technical term it is applied to uncertainty about the ultimate outcome of a contract, which may lead to dispute and litigation. A contract is presumed to suffer from *gharar* if it is about:

> (a) an occurrence about which the parties are unaware whether such an event will take place or not;

> (b) a thing that is not within the knowledge of the parties.

> (c) a thing about which it is not known whether it exists or not;

> (d) a thing whose acquisition is in doubt; and

> (e) a thing whose quantum is unknown.

Examples of transactions based on *gharar* are: sale of fish in water, birds in the air, a fetus in the womb, and fruits of trees at the beginning of season when their quality cannot be established.

Prohibition of *gharar* has occurred in a large number of *aḥādīth* such as:

---

[3]Muḥammed ibn yazīd ibn Mājah, ,*Sunan*, Istanbūl:

　　Dār al -Da'wah,1952 Ḥadīth no. 2245.

[4]Nūr al-Dīn 'Alī Haythamī ,*Majma' al-zawā 'id*, Beriut:Dār al-Kitāb

　　al-' Arabī,1982,vol.6,p.250.

(a) Abū Hurairah (r.a.t.a.) narrated that the Holy Prophet (s.a.w.s.) forbade sale by pebbles and the *gharar* sale i.e. indeterminate and speculative transactions[5].

(b) It is narrated by Anas ibn Mālik that God's Messenger forbade the sale of fruits till they were ripe.

(c) Allah's Messenger further said:" If Allah spoiled the fruits what right would one party have to take the money of his brother"?[6]

(d) 'Alī reported that the Messenger of Allah forbade forced purchases from a needy person and *gharar* purchase and the purchase of fruit before it reached maturity.[7]

3. Prohibition of Ribā

Another principle that governs transactions is that of prohibition of *ribā*. *Ribā* is defined as "an increase that has no corresponding consideration in an exchange of property for property".[8]

A contemporary scholar, Nabīl Ṣālih has defined it as "an unlawful gain derived from the quantitative inequality of the counter-value in any transaction purporting to affect the exchange of two or more species which belong to the same genus and are governed by the same efficient cause".[9]

The prohibition of *ribā* appears in a large number of texts of the Qur'ān and the Sunnah.

---

[5] Muslim ibn al-Ḥajjāj Muslim, *Saḥīḥ,* Beriut: Dār iḥyā al-Turāth al-Islāmī, Kitāb al-Tijārāt, no.1513, vol.3, p.454 .

[6]. Ibid., *Kitāb al-Buyū',* no.1554, vol. 3, p.1190.

[7] Sulaymān ibn al-Ash'ath al-Sijistānī Abū Dāwūd, *,Sunan,*

Cairo: Iḥyā al-Sunnah al-Nabawiyyah,1975, no. 3382, vol. 3, p.676.

[8] Muḥammad ibn Maḥmūd Bābartī, *al- 'Ināyah 'alā al-Hidāyah,* Cairo:Muṣṭafā al-Bābī al-Ḥalabī,1970,vol.7,p.3.

[9] Nabīl Ṣālih, *Unlawful Gain And Legitimate Profit In Islamic Law,* London: Kluwer law international,1992, p.16.

Says the Qur'ān:

$$وَأَحَلَّ ٱللَّهُ ٱلْبَيْعَ وَحَرَّمَ ٱلرِّبَوٰاْ$$

And Allah has permitted sale and prohibited usury.[10]

$$يَٰٓأَيُّهَا ٱلَّذِينَ ءَامَنُواْ ٱتَّقُواْ ٱللَّهَ وَذَرُواْ مَا بَقِىَ مِنَ ٱلرِّبَوٰٓاْ إِن كُنتُم مُّؤْمِنِينَ ۝ فَإِن لَّمْ تَفْعَلُواْ فَأْذَنُواْ بِحَرْبٍ مِّنَ ٱللَّهِ وَرَسُولِهِۦ ۖ وَإِن تُبْتُمْ فَلَكُمْ رُءُوسُ أَمْوَٰلِكُمْ لَا تَظْلِمُونَ وَلَا تُظْلَمُونَ$$

O you who believe: Fear God and give up what remains of your demand for usury if you are indeed believers. If you do it not, take notice of war from God and His Apostle, but if you turn back you shall have your capital sums. Deal not unjustly and you shall not be dealt with unjustly.[11]

The Holy Prophet (s.a.w.s.) cursed one who charges *ribā*, gives it, records it, and witnesses it. He said, "They are all equal".[12]

4.　Prohibition of Qimār (Gambling) and Maysir (Games of Chance)

Qimār includes every form of gain or money the acquisition of which depends purely on luck and chance. As opposed to others equally eligible, one may acquire income as a result of lottery or lucky draws. It also includes any receipt of money, benefit or usufruct that is

---

[10]Qur'ān 2:275.

[11]Qur'ān 2:278.

[12]Muslim, *Ṣaḥīḥ, Kitāb al-Musāqāt*, no.1598, vol. 3, p.1219.

at the cost of the other party or parties having equal entitlement to that money or benefit.[13]

Maysir literally means getting something too easily or getting a profit without working for it. The form most familiar to the Arabs was gambling by casting lots by means of arrows on the principle of lottery. The arrows were marked and served the same purpose as a modern lottery ticket. An item e.g. the carcass of a slaughtered animal was divided into unequal parts. The marked arrows were then drawn from a bag. Those who drew blank arrows got nothing while other arrows indicated prizes big or small. Whether one got a big share or a small share or nothing, depended on pure luck. Dicing and wagering are rightly held to be within the definition of gambling and *Maysir*.[14] The Qur'ān has explicitly prohibited this practice. It says:

$$\text{يَـٰٓأَيُّهَا ٱلَّذِينَ ءَامَنُوٓاْ إِنَّمَا ٱلْخَمْرُ وَٱلْمَيْسِرُ وَٱلْأَنصَابُ وَٱلْأَزْلَـٰمُ رِجْسٌ مِّنْ}$$

$$\text{عَمَلِ ٱلشَّيْطَـٰنِ فَٱجْتَنِبُوهُ لَعَلَّكُمْ تُفْلِحُونَ ﴿٩٠﴾}$$

O you who believe: Intoxication and gambling, dedication of stones, and divination by arrows are an abomination of satan's handiwork. Eschew such abomination, that you may prosper.[15]

5. Prohibition of Khilābah and Ghishsh (Fraud and Deception)

The Qur'ān and the Sunnah disapprove of fraud, cheating and deception in whatever form they might be. The words *khilābah*, *ghishsh* and *tatfīf* have been used in the Qur'ān and the Sunnah to convey the meanings of fraud and cheating. Fraud refers to manoeuver practised by one of the parties to induce a person to a contract without

---

[13] Mahmood Ahmad Ghazi, *Mudārabah Financing: an appraisal.*
Paper presented in the Conference on Islamic Corporate Finance: Sharī'ah based Solutions, Nov. 21-22, 1998 at Karachi.

[14] 'Abdullah Yūsūf 'Alī, The Holy Qur'ān: Translation and Commentary, al-Rājiḥī company , Saudi Arabia: 1983, p111.

[15] Qur'ān 5:90.

which he would have not entered it. It also refers to concealing the defects of and adulteration in merchandise.

Fraud and cheating have been strongly condemned in the Qur'ān and the Sunnah. Fraud includes a number of practices such as giving short measure and short weight (*taṭfīf*), false bidding to raise price of an item (*najash*), leaving an animal unmilked for a long time to give false impression to buyer about its milk yield (*taṣriyah*), the practice of meeting villagers at the outskirts of the town in order to purchase their merchandise before they reach the market place (*talaqqī al-rukbān*), false swearing and hiding defects in sale.

Some texts of the Qur'ān and the Sunnah dealing with the topic are as follows:

وَيْلٌ لِّلْمُطَفِّفِينَ ۝ ٱلَّذِينَ إِذَا ٱكْتَالُواْ عَلَى ٱلنَّاسِ يَسْتَوْفُونَ ۝ وَإِذَا كَالُوهُمْ أَو وَّزَنُوهُمْ يُخْسِرُونَ ۝ أَلَا يَظُنُّ أُوْلَٰٓئِكَ أَنَّهُم مَّبْعُوثُونَ ۝ لِيَوْمٍ عَظِيمٍ ۝

Woe to those that deal in fraud, those who, when they have to receive by measure, exact full measure, but when they have to give by measure or weight to men, give less than due. Do they not think that they will be called to account on a Mighty day.[16]

The Prophet (s.a.w.s) is reported to have said: "If both the parties spoke the truth and described defects of the goods, then they would be blessed in their transactions, and if they told lies and hid something, then the blessing of their transaction would be lost."[17]

The Holy Prophet (s.a.w.s) also said: "False swearing (by the seller) is beneficial to the trade, i.e. it may persuade the

---

[16]Qur'ān 83: 1-6.

[17]Muḥammad ibn Ismā'īl Bukhārī, *Ṣaḥīḥ*, Beriut: Dār al-Kitāb al-'Arabī,,1323 AH, no.2079, p.410.

buyer to purchase the goods, but in that way he will be deprived of God's blessing to the earnings"[18].

It is reported that a person came to Holy Prophet (s.a.w.s.) who was always defrauded in buying. The Holy Prophet (s.a.w.s.) instructed him to say at the time of buying: "There should not be any attempt to deceive, and I have the right to cancel it within three days"[19]

"The truthful merchant will be on the day of resurrection together with the Prophets, the faithful ones, the martyrs and the pious people".[20]

The Holy Prophet (s.a.w.s.) once happened to pass by a heap of grain in a market place and on examination found that the grain beneath the surface was wet while that on surface was dry. He chided the seller for resorting to such deceptive tactics and said: "He who deceives is not one of us"[21]

6. Prohibition of Two Mutually Inconsistent Contracts or Contingent Contracts

This is another principle that relates to transactions. Two mutually inconsistent contracts have been prohibited by the Holy Prophet (s.a.w.s) in a number of *aḥādīth*.

It is narrated by Abū Hurayrah (may Allah be pleased with him) that the Holy Prophet (s.a.w.s.) prohibited from two sales in one sale (*bay'atān fī bay'*).[22] The *ḥadīth* of two sales in one sale has been interpreted in a number of ways ,e.g.

[18]Ibid., no.2087, p.412.

[19]Ibn Mājah, *Sunan*, no.2205, vol.2, p. 743.

[20]Ibid. , no. 2139, vol. 2, p. 724.

[21]Muslim, *Ṣaḥīḥ*. no.102, vol.1, p. 99.

[22]Abū Dāwūd. *Sunan*, no.3540, vol.3 ͏

1. *The sale of two articles for two prices:* This occurs where one person says to other "I sell you this article at this price on the condition that you sell your house at this price"

2. *Contingent sale:* It occurs when a contract is made contingent upon another contract when both are mutually inconsistent for example, A says to B, "I sell you my house if C sells his house to me". Here the completion of first contract is contingent upon the second contract.

3. *The sale of a single object for two prices:* This kind of sale has been understood in two ways: In the first way: one of the two prices is payable in cash and the other is payable later.For example: A says to B "I sell you this commodity for one hundred in cash and one hundred and fifty on credit. " In the second way: one of the contracting party says: "I sell this garment cash down for such and such a price on the condition that I will buy it back after a certain delay at a certain other price"[23].

7. Conformity of Contract With the Maqāṣid al-Sharī'ah (Objectives of the Sharī'ah)

The aim of the *Sharī'ah* in regard to man is five fold: to preserve his religion, life, progeny, intellect and material wealth. All the injunctions of the *Sharī'ah* are directed towards the realisation of five objectives known as the *maqāṣid al -Sharī'ah*.These are:

1. Preservation of *Dīn* (Religion)

2. Preservation of *Nafs* (Life)

3. Preservation of *Nasl* (Progeny)

4. Preservation of *'Aql* (Intellect)

5. Preservation of *Māl* (Property)

---

[23] See Nayla comair-obeid,*The Law of Business Contracts in the Arab Middle East* , London: Kluwer law international,1996 p.61.

Any transaction or contract that offends or jeopardizes any of these objectives is invalid in the *Sharī'ah*. It is pertinent to note here that the *maqāsid al-sharī'ah* are alternately referred to as *ḥuqūq Allāh* (rights of God) in Islamic Law. The right of God in *Sharī'ah* refers to every thing that involves the benefit of the community at large. *Taftāzānī* defines *ḥuqūq Allāh* in the following words: "By rights of. God is meant that which comprehends a public benefit, not peculiar to any individual. It is referred to God because of the greatness of its significance and generality of benefit"[24].Thus, *ḥuqūq Allāh* in this sense corresponds with public rights, or public policy in the modern law. The objectives of *Sharī'ah* or *ḥuqūq Allāh* have been emphasised in a large number of texts of the Qur'ān and the Sunnah. The following verses on this topic can be cited.

مِنْ أَجْلِ ذَٰلِكَ كَتَبْنَا عَلَىٰ بَنِىٓ إِسْرَٰٓءِيلَ أَنَّهُۥ مَن قَتَلَ نَفْسًۢا بِغَيْرِ نَفْسٍ أَوْ فَسَادٍ فِى ٱلْأَرْضِ فَكَأَنَّمَا قَتَلَ ٱلنَّاسَ جَمِيعًا وَمَنْ أَحْيَاهَا فَكَأَنَّمَآ أَحْيَا ٱلنَّاسَ جَمِيعًا

On that account, we ordained for the children of Israel that if any one slew a person, unless it be for murder or for spreading mischief in the land, it would be as if he slew the whole people, and if anyone saved a life, it would be as he saved the life of whole people.[25]

وَلَكُمْ فِى ٱلْقِصَاصِ حَيَوٰةٌ يَٰٓأُو۟لِى ٱلْأَلْبَٰبِ لَعَلَّكُمْ تَتَّقُونَ

In the law of equality, there is saving of life to you, O men of understanding.[26]

---

[24] Mas'ūd ibn' Umar Taftazānī, ,*al-Talwīh*, Cairo: Maktabah Muḥammad 'Alī Ṣabīh, 1957, vol.2, p.151.

[25] Qur'ān 5:32.

[26] Qur'ān 2:179.

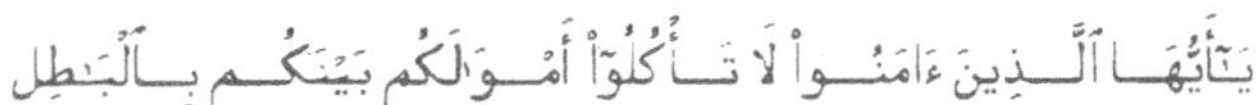

O you who believe: Devour not your property among yourselves in vanities.[27]

In a *ḥadīth* the Holy Prophet (s.a.w.s.) said: "Allah has made the life, and property and honour of each one of you unto the other sacred and inviolable like this day of this month in this territory"[28]

The requirement of the conformity of contract with the objectives of the *Sharī'ah* is similar to the requirement of modern law that an agreement should not be against public policy.

8. Principle of Liability for Loss and Entitlement to Profit

Another principle that governs contracts and commercial transactions is the principle of liability for loss and entitlement to profit. This principle has been enunciated in the following texts. The Holy Prophet (s.a.w.s) said:

1. " *Usufruct* devolves with liability"[29]

2. "A loan with a sale is not permitted, nor two conditions in a sale nor a profit of a thing allowed which is not in one's liability, nor the ṣale of what you do not have in your possession."[30]

This principle provides that a person is entitled to profit only when he bears the risk of loss. The principle operates in a number of contracts such as a contract of sale, hire or partnership. A businessman is entitled to profits and gain in his business because he is ready to bear loss. Similarly, the landlord of a house is entitled to rent of his

---

[27]Qur'ān 4:29.

[28]Bukhārī, *Ṣaḥīḥ*, no.7447, p.1562, no.7447, p.1562.

[29]Abū Dāwūd,, *Sunan*, no.3508, vol. 3, p.777.

[30]Abū 'Abd al-Raḥmān ibn Shu'ayb Nasā'ī, *Sunan*, Istanbūl: Dār al-Da'wah ,Kitāb al-tijārah, no.4625, 4644, vol. 7, p.33.

house in the hiring contract because he subjects himself to the risk of its destruction and damages to it. This risk makes him the rightful owner of its rent.

All profit that has accrued to the partners in a partnership contract is also attributable to this principle of liability. On the other hand, any excess over and above the principal sum paid to the creditor by the debtor is prohibited because the creditor does not bear any risk with regard to the amount lent.

9. Permissibility as a General Rule

In the field of transactions and contracts every thing that is not prohibited is permissible. This rule has been emphasised in a number of verses of the Qur'ān. Some of which are as follows:

وَسَخَّرَ لَكُم مَّا فِى ٱلسَّمَٰوَٰتِ وَمَا فِى ٱلْأَرْضِ جَمِيعًا مِّنْهُ

And God has made of service unto you whatever is in the heavens and whatsoever is in the earth; it is all from him"[31]

قُل لَّآ أَجِدُ فِى مَآ أُوحِىَ إِلَىَّ مُحَرَّمًا عَلَىٰ طَاعِمٍ يَطْعَمُهُ إِلَّآ أَن يَكُونَ مَيْتَةً أَوْ دَمًا مَّسْفُوحًا أَوْ لَحْمَ خِنزِيرٍ فَإِنَّهُۥ رِجْسٌ أَوْ فِسْقًا أُهِلَّ لِغَيْرِ ٱللَّهِ بِهِۦ فَمَنِ ٱضْطُرَّ غَيْرَ بَاغٍ وَلَا عَادٍ فَإِنَّ رَبَّكَ غَفُورٌ رَّحِيمٌ ﴿١٤٥﴾

Say: I find not in that which is revealed unto me prohibited to an eater that he eats thereof, except it be carrion, or abomination which was immolated to the name of other than God. But who is compelled (thereto) neither craving

---

[31]Qur'ān 45:13.

nor exceeding the limit, Lo, your Lord is forgiving, merciful.[32]

قُلْ مَنْ حَرَّمَ زِينَةَ ٱللَّهِ ٱلَّتِىٓ أَخْرَجَ لِعِبَادِهِۦ وَٱلطَّيِّبَـٰتِ مِنَ ٱلرِّزْقِ

Say (O Muhammad): Who has forbidden the adornment of God, which he has brought forth for His bondsmen, and the good things of His providing.[33]

The principle of permissibility referred to above establishes the fact that all agreements and conditions contained in them are permissible as long as they do not contradict any explicit text of the Qur'ān and the Sunnah. This broad principle gives ample scope to different communities to frame laws for themselves in order to meet new and changed situations.

"He has explained to you that which is forbidden"[34]

The *aḥādīth* of the Holy Prophet (s.a.w.s.) also highlight permissibility as a general rule to be adhered to in the sphere of *mu'āmlāt* .The Holy Prophet (s.a.w.s) says: "Muslims have to abide by their conditions except those that make the unlawful lawful or the lawful unlawful."[35]This *ḥadīth* points to the fact that every agreement is basically lawful so long as it does not oppose any explicit text of the Qur'ān and the Sunnah.

The Quranic commandment of the fulfilment of contractual obligations contained in the first verse of Surah al-Māidah[36] also provides that subject to any prohibition and limitation set down in the Qur'ān and the Sunnah all contracts are to be fulfilled. Ibn Taymiyyah writes."If proper fulfilment of obligations and the respect for covenants are prescribed by the Lawgiver, it follows that the general

---

[32]Qur'ān 6:145.

[33]Qur'ān 7:32

[34]Qur'ān 6:119.

[35]Haythamī, *Majma' al-Zawā'id*, vol. 4, p.205.

[36] O believers: fulfill your contracts. Qur'ān 5:1

rule is that contracts are valid. It would have been meaningless to give effect to contracts and recognize the legality of their objective, unless these conditions were themselves valid".[37]

Conclusion

The Qur'ān and the Sunnah have dealt with *'ibādāt* (devotional acts and the matters of ritual obedience) in detail and *mu'āmlāt* (civil transactions) in general terms.

Some important principles governing commercial contracts and transactions are as under:

(a) The contract should be by free mutual consent.

(b) It should be devoid of *gharar* (uncertainty, indeterminacy)

(c) It should be free from *ribā*.

(d) It should not contain an attribute of *qimār* (gambling) and *maysir* (games of chance)

(e) It should be free from *ghishsh,*and *khilābah* (fraud and cheating)

(f) Two mutually inconsistent contracts are not permissible.

(g) A contract should not be contrary to objectives of the *Sharī'ah*.

(h) Entitlement to profit depends upon liability for risk.

(i) What is not explicitly prohibited is permissible. All the agreements are permissible unless they contradict any text of the Qur'ān or the Sunnah, or oppose the objectives of the *Sharī'ah*.

[37] Ibn Taymiyyah, *Fatāwā*, vol.3, p.387.

CHAPTER- 2

MEANING OF 'AQD (CONTRACT) AND OTHER SIMILAR TERMS

Meaning of the terms: Mīthāq, 'Ahd and 'Aqd

Three Arabic terms are used to designate contract and convey the sense of undertaking and obligation: *Mīthāq, 'Ahd* and *'Aqd*.

Mīthāq

Mīthāq is a contract that signifies earnestness and firm determination on the part of parties to fulfill the contractual obligation. In other words *mīthāq* is a contract, which is considered to be sacred by the contracting parties, and has more sanctity than the ordinary contracts. The examples of *mīthāq* include; the very first covenant between man and God at the outset of creation, treaties by the Muslims with other nations, and the contract of marriage. The word *mīthāq* has been used in the Qur'ān in a number of verses.

$$ ٱلَّذِينَ يُوفُونَ بِعَهْدِ ٱللَّهِ وَلَا يَنقُضُونَ ٱلْمِيثَٰقَ ، $$

These who are true to their bond with God and who
never break their covenant.[1]

$$ وَإِنِ ٱسْتَنصَرُوكُمْ فِى ٱلدِّينِ فَعَلَيْكُمُ ٱلنَّصْرُ إِلَّا عَلَىٰ قَوْمٍ بَيْنَكُمْ $$
$$ وَبَيْنَهُم مِّيثَٰقٌ وَٱللَّهُ بِمَا تَعْمَلُونَ بَصِيرٌ $$

But if they seek your aid in religion, it is your duty to
help them except against a people with whom you
have a treaty of mutual alliance.[2]

---

[1] Qur'ān. 13:20.

[2] Qur'ān. 8:72.

$$\text{إِلَّا ٱلَّذِينَ يَصِلُونَ إِلَىٰ قَوْمٍ بَيْنَكُمْ وَبَيْنَهُم مِّيثَـٰقٌ}$$

Except those who join a group with whom a you have treaty.[3]

$$\text{وَكَيْفَ تَأْخُذُونَهُۥ وَقَدْ أَفْضَىٰ بَعْضُكُمْ إِلَىٰ بَعْضٍ وَأَخَذْنَ مِنكُم}$$

$$\text{مِّيثَـٰقًا غَلِيظًا}$$

For how can you take it back (dower), when you have lain
  with each other, and entered a firm contract?[4]

The commentators of the Qur'an hold that the word *mīthāq* in this last verse refers to the contract of marriage. Thus marriage is a sacred contract enjoying the sanctity of religion.

'Ahd

'Ahd means a unilateral promise or undertaking although it also includes a bilateral obligation. The Qur'an has used this word in both senses. Some verses in which the word has occurred are given below:

$$\text{وَأَوْفُوا بِٱلْعَهْدِ إِنَّ ٱلْعَهْدَ كَانَ مَسْئُولًا}$$

And fulfill every engagement, for every engagement will be
enquired into (on the day of reckoning).[5]

$$\text{وَأَوْفُوا بِعَهْدِى أُوفِ بِعَهْدِكُمْ}$$

And fulfill your covenant with me as I fulfil my covenant
with you.[6]

---

3 Qur'ān. 4:90.

4 Qur'ān. 4:21.

5 Qur'ān. 17:34.

6 Qur'ān. 2:40.

وَٱلۡمُوفُونَ بِعَهۡدِهِمۡ إِذَا عَـٰهَدُواْ

(But righteous) are those who fulfil the contracts, which they have made.[7]

'Aqd

'Aqd is synonymous with the word "contract" found in modern law. It is of common occurrence in Islamic legal literature. It implies obligation arising out of a mutual agreement.

The literal meaning of the word *'aqd* is "to join" and "to tie". The term *'aqd* has an underlying idea of conjunction as it joins the intentions and declarations of two parties. The Qur'ān has used the word in this sense in different places.

وَلَا تَعۡزِمُواْ عُقۡدَةَ ٱلنِّكَاحِ حَتَّىٰ يَبۡلُغَ ٱلۡكِتَـٰبُ أَجَلَهُۥ

And resolve not on the marriage tie until the prescribed period (*'Iddat*) reaches its end.[8]

لَا يُؤَاخِذُكُمُ ٱللَّهُ بِٱللَّغۡوِ فِيۤ أَيۡمَـٰنِكُمۡ وَلَـٰكِن يُؤَاخِذُكُم بِمَا عَقَّدتُّمُ ٱلۡأَيۡمَـٰنَ

Allah will not call you to account for what is void in your oaths, but will call you to account for the oath, which you take in earnest.[9]

يَـٰٓأَيُّهَا ٱلَّذِينَ ءَامَنُوٓاْ أَوۡفُواْ بِٱلۡعُقُودِ

O you who believe! Fulfil your contracts.[10]

---

[7] Qur'ān 2:177.

[8] Qur'ān, 2:235.

[9] Qur'ān, 5:88.

[10] Qur'ān, 5:1.

Definition of 'Aqd

In Islamic legal literature 'aqd is used in two senses i.e. general and specific

In the general sense, 'aqd is applied to every act which is undertaken in earnestness and with firm determination regardless of whether it emerges from a unilateral intention *(irādah munfaridah)* such as *waqf*, remission of debts, divorce, undertaking an oath, or it results from mutual agreement, such as sale, hire, agency and mortgage.[11] 'aqd in this sense is applied to an obligation irrespective of the fact that the source of this obligation is a unilateral declaration or agreement of two declarations

In the specific sense it has been defined in different ways. However, the common feature of all definitions is that it is a combination of an offer and acceptance which gives rise to certain legal consequences.

It is pertinent to note that modern Muslim scholars are inclined to apply 'aqd only to bilateral contracts as it is the case in Western Laws. Rayner attributes this inclination to an increasing tendency towards uniformity with the West in the field of obligations. In the view of this author, it is an evidence of the fact that Muslim Scholars are clearly moving away from the wider Islamic interpretation of the term towards the more precise definitions employed in Western systems.[12]

Now we take up some important definitions of 'aqd in the modern sense of bilateral obligations.

---

[11] See Wahbah al-Zuḥaylī, *al-fiqh al-Islāmī wa adillahtuhū*, Damascus: Dār al-Fikr,1984,vol. 4, p.80

[12] Rayner, *The Theory of contracts in Islamic Law*,London: Graham and Trotman,1991, P 80

a) Murshid al-Ḥayrān: "Conjunction of an offer emanating from one of the two contracting parties with the acceptance of the other in a manner that it affects the subject-matter of the contract".[13]

b) Majallat al-Ahkām al-'Adliyyah: "It is where the two parties undertake obligations in respect of any matter. It is affected by the combination of an offer (*ī jāb*) and acceptance (*qabūl*)"[14]

In'iqād (making of *'aqd*) has been defined in Section- 104 of the *Majallah* It reads: "*In'iqad* is to connect an offer with acceptance in a legal manner from which flow legal consequences with respect to subject matter".[15] It seems that the term *'aqd* as used in the *Majallah* is equivalent to the term "agreement" in the contract Act of 1872. Law considers a simple agreement contract only when it is enforceable. *In'iqad.* on the other hand, signifies that the contract has actually taken place. Thus the difference between *'aqd* and *in'iqad* is that the latter expresses the additional condition of being legal, i.e., enforceable by Law.

c) Al-'Ināyāh: "Legal relationship created by the conjunction of two declarations, from which flow legal consequences with regard to the subject matter".[16]

d) Shaykh Abū Zahrah: "*'Aqd* is a conjunction between two declarations or that which substitutes them" (i.e., conduct creating a legal effect"[17]

e) Abd al- Razzāq al-Sanhūrī: "Contract is concurrence of two wills to create an obligation or to shift it or to relinquish it".[18]

---

[13] Qudrī pasha. *Murshid al-Ḥayrān.* Cairo: 1933.art. 186. P.27

[14] Commission of Ottoman Jurists (1867-77) *Majallat al-Ahkām al-'Adliyyah.* Istanbūl. 19305A.H.. art. 153.

[15] Ibid.. art. 154

[16] Bābartī. *'Ināyah 'alā Fath al-Qadīr.* vol.5. p.47.

[17] Abū Zahrah. *al-Milkiyyah wa-Nazariyya al-'Aqd.* Cairo: Dār al-'Arabī.1939. p.171

[18] Abd al-Razzāq al-Sanhūrī. *al-Wasīt.* Cairo: Dār al-Nahdah 'Arabiyyah.1964.p.138

Sale and hire contracts are examples of contract meant for creating an obligation. The contract of *ḥawālah*, i.e., assignment of debt serves as a means of shifting liability from a principal debtor to a third party, which assumes the role of new debtor.

Preferred Definition

Contemporary Muslim scholars prefer the definition of *al-'Ināyah* referred to above, because it is much more comprehensive, and covers all the ingredients of contract: (1) agreement based on offer and acceptance; (2) contracting parties; (3) completion of offer and acceptance in a legal manner; and (4) subject matter.

Analysis of the Definition

The definition offered by the author of *al-'Ināyah* can be broken into the following ingredients:

- Existence of two parties: The definition implies that there must be two parties to the contract. Thus a contract cannot be concluded through a unilateral declaration although such declaration may have legal effects. An example of a unilateral declaration is divorce *(ṭalāq)*, which issues forth from the husband only but has legal consequences. An endowment (*waqf*) also comes into being through a unilateral declaration. Thus, though a unilateral declaration may have legal consequences in many cases, it cannot be called a contract ('*aqd*) on the basis of this definition.

- Issuance of outward act depicting internal willingness There must issue forth from the contracting parties that which makes manifest the intention or willingness of parties to enter into a contract. Such willingness may be communicated by way of speech, an action or any other indication. What issues forth first from either of the parties is termed the offer (*ījāb*) while that which follows is termed the acceptance (*qabūl*). The offer and acceptance are declaration of the internal willingness of the parties.

- There must be a legal (*Shar'ī*) union between the two declarations: The offer and acceptance must agree with each other in the manner prescribed by the *Sharī'ah*. This agreement or conformity or union cannot take place unless certain conditions are fulfilled, like the issuance of *ījāb* and *qabūl* in the *majlis*, the conformity of the offer to the acceptance, the existence of the offer till the acceptance is linked with it.

- The appearance of the effects of the conjunction of the offer and acceptance in the subject matter: The contract when formed produces legal effects in the subject matte. Thus the legal status or position of the subject matter either stands modified or shifts from one state to another. In the contract of sale, for example, the ownership of the goods stands transferred from the seller to the buyer, while in a mortgage the possession of the property passes from one party to another.[19]

Conclusion

The preceding discussion may be summarized as follows:

1. Three Arabic terms *mīthāq, 'ahd" and 'aqd* are used to convey the sense of undertaking and obligation.

2. *Mīthāq* is a contract that signifies earnestness and firm determination on the part of parties to fulfil a contractual obligation. *Mīthāq* has been used in Qur'ān in the sense of covenant, treaty of mutual alliance with non-believers and for marriage contract.

3. *'Aqd* conveys the sense of unilateral promise or undertaking.

4. *'Aqd* implies obligation arising out of mutual agreement. *'Aqd* is defined as legal relationship created by the conjunction of two declarations, from which flow legal consequences with regard to the subject-matter.

[19] Ḥassān, al-*Makhal li Dirāsāt al-Fiqh al-Islāmī*, Cairo: Maktabah al-Muthanna,1979,pp.235, 236.

CHAPTER-3

ELEMENTS OF CONTRACT:
Form (Ṣīghah)

The majority of the Muslim Jurists hold that the essential elements of a contract are three: the form i.e. offer and acceptance (*ṣīghah*); the contracting parties (*'āqidān*); and the subject matter (*ma'qūd 'alayh*). Hanafi jurists hold that there is only one element of a contract: namely, the *ṣīghah* (form). This, however, implies the existence of other elements. From the practical point of view, there is not much difference between the opinion of the Hanafīs and that of the majority. It is pertinent to note that some modern Muslim jurists have dealt with the object of contract or the motivating cause of contract as an independent element of contract. They did not consider it a part of the subject matter. As such the elements of a contract are four instead of three.[1]

Sanhūrī, an eminent contemporary Muslim jurist, has cited seven component elements in a contract: They are (1) the concurrence of offer and acceptance; (2) the unity of the *majlis* of contract; (3) plurality of contracting parties; (4) reason (*'aql*), or the power of distinction (*tamyīz*) of the contracting parties; (5) That the subject (*maḥall*) is susceptible to delivery; (6) the object *(mahall)* defined; and (7) the beneficial nature of the object in that it is permitted for trade in.[2] We have however, followed the scheme of the earlier jurists.

Form of Contract

Form is the instrument or the means by which a contract is made. It consists of *ījāb* (offer) and *qabūl* (acceptance).

---

[1] See Zuhaylī, *al-Fiqh al-Islamī wa Adillahtuhū*, vol.4. p. 94.

[2] Sanhūrī, *Maṣādir al-Ḥaq*, vol.4. pp. 134-135.

MEANING OF ĪJĀB AND QABŪL

In the Majallah. *ījāb* has been defined as "a declaration that is made first with a view to creating an obligation, while the subsequent declaration is termed *qabūl*.[3]

In Islamic Law, *ījāb* signifies the willingness of a party to do something positive. Islamic Law is silent on whether the willingness of a party to abstain from a thing also constitutes *ījāb* or not. The Council of Islamic Ideology in Pakistan is of the view that only the commission of an act forms *ījāb*. Abstinence from an act cannot be regarded as *ījāb*.[4] The Federal Shariat Court, on the other hand, has held a different viewpoint. It is of the opinion that a contract may be to do anything or to abstain from doing it.[5] This meaning of *ījāb* conforms to the meaning of *ījāb* in the Contract Act of 1972. The Contract Act defines it in the following words "When one person signifies to another his willingness to do or to abstain from doing anything, with a view to obtaining the assent of that other person to such an act or abstinence. he is said to make a proposal".[6]

Different Kinds of Form (Ṣīghah):

In Islamic Law offer and acceptance can be conveyed in a number of ways namely:

a) By Words: There is no dispute amongst the jurists as regards the conclusion of contracts through words. The reason for this is that words are considered to be the basis of all kinds of expression and other things can only take their place in cases of necessity.

A basic rule in Islamic Law, however. is that the basis to be considered in contract is the meaning and not words and forms.[7] It is

---

[3] *Majallah*, Art. 101.
[4] Council of Islamic Ideology. *14th report on Contract Act 1872, 1984,*
[5] Federal Shariat Court, *Suo moto examination of laws in the contract Act. 1986.* p.5.
[6] Mullah.D.F..*The Contract Act,* 1872.Lahore: Mansoor Book House.1987.Section 2.
[7] 'Abd al-Karīm Zaydān, *al-Madkhal li Dirāsāt al-Sharī'ah al-Islāmiyyah.* Bughdād: Maktaba al-Quds.1982. p.92.

Elements of Contract: Form *(Sīghah)*

for this reason that the jurists have not fixed particular words for the formation of particular contracts. Whatever conveys the meaning with clarity is considered sufficient for the formation of the contract. It is all the same whether the words are explicit or implicit. However the Shāfi'īs and Ḥanbalīs exempt from the above rule certain contracts. Thus, the words used for the contract of marriage are *nikāḥ* or *ziwāj* rather than gifting or ownership. Thus if a woman were to say "I gift myself to you", or "I make you my owner" then the contract of marriage will not be deemed to have been concluded according to these schools.[8] From another viewpoint such postulation creates a difficulty for those witnessing such contracts. The Ḥanafīs and Mālkīs do not recognise the above exceptions.[9]

Tense: In order to avoid any degree of uncertainty, Islamic Law requires that the words must convey the past tense. Thus, if A says to B: "I have sold this house to you for Rs. 100,000 and B replies I have accepted", a contract is said to have taken place. A contract concluded in the future tense is invalid. A contract made through the present tense can be concluded if it is accompanied by some other evidence (circumstantial) showing that the intention is to conclude the contract presently and not in the future

As regards *amr* (command) the Jurists disagree as to whether the *sīghah* in the form of a command or order *(amr)* is sufficient to constitute an offer. Majority of them are of the opinion that it does as it expresses the intention of the parties quite clearly.[10] Ḥanafī jurists, on the other hand, hold the opinion that it is not to be allowed even if it is accompanied by circumstantial evidence. These Jurists consider the imperative form of *sīghah* as a demand for an offer.[11]

---

[8] Shirbīnī.*Mughnī al-Muhtāj*.Cairo: Sharikah wa Maṭba'ah
Muṣṭafā al-Bābī al-Ḥalabī.1933. vol.3. p.532.

[9] Ibn al-Humām.*Fath al Qadīr*.Cairo: Muṣṭafā al-Bābī
al-Ḥalabī.1387/1968.vol. 5 p.76.

[10]Ḥattābal-malkī.*Mawāhibal-jalīl*.Tripoli:1329:4:228.
Muḥammad ibn Ahmad Dusūqī. 'Arafah. *Ḥāshiyah 'ala al-Sharh
al-Kabīr*.Cairo: 'Īsā al-Bābī al-Ḥalabī.1931. vol. 3 p 3:
Ibn Rushd. *Bidāyat al-Mujtahid* .Lahore: Maktabah al-
'Ilmiyyah.1984.vol.2:p 168

[11]Abū Bakr ibn Mas'ūd Kāsānī. *Bādā'i' al-Sanā'i'* .Cairo:Sharikh al-
Matbū'āt al- 'Ilmiyyah.1909-1910.vol 5. p.133.

b) Writing: The majority of jurists (except the Ḥanbalīs) are of the view that contracts can be concluded through writing, irrespective of whether the parties are present in one *majlis*, i.e., contracting session or one of them is missing. It is customary in event of absence of one party that an offer may take the form of a letter.

Some of the Shāfi'ī jurists have opposed this opinion maintaining that the one who is capable of contracting through spoken words must not resort to writing. According to these jurists, contract in writing is allowed only when the person is unable to speak.

c) Gesture or Indication: The Ḥanafīs and Shāfi'īs are of the opinion that forming contracts through gestures or indications is not allowed for one who can speak or write, because spoken words and writing serve a more powerful form of expression of willingness than gesturing. The Mālikī jurists, however, permit such contracts as the rule according to them is that, whatever conveys the willingness of the parties is sufficient, irrespective of whether words are used or not.

d) By Conduct: This is termed as *mu'āṭāh* in Islamic Law. For example, A says to B: "I sell you this book for Rs.10 B places Rs.10 on the counter and picks up the book. The majority of jurists allow this form of concluding a contract, but with the following conditions:

i- Conduct must be from both sides: Delivery of counter values must be from both sides. Like a buyer asks the seller the price of an item and the seller mentions a price. The buyer then hands over the money and the seller delivers the item to him.

ii- There must be an intention: Conduct should be based on consent of the parties to the extent that no presumptive evidence that exists negates the existence of consent.

iii- That the item must be of small value:The Muslim jurists are of the view that in order to form a contract through conduct it is necessary that the subject matter of the contract must of a small value like bread meat etc. and not expensive, like house, land, gold or silver. However, Mālikī jurists allow even in expensive items. The above conditions depend mostly on customs prevailing in the area. [12]

---

[12] Ibn Qudāmah, *al-Sharḥ al-Kabīr*.Beiut: Dār al-Fikr.1405/1985.vol.3 p.3

Elements of Contract: Form *(Sīghah)*

The Shāfi'ī Jurists do not allow the formation of contracts through conduct.[13]

Condition necessary for Ṣīghah (Form)

As stated earlier, the *ṣīghah* (form) comprises an offer *(ījāb)* from one party and an acceptance (*qabūl*) from the other. Muslim jurists, however, have laid down certain conditions for offer and acceptance without the fulfilment of which the contract cannot be concluded. These conditions are:

a) conformity of the offer and acceptance on the same subject matter; and

b) issuance of the offer and acceptance in the same session (*majlis*).

(1) Conformity of the offer and acceptance on the same subject matter: It is necessary that the acceptance must conform to the offer in all its details irrespective of whether such conformity is express or implied.

(2)Issuance of the offer and acceptance in the same session of Contract: According to the jurists when an offer is made, it must be accepted in the same meeting. However, the promisee is allowed to think over the offer for some time. The basis of this viewpoint is a precept of the Holy Prophet (s:a w.s.). "The contracting parties have the right of option until they separate".[14]

Opinion is divided among scholars in regard to the interpretation of the phrase "until they separate". According to Imām Abū Ḥanīfah it is the separation from a particular topic and not from the place of session. This means that if the parties complete the offer and acceptance and then start discussion on some other topic, the contract is not liable to be cancelled at option. Ḥaḍrat 'Umar said: "Sale is either a concluded deal or deal subject to option". Imām Shāfi'ī and Imām Aḥmad, on the other hand, hold that separation should be bodily separation from the place of negotiation.

---

[13] Shirbīnī. *Mughnī al-Muḥtāj* vol.2, p.3.
[14] Bukhārī. *Ṣaḥīḥ, Kitāb al-Buyū.'* no.2112. p.417.

However, both these group are unanimous on the point that a contract must be completed by offer and acceptance in the same meeting unless one party reserves for itself the right to think over to ratify or to revoke the contract later.

Commenting on the condition of unity of contract session the Federal Shariat Court has observed the following:

> A narrow interpretation of *Majlis* would mean that the offer of the promisor should be accepted without any delay and without giving the promisee any opportunity to think or consult someone in order to make up his mind. This may be practicable in small transactions but will fail in bigger transactions. which may require considerable inquiry. Thus. if an offer is made for sale of a factory. it will require inquiry into the title. power to sell, value of machinery. value of building, its liabilities, if any, profitability etc. If the *Majlis* is interpreted to mean single session. no one will consider purchasing a property.[15]

The Court further noted:

> The language of the above-mentioned tradition demonstrates that it was only meant to denote the law of revocation. thus if two parties agree to enter into a contract in one meeting. each of them shall have a right to retract from it till they separate. This appears to be the object. Its other object is that the offer must be taken seriously. To some modern scholars the word "meeting" is only a legal fiction in that whatever time is taken by the promisee to communicate his acceptance may be called the continuance of the same meeting [16]

Does this *ḥadīth* pose a practical problem for entering into bigger transactions as the Federal Shariat Court has observed? The answer is 'No'. The reason is that even if the contracting parties conclude the transaction in one session and observe the requirement of *majlis*, they still have the right to think over the transaction and revoke it within a specified time. This right is known in Islamic Law as "option of stipulation" (*Khiyār al-Sharṭ*). The option of stipulation is

---

[15] *Federal Shariat Court of Pakistan, Suo-Moto examination of Laws in the Contract Act. 1986 p 8.*

[16] Ibid.

the power by virtue of which one of the two contracting parties can give his final assent to the contract within a specified time. Islamic Law recognizes this right for the contracting parties. As such, if a purchaser, while giving his consent to the offer, retains the right to accept or reject it within three days, the contract will not be binding on him during that period. This means that Islamic law provides a mechanism to overcome the problem caused by the restriction of unity of session.

It is pertinent to point out here that the requirement of unity of session does not apply to contract of agency, making bequest and appointment of an executor (*waṣī*) for the property of minor.

LAPSE OF OFFER IN MODERN LAW

The Contract Act of Pakistan does not fix any time or place during which or when the offer remains effective for the promisee to accord his acceptance. Section 5 and 6 deal with the question of revocation of offer. Section 5 provides that the revocation of proposal can be made before communication of the acceptance to the proposer by the promisee. Similarly, the acceptance can be revoked before its communication. Section 6 deals with the modes of revocation. Thus revocation can be affected:

(1) through communication of a notice of revocation;

(2) by lapse of time prescribed for acceptance in the proposal for acceptance;

(3) by lapse of reasonable time;

(4) by failure of the acceptor to fulfil a condition precedent to acceptance; and

(5) by death or insanity of the proposer, when the fact of his death comes to the knowledge of the acceptor before his acceptance.[17]

This method can be followed by Islamic Law also since it facilitates the contract. Moreover, it is in the interest of the public It goes without saying that realisation of the public interest is an

---

[17] See *Contract Act, 1872*, Section 5,6.

objective of the Sharī'ah. Such methods may also be justified under the rule "Hardship causes giving of facility"[18] and the rule: "What is not prohibited is permitted".[19]

Causes of Cancellation of Offer (Ījāb)

There are five causes due to which an offer ceases to exist. These are:

1. Withdrawal of offer by the maker: The majority of Muslim jurists are of the opinion that an offer can be withdrawn at any time before its acceptance by the other party. The Hanafīs call this the "option of withdrawal" It is permissible to them, as the rights of the other party have not been linked with the subject matter as yet. The Mālikīs on the other hand do not give the maker of an offer the right of withdrawal. If the other party accepts the offer after the withdrawal but within the same session, the contract becomes binding.

2. Death of a party or loss of its capacity: The death of either party before acceptance causes the offer to lapse. Similarly, if there occurs a loss of capacity or the party becomes insolvent, the offer ceases to exist. The 'Ibādiyyah, a sect of the Khawārij, however, hold that the offer once issued does not cease to exist due to death or loss of capacity but can be accepted by the other party to complete the contract. They also maintain that an acceptance can be made by survivors of a party to whom the offer was made. In other words rights can be inherited.

3. Refusal of the offer: The offer can be rejected by words or conduct.

4. Termination of the majlis: The offer will be deemed cancelled by the termination of *Majlis* before acceptance from the other party.

5.Destruction of the subject matter: The destruction of the subject matter wholly or in part leads to the lapse of the offer. Thus the

---

[18] Mohammad Sidqī al-Būrnū, *al-wajīz fī- īdāh Qawā 'id al-Fiqh al-Kulliyyah*. Beriut:Mu'ssasah al-Risālah.1ˢᵗ edition 1404/1983, p.129.

[19] Ibid. p.109.

existence of the subject matter is a condition for the existence of an offer.[20]

Conclusion

The above discussion leads to the following conclusions:

1. A Contract has three elements: form (offer and acceptance), the contracting parties and subject matter.

2. *Ijāb* (offer) in juristic literature signifies the willingness of a party to do something positive. The literature is silent on whether abstinence of a party from doing some thing also forms *ijāb* or not. In our view *ijāb* in the sense of abstinence is also acceptable in the *Sharī'ah* on the basis of the rule of permissibility discussed in the first chapter of this book, which provides that every thing is permissible unless explicitly prohibited.

3. Offer and acceptance can be conveyed by spoken words, in writing or through indication and conduct.

4. It is a requirement of Islamic Law that acceptance should conform to offer in all its details and that the offer should be accepted in the same meeting.

5. The requirement of unity of session has been interpreted in different ways. To the modern jurists, whatever time is taken by the promisee to communicate his acceptance may be called continuance of the same meeting.

6. Option of stipulation (*Khiyār al-Shart*) is a mechanism provided by Islamic Law to overcome the problem caused by the restriction of unity of session. This option or right makes a contract non-binding for the party, which has reserved that right within a specified period.

---

[20] Hassān. Hussain Hāmid. *al-Madkhal li Dirāsah al-Fiqh al-Islāmī.* pp.252-254.

CHAPTER -4

ELEMENTS OF THE CONTRACT: SUBJECT-MATTER

The second essential element of a contract is its subject matter, which includes a number of things; namely, commodity, performance, consideration and object of the contract. The term "subject-matter" is applied to all of these things. Islamic law does not hold consideration as an independent element of contract. The reason is that the contractual obligation of one party according to Islamic law is consideration for the contractual obligation of another party. In a contract of sale, the commodity is the consideration for the purchaser and the price is the consideration for the seller. The object of the contract is also covered under subject matter.

Condition Relating To Subject-Matter

Islamic law has laid down the following conditions for the subject matter.

1. Legality of subject-matter

The commodity, service or performance must not include things prohibited by the *Sharī'ah* like wine, pork, intoxicants, and prostitution. It is forbidden for a Muslim to acquire or transfer through contract any thing that the *Sharī'ah* has declared *harām*. Since adultery, obscenity and immorality are prohibited by the *Sharī'ah*, any contract or transaction that entails these evils or promotes them in any way is also forbidden. From this it is established that the subject matter of a contract must be such in which transactions are legally permissible. The list of things prohibited by the *Sharī'ah* has been affirmed in the Qur'ān and the Sunnah. This includes wine, flesh of swine, blood or animals, which have died naturally or have not been slaughtered according to Islamic teachings. Contracts involving such things are not permissible, especially when the contracting parties are Muslims. Muslim Jurists are divided on the sale of milk of a woman and the hair of human beings. Some Jurists allow it because according to them, milk and hair are pure and beneficial. Other Jurists disallow this sale on the basis that these are a part of man. Musical instruments are also included in the things proscribed by Islamic Law, provided the contracting parties are Muslims.[1] Contracts for wine, swine and musical instruments are, however, allowed for non-Muslim citizens of an Islamic state. Sale of human blood today for the purpose of transfusion and donation and the sale of human eyes can be covered by the principle of necessity.

Articles of public property also constitute forbidden commodities in private transactions. Thus, a mosque cannot constitute the subject matter of a contract of sale, because its use cannot be passed on to an individual.[2]

The legality of subject matter further requires that the commodity should be owned by some one. Thus, public property is excluded and cannot be the subject matter of a contract. The same applies to other things, which are yet to be owned like fish in the sea etc. As regards public property, however, the state is nowadays considered similar to a person capable of owning property.

Legality of subject matter also requires that there should be no encumbrance or right attached to it. An example in this regard is sale of mortgaged property to which the rights of the creditor/mortgagee are linked.

2. Existence of subject matter

The subject matter should either be in actual existence at the time of contract or it should be capable of being acquired and delivered to a prospective buyer in the future. Transactions, which involve an element of uncertainty and risk with regard to the existence and acquisition of the subject matter, are forbidden in Islamic Law. Examples of such transactions are as follows:

    a) fruits on tree at the beginning of the season when their quality is yet to be established;

---

[1] Kāsānī, *Badā'i' al-Sanā'i'*, vol. 5, p.144.
[2] Abū Zahrah, *al-Milkiyyah wa Nazriyyat al-'Aqd*, p.255.

b) sale of fish still in water;

c) milk in the udders of an animal;

d) sale of standing crops (which are not free from getting spoiled);and

e) foetus yet in the mother's womb.

Commenting on the practice of selling fruit trees before they begin to blossom, Anwar Iqbal Qureshi writes:

> It is unfortunately a custom with us that fruit trees are sold before they begin to have blossoms upon them. This is known as spring sale. This spring sale, for instance, of mangoes is affected before trees begin to have blossoms. The natural consequence of this is a definite loss to one of the parties to the transaction. What happens usually in such transactions is that people make a general estimate of the produce in fruits. But no one can be aware of the unknown in which case this amounts to a form of gambling.[3]

As regards non-existent object, Muslim Jurists, in general, hold the view that their sale is invalid. They base this opinion on the following tradition of the Holy Prophet (s.a.w.s): 'Sell not what you do not have'.[4] The only exception to this rule is *salam* sale where the purchaser pays price in advance while delivery of the subject matter is postponed to a specified future date. They restrict *salam* to those commodities, which can be determined in terms of quality and quantity. This means that future goods are not saleable in ordinary sale.

Wahbah Zuhāylī explains the viewpoint of the *fuqahā'* on this issue in the following words:

> The object of contract must be present during the contracting session. Contracting over a non-existent object is invalid, like selling crop before it is visible, on the assumption that the crop might not appear. Equally prohibited are cases involving what is known as "the fear of

---

[3] Anwar Iqbal Qureshi, , *Islam and Theory of Interest*,Lahore;Sh.Muhammad Ashraf publishers,*1991*, p.90.

[4] Abū Dāwūd, *Sunan*, no.3503.

non-existence (*khaṭar al-'adam*) like the assumption that a foetus might not survive upon birth…This requirement is mandatory in the Ḥanafī and Shafi'ī schools, regardless of whether the transaction involves commutative (*mu'āwaḍāt*) or gratuitous (*tabarru'āt*) contracts.[5] Any transaction involving *ma'dūm* is void whether the case is sale (bay'), gift (*hibah*) or pledge (*rahn*). This view is based on a tradition of the Prophet (s.a.w.s.) wherein he is reported to have prohibited the sale of the foetus of an animal (bay' *ḥabal al-ḥablah*)[6] as well as the sale of an embryo (*al-maḍāmīn*)[7] and sperm (*al-malāqīḥ*).[8] He is also reported to have prohibited people from dealing in transactions where the seller did not possess the object. This is because object was treated as *ma'dūm* during the contract. They have established an exception to this general rule, i.e., the prohibition of *bay' al-ma'dūm* in cases pertaining to sale by advance (*salam*), contract of manufacturing (*istiṣnā'*). These transactions are approved, despite the absence of the object of contract, by way of *istiḥsān* (juristic preference) in order to cater for the needs of mankind".[9]

Ibn al-Qayyim, an eminent Ḥanbalī Jurist, has differed with the majority opinion. He is of the view that non-existence of an object does not constitute a reason for prohibition. He tries to denounce the confusion between uncertainty and non-existence. He says:

"There is nothing in the Qur'ān nor in the Sunnah that asserts the view that contracting over a *ma'dūm* (non-existing object) is disallowed. What is available in the *Sunnah* regarding transactions involving existent commodities is contained in the *ḥadith* : "do not sell what is not with you (i.e. not in your possession)". The *ḥadith* indicates that the *'illah* (legal effective cause) here is not *'adam* or non-existence but *gharar* (uncertainty). The uncertainty is due to the inability to deliver the subject

[5] Kāsānī, *Badā'i' al-Ṣanā'i'*, vol. 5, p.187,Shiribīnī , *Mughnī al-Muḥtāj*, vol. 2, p.20.

[6] Shawkānī, *Nayl al-Awṭār*, Lahore;Anṣār al- Sunnah al-Muḥammadiyyah,n.d.vol. 5, p.156.

[7] Haythamī, *Majma' al-Zawā'id*, vol.4, p.104.

[8] Ibid, vol.4, p.104 .

[9] Zuhaylī ,*al-Fiqh al-Islāmī wa Adillahtuhū*, vol.4, pp.173-174.

matter of the contract, for instance a runaway camel (*al-ba'īr al-shārid*). Whenever the *'illah* is removed the *hukm* too stands removed, for are you not aware that the Lawgiver has permitted *'ijāara* and *al-musāqāh* because of the absence of uncertainty? The Lawgiver, instead, disallowed the sale of a runaway camel because of the element of *gharar* inherent in it even though it is in existence. Similarly, the lawgiver has disapproved the hire of a camel in cases where the owner of the camel cannot deliver the animal for use. Above all, this principle applies to all forms of commutative contract in contrast with *al-waṣiyyah* (bequests). *Al-Waṣiyyah* is a pure gratuitous contract to which *gharar* does not apply. Thus a contract concerning a will created over an absent subject-matter is a valid contract.[10]

As regards the ḥadith: "Sell not what is not with you", other jurists have advanced three different interpretations, which are as follows:

1. "Sell not what is not with you" means not to sell what you do not own at the time of sale. Many prominent 'Ulamā of the various schools have recorded the view that the seller must own the object of sale when he sells it, failing which the sale will not be concluded, even if the seller acquires ownership afterwards. The only exception to note in this context is the forward sale of *'salam'* where ownership is not a pre-requisite.

2. The jurists and 'Ulamā of *ḥadīth* have generally held the view that the ḥadīth under discussion applies only to the sale of specified objects but not to fungible goods as these can easily be substituted and replaced. It is thus stated that prohibition in question is confined to the sale of objects in rem *(buyū' al-a'yān)* and does not apply to sale of goods by description. Hence when *Salam* is concluded over fungible goods that are commonly found in the locality, it is valid even if the seller does not own the object at the time of contract. Imām Shāfi'ī has also held that one may

---

[10] Ibn al-Qayyim, *I' lām al-Muwaqqi'īn* Cairo:Maktabah al-Kulliyyah al-Azhariyyah,1968,vol. 1, p.358.

sell what is not with him provided that it is not a specified object, for delivery of a specified object cannot be guaranteed if the seller does not own it.

3. The third position some 'Ulamā have taken on the interpretation of this *ḥadīth* is that sale of 'what is not with you' means sale of what is not present and the seller is unable to deliver. This is the view of Ibn Taymiyyah and the Mālikī jurist al-Bājī.[11] They contend that the emphasis in the *ḥadīth* is on the seller's inability to deliver, which entails risk-taking and uncertainty. If the *ḥadīth* were to be taken on its face value, it would proscribe *Salam* and a variety of other sales, but this is obviously not intended. It is quite possible that the seller owns the object and yet is unable to deliver it or that he possesses the object but does not own it ; in either case he would fall within the purview of this hadith. The emphasis in the *ḥadīth* is, therefore, not on ownership, nor on possession, rather it is on the seller's effective control and ability to deliver. Thus the effective cause ('illah) of the prohibition is *gharar* on account of inability to deliver.[12]

Among modern writers, Yūsuf Mūsā, 'Alī abd Al-Qādir and Yūsuf Al-Qaradāwī have drawn attention to the fact that the market place of Madīnah during the Prophet's (s.a.w.s.) time was so small that it did not offer assurance of regular supplies at any given time. The hadīth, therefore, prohibited sale of objects that were not available at the time of sale. This is perhaps, what is indicated, in the hadīth in which Ḥakīm b. Ḥizām said that people would come to him asking to sell them what he did not have. In contrast, the modern markets are regular and extensive which means that the seller can find goods at almost any time and make delivery as may be required. We also note that the contract normally operates on a deferred basis that gives the

---

[11] Abū al-Walīd Muhammad ibn Ahmed.
    Ibn Rushd. *al-Muqaddimāt*, Cairo:Matba'ah al-Sa'ādah,1325/1907, vol.2, p.221: Ibn Taymiyyah. *al-Qiyās fi al-Shar' al-Islāmī* Cairo:Maktabah al-Salafiyyah,1328AH. pp. 26-27.
[12] Zainuddin Zafar, *"Bay' al-Ma'dūm: An analysis*, paper presented in International Islamic Capital Market Conference Malaysia 1997.

seller a fair amount of time to buy what is required in order to make delivery, if necessary, within the contract period. When we compare the Madinah market at the time of the Prophet (s.a.w.s) with a modern market, we are faced with a different reality. Given the means and facilities that are available today, the fear of failure to find the goods and make delivery, which was the basic rationale behind the original prohibition, no longer exists.[13]

3. Certainty of delivery

The ability or capacity to deliver the subject-matter of the contract at the time of conclusion of a contract is an essential condition to make a valid contract. If such a capacity is lacking, the contract is void and this position is not altered by the fact that the seller was able to deliver the goods after the time of contract. This condition is applicable to contracts of sale as well as mortgages and pledges. The condition is dictated by the nature of the contract and the purpose, which such contract is supposed to serve. Thus, in a contract of sale the purpose is that the buyer should be able to exercise the authority and benefits of an owner. If such a capacity is lacking the purpose fails. The Muslim Jurists, therefore, prohibit the sale of a stray animal, whose whereabouts are not known, or fish in the sea or birds in the air.[14]

4. Precise determination of Subject Matter

The general principle in Islamic Law is that the subject matter must be precisely determined as regards its essence, quantity and value. Similarly, if the subject matter is an obligation or performance, it must be precisely determined at the time of the contract otherwise the contract will be invalid. Indetermination in a contract belongs to variety of things i.e. genus, specie, quality, price, and value. An example of indetermination with regard to genus is where a seller was to say: "I am selling you an ewe from this flock or a dress from this bundle". Such sale is irregular (*fāsid*) because the particular ewe or dress has not been indicated.[15] Similarly, if price of an item is not

---

[13] Ibid.

[14] kāsānī, *Badā'i' al-Sanā'i'* vol. 5, p.147.

[15] See Siddīq al- Darīr, *al-Gharar fī al-'Uqūd*, Islamic Development Bank ,Jeddah, p.20.

fixed or its fixation is left to the arbitration of a third party, this too is indetermination. This indetermination renders a contract *fāsid*. The subject matter is ascertained by the acquisition of such knowledge that does away with all uncertainty and vagueness likely to lead to dispute among contracting parties.

There are two ways, in the opinion of the Jurists, to determine subject matter.[16]

First Method: Examination

The subject matter becomes known and specified when the parties to a contract see and examine it at the time of contract. If the subject-matter is present at the session (*majlis*) of a contract then the majority holds its examination to be necessary. Failure of the parties to examine the subject-matter while it is present invalidates the contract.

Second Method: Sale by description

The second method of sale acknowledged by the Jurists is sale by description. Such description must be detailed enough to do away with any vagueness and uncertainty. If the goods or property to be sold are already known, like a house or horse of a seller who has only one house or horse, a description highlighting its specification or characteristics would be deemed to be sufficient. But if the sale is of fungible (*mithlī*) goods then genus, kind and quantity must bedescribed. This method is applicable where the goods are not present in the *majlis* of the contract. The majority of the jurists allow it. The Shāfi'īs, however, do not allow it and stipulate actual examination at the time of the contract as a necessary condition. Examination is the sole medium through which sale is possible according to these. [17] jurists.

Some jurists allow a sale even if the goods have not been examined or described. This is achieved by granting to the buyer the option of sight or examination after the contract. In this case the buyer can reject the goods on examination. This option can also be exercised when the goods have been sold by description only. Some of the jurists give an absolute right to reject the goods on sight even if they

[16] Ḥassān, *al-Madkhal*, p.311.
[17] Shīrāzī, *al-Muhadhdhab*, vol. 1, p.263.

conform to the description.[18] Others restrict such right to a case where the goods do not conform to the given description.[19]

We can conclude from the above that the majority of the jurists allow sale by description and it is only the Shāfiʿīs who insist on examination and sight at the time of the contract. The jurists distinguish between fungible goods and non-fungible goods.

5. Legality of Object and Underlying Cause

The validity of contract requires that the object and the underlying cause must be legal. Thus a contract made for the use of a property in commission of an offence, when the parties know this fact, is unlawful. Similarly, selling a weapon to a person who will kill an innocent man with it is illegal if the seller has knowledge of this fact. It means that the intended objectives of the contract should not oppose the will and intention of the Lawgiver.

Modern law also lays emphasis on this point. Thus, all contracts which promote immorality, or are against public policy, or harmful to a person or property of a third party, or which are forbidden by law are deemed void and of no legal effect. It is for this reason that courts do not countenance a claim to enforce a promise to pay for any criminal act.[20] Under Kuwaiti law, this concept is contained in Article 167 that governs *maḥall* (subject-matter). It reads: "The motivating purpose must be legal".[21]

The Egyptian Civil Law provides that if there is no cause of obligation, or if a cause is contrary to the general system or morals the contract will be invalid. Thus, the sale of weapons whose import is prohibited is invalid on account of the illegality of the cause and knowledge of the seller regarding this prohibition. Likewise a contract of loan intended for getting money for gambling is invalid, when the moneylender knows about this intention. The sale or leasing of a house

[18]kāsānī, *Badāʾiʿ al-Ṣanāʾiʿ* vol. 5, p. 292.
[19]Dasūqī , *Ḥāshiyah al-Dasūqi* vol.3, pp.23-24, Shīrāzī, *al-Muhadhdhab* vol.1, p.264.
[20] *Business Law*, London: Cavendish publishing ltd. p.73.
[21] *Kuwaiti Civil Code, 1980,* section 167.

is also invalid if the purchaser or lessee intends to turn it into a brothel when the seller or lessor knows of this intention".[22]

In declaring a contract invalid on account of illegality of cause, Islamic law stipulates that both the contracting parties must have knowledge of such illegality. Thus, ignorance of such a fact on the part of either of the contracting parties would not render the contract invalid. This is to ensure the security and stability of contracts.

Muslim Jurists have decided on the above basis that the sale of grapes to a person, who will extract wine from them, is invalid, because the intention and motivating cause is unlawful. Likewise, a contract of marriage to facilitate re-marriage between divorced couple is invalid, because such a contract does not intend to bear the consequences of marriage. At the same time intention in such a contract disagrees with the intended objectives of the Lawgiver. On the same grounds, a contract to sell something on credit say, for Rs. 100/- and buy it back for say, Rs. 80/- with immediate payment, is held to be invalid, because the purpose of the parties is to conclude a usurious transaction which is prohibited in the *Shari'ah*. The mere form of the sale does not exclude it from purview of usurious loan contracts.

In this regard the eminent jurists, Imam Ibn al-Qayyim writes:

> The proofs and rules of the Shari'ah indicate that intentions are taken into account in contract, that affect their validity and invalidity, and lawfulness and unlawfulness of a contract, but more seriously that it affects the action which is not a contract with respect to making it lawful and unlawful. The same item becomes lawful sometimes and unlawful at other times depending on variation of intention and intended objectives.[23]

---

[22] See 'Abd al-Razzāq Sanhūrī, ‚*Maṣādir al-Haq,*Cairo:Dar al- Marifah,1968 vol.4, p.30.

[23] Ibn al- Qayyim , *I'lām al-Muwaqqi'īn*, vol. 3, p.96.

Conclusion

1. The subject- matter, i.e., commodity or performance or service should be lawful.

2. The object of contract should be either in actual existence at the time of contract or it should be capable of being delivered in future.

3. Contracting over a non-existent object is disallowed only when there is grave uncertainty regarding its acquisition and delivery to the buyer.

4. The object of contract should be deliverable.

5. The subject-matter should be precisely determined at the time of contract.

6. The subject-matter can be determined either by the examination or by the description.

7. The validity of contract requires that its motivating cause should also be according to requirements of the *Sharī'ah*.

CHAPTER -5

ELEMENTS OF CONTRACT: CONTRACTUAL CAPACITY OF CONTRACTING PARTIES

A basic requirement for conclusion of a valid contract is the necessity that the contracting parties should be qualified to enter a contract. Thus, such parties are required to possess legal capacity *(ahliyyah)* for this purpose.

Capacity for execution or *Ahliyyat al-Adā*

The capacity for execution is defined as the "capacity of a human being for the issuance of words and performance of deeds to which the lawgiver has assigned certain legal effects."[1] On the basis of this definition the capacity for execution is considered by the jurists to be of three kinds.

i) Capacity for the *Khiṭāb Jinā'ī:* This is the capacity for the issuance of words and the performance of deeds the legal effects of which are worldly punishments. In other words whosoever possesses such a capacity can acquire through his words and deeds a liability for punishment. This is termed as the capacity for punishment or the capacity for the *khiṭāb jinā'ī.*

ii) Capacity for the *Khiṭāb of 'Ibādāt:* It is the capacity for the issuance of words and performance of deeds the legal effects of which are produced in the shape of reward or *thawāb* in Hereafter and as well as the fulfillment of one's obligation in the present world. This is termed as the capacity for *'Ibādāt* or the capacity for the *khiṭāb* of *'Ibādāt.*

---

[1] Ḥassān ,al-*Madkhal,* p.320.

iii) Capacity for the *Khiṭāb of Mu'āmlāt:* This is the capacity for issuance of words and performance of deeds the legal effects of which are exercise of rights and fulfillment of obligations for contracts and other transactions. It may be called the capacity for transactions or the capacity for the *khiṭāb* of *mu'amalāt.*[2]

The Condition oı *Ahliyyah-al-Adā*: The requirement for *ahliyyah al-adā*` is reason and discretion. The method to check whether a person possesses faculties of reasons and discretion the lawgiver has associated such powers with puberty. This is the view of the majority.

The Ḥanafīs on the other hand acknowledge a deficient capacity of execution for purposes of some transactions for a person who has attained some degree of discretion though his mental faculty is not fully developed. Thus, a minor who possesses discretion can be assigned such a capacity. Here, again there is no certain way of determining that the minor has attained this capacity. TheḤanafī jurists ,however, fix the age of seven years for the assignment of such a capacity. Anyone over seven who has not attained puberty may be assigned such a capacity.A deficient capacity is also assigned by the Ḥanafīs to one who has attained puberty but his mental faculty is not fully developed mentally, like the *ma'tūh* (lunatic).

Complete and deficient capacities of execution:

The capacity of execution is then divisible into two kinds:

Deficient capacity is assigned to a non-pubert who possesses some discretion and to the *ma'tūh* (lunatic) who has attained puberty yet lacks complete mental development.

A person who possesses a deficient capacity is not subject to the *khiṭ āb jinā 'ī*. Thus he cannot be held criminally liable. The reason for this is that the *khiṭ āb jinā 'ī* is applicable only to that person who can understand the *Khiṭ āb* fully.

As regard *'ibādāt* the *fuqahā'* are unanimous that the communication of Lawgiver addressed to the minor is by way of recommendation and that there ıs reward (*thawāb*) for the performance

---

[2] Ibid, p.328.

of the '*ibādāt* by such person. We are now concerned with the capacity of such persons for the purpose of transactions. The Ḥanafīs divide transactions into three kinds:

a) Purely Beneficial Transactions: These are like the acceptance of a gift or of *ṣadaqah* and are allowed to a non-pubert who can discriminate and has been permitted to do so by his guardian.

b) Purely Harmful transactions: The granting of divorce, manumission, *ṣadaqah, qarḍ, hibah, waqf* and *waṣiyyah* are not to be entered into by the *sabī mumayyaz* (minor possessed with discretion).

c) Transactions equally likely to result in profit or in loss: These are the sale, hire, and partnership. They are considered as valid if permission of the guardian is granted. Thus, a deficient capacity for execution is granted by the Ḥanafīs to the *ṣabī mumayyaz*. Other jurists refuse to acknowledge any kind of capacity for the *ṣabī mumayyaz*. The *Khiṭ āb* according to them is not directed towards the non-pubert at all; hence it makes no difference whether the transactions are beneficial or harmful[3].

Complete Capacity

Complete capacity is established for a human being when he attains full mental development and acquires the ability to discriminate. Thus, the requirement of this capacity is reason ('*aql*) and discretion (*rushd*). Such a stage has been associated with an external standard by the Lawgiver. This standard is puberty. The sign of puberty is ejaculation in a male, and menstruation in a female. In the absence of these signs puberty is presumed to have occurred by the age of 15 in both male and female according to the majority of the jurists and at 18 years for a male and 17 years for a female according to Imam Abū Ḥanīfah.

Attaining puberty in itself alone is not sufficient evidence that a person has acquired complete capacity for execution. In addition to puberty, the possession of *rushd* or maturity of action is also deemed necessary.

---

[3] Aḥmad Ibrahīm Bik, *al-Iltazāmāt fī al-Shar' al-Islāmī*, Cairo: Dār al-Anṣār, *1944*, pp.120-121.

Circumstances which affect the legal capacity of a person

There are certain factors, which impair legal capacity of a person and prevent him from concluding contracts and making dispositions in his property. These are as follows:

1. **Junūn (Insanity):** "*Junūn* is the mental derangement which, except in rare cases, prevents a person from and dispositions utterances". It is divided into two kinds:

    i-Aṣlī (regular) when a person attains puberty during his lunacy.

    ii- Ṭārī' (casual): which appears after a person has attained puberty and developed sanity together with mature understanding.[4]

    Insanity eliminates the legal capacity of an individual because its basis is intelligence and discrimination, and Insane is destitute of that. As regards legal effects of the utterances and dispositions of Insane, he is like a minor without discretion *(ṣabī ghayr mumayyaz)*, which do not produce any effect. Islamic Law puts an insane person under a guardian who looks after his affairs.

2. **'Atah (lunacy or partial insanity):** *Ma'tūh* is partial or temporary insane person who acts some times like a sane person and some other times like an insane person.

    " '*Atah* is defined as 'the mental derangement of a person who is confused in his speech and who speaks sometimes like sensible person and sometimes like lunatics".[5]

    Ma'tūh is treated like a minor possessed with discretion *(ṣabī mumayyaz)*. Thus, he is not allowed to enter contracts, which are disadvantageous for him. However, he is allowed to conclude beneficial transaction. As regards transactions that may equally result in benefit and loss, his transactions will be considered valid subject to verification by his guardian.

---

[4] Zaydān, *al-Madkhal*, p.317.

[5] 'Ubaid Allah ibn Mas'ūd , Sadr al-Sharī'ah, , *al-Tawḍīḥ*, al-Maktabah al-Khayri yyah1322 H., vol. 2, p.168.

3. Forgetfulness: Forgetfulness is defined as: "A circumstance that befalls a man without his volition causing loss of remembrance of something.[6]

The majority of jurists are of the opinion that a contract concluded through mistake or forgetfulness is not a contract at all. They rely for this on the words of the Holy Prophet (s.a.w.s) contained in a Hadīth in which he said: "My Ummah is forgiven for that which they have done through mistake or forgetfulness or under coercion".[7]

The Hanafis oppose the majority and declare that statements made by mistake or forgetfullness are valid for the formation of contracts. They maintain that the door will otherwise swing open for setting up false defences and the security of transactions demands that this should not be allowed.

4. Safah (Prodigality and Weakness of Intellect): *Safah* has been defined as follows:

> *i-* "*Safah* is that weakness of intellect which urges a person to act with respect to his property contrary to the dictates of intellect with the non-existence of mental disorder."[8]

> *ii-* "*Safah* is the disposition of one's property contrary to the dictates of the intellect and the *Shari'ah* by spending it without righteous purpose, squandering and using of more of it than necessary despite the persistence of one's intellect in reality."[9] *Safah* is opposite of the word *rushd* which signifies the handling of financial matters in accordance with the dictates of reason. Thus, *rashīd* is a person who can identify avenues of profit as well as loss and act accordingly to preserve his wealth. This is majority viewpoint. The Shāfi'ī

---

[6] Ḥassān, *al-Ḥukm al-Shar'ī 'inda al-Uṣūliyyīn*, Dār al-Nahḍah al-'Arabiyyah, 1972, p.186.

[7] Haythamī, *Majma' al-Zawā'id*, vol. 6, p.250.

[8] Amīr Badshah, *Taysīr al-Taḥrir*, Cairo: Muṣtafā al-Bābī al-Ḥalabī, 1351 AH, vol.2, p.300.

[9] Ḥassān, al-*Ḥukm al-Shar'ī 'inda al-Uṣūliyyīyn*, p.210.

Jurists, on the other hand, maintain that *rushd* is maturity of actions not only with regard to financial matters but also in matter of *dīn*. Thus, a person who attains puberty and handles his business sensibly but he doesn't abide by the rules and prohibitions of Lawgiver,is not *rashīd* in the opinion of Imām Shāfi'ī. An eminent Shāfi'ī Jurist Imām Nawawī declares *rushd* to be present in a person in the following circumstances:

i)   when he is able to perform his religious duties properly;

ii) when he behaves reasonably in his personal affairs;

iii) when he abstains from every thing that brings him reproach; and

iv) when he is not a spendthrift, i.e., he does not waste his wealth by allowing himself to be deceived in commercial transactions by obvious fraud.[10]

A person is considered eligible to take charge of his wealth if he is both *bāligh* and *rashīd*. This is the general view. However, Imām Abū Ḥanīfah maintains that a person who attains the age of 25 years, must be given his property irrespective of the fact that he attained *rushd* or not. He also maintains that if property is given to one who attains majority and *rushd* and subsequently loses his *rushd* while yet under 25, will not be subjected to interdiction (*ḥajr*).[11] Kuwaiti Civil Code provides that transactions of the *safīh* will, after determination of the judgement be treated in the same way as that of a minor without discernment. Any transaction arising from him before he is proclaimed *Safīh* is neither *Bāṭil* nor voidable except where the contract has been concluded in collusion with anticipation of the restriction, that is fraudulently and with knowledge of the impending lack of capacity.[12] The *safīh* may validly make *waqf* or bequest dispositions if the court authorizes him to do so.[13]

---

[10] Nawawī ,Muḥiyyuddīn Abū Zakariyyah, Minhāj al-Ṭālibīn, translated into English by: E.C.Howard,London:1977,p.167.

[11] 'Abd al- Sattār al-Jibālī, *A ḥkām 'Aqd al-Bāy'*. Cairo: Jami'ah al-Azhar,1993, P.49

12 *Kuwaiti Civil Code,* Art, 101 (1)

13 Ibid, 102.

The court has the power to give absolute or limited authorization to a *safih* to handle his affairs whether wholly or in part. In special cases it may require the *safih* to give account of his affairs.[14] The court may also restrain or withdraw his authorization if it sees just grounds for doing so.[15]

A *safih* who has been given permission to administer personal affairs, also has capacity to enter into transactions out of the bounds of that permission set by the court especially for him.[16]

Procedure for exercise of interdiction:

The opinion of Ḥanafī jurists is divided on the issue as to whether the interdiction should be by orders of court or the existence of (*safah*) itself.

Imām Muhammad holds that a *safih* should be prevented from disposing his property by the mere existence of *safah* without necessitating the order of the court. Therefore, the existence of stupidity in a person presupposes interdiction and its non-existence requires its removal.

According to Abū Yūsuf interdiction will be imposed and lifted by the order of the court. The result of this disagreement becomes manifest in the dispositions of a *safih* prior to placing him under interdiction. These dispositions are valid and enforced according to Imām Muḥammad. According to Abū Yūsuf they remain suspended until the decision of the court.

The Iraqi Civil Code favours the opinion of Imām Abū Yūsuf, hence, when a *safih is* placed under interdiction by the court, he becomes like a minor possessed with discretion. Iraqi Law allows him to make bequest to the extent of one-third of his property.

5. **Death-illness (*maraḍ al-Mawt*):** Death-illness has been defined as follows:

> Death-illness is that form of illness from which death is to
> be apprehended in most cases, and illness which disables

---

[14] Ibid., 103 (1).

the patient from looking after affairs outside his house if he is a male, and the affairs within her home if she is female, provided the patient dies in such condition before a year has passed.[17]

It is clear that death-illness means an illness from which death is ordinarily apprehended in most cases.

To constitute a malady, death-illness (*marad al-mawt*) there must be: (a) proximate danger of death, so that there is a preponderance of apprehension of death; (b) some degree of subjective apprehension of death in the mind of sick person; and (c) some external indication, chief among which would be inability to attend to ordinary avocations.[18]

Death-illness is considered one of the impediments to disposition made to protect a specific public benefit such as prohibiting a pledgee from disposing of the property pledged as security with him in the interest of debtor.

Transactions of *Marīd marad al-Mawt*: Transactions undertaken by a person on his deathbed are of two types:

a) **Transactions without Consideration:** A person seized with a death illness is prohibited from disposing of his property without any return within the limit of two thirds to protect the interest of heirs, because his dispositions without any return such as donation, *waqf,* alms are considered a bequest, which is permissible to the extent of one-third of the property only. If he is in debt, he is prohibited to donate his property for it is needed to pay his debt. He is, however, allowed to dispose of property exceeding debt on the condition that it is taken out of one-third of the property; failing which his heirs have the right to nullify it.[19] But if he is not in debt, or his debt is

---

[17] Ahmad Hassan, *Principles of Islamic Jurisprudence*, Islamabad: Islamic Research Institute ,1993, p. 323.

[18] Mulla, *Mahomedan Law,* p. 148.

[19] Hassan *Introduction to the study of Islamic Law,* Sharī'ah Academy, Islamic international Islamic University, p.373.

less than his legacy, these dispositions will not be effective with respect to his heirs except within one-third of the whole legacy if there is no debt or within one-third of the remaining property after the payment of debts. The reason is that these dispositions are treated as will or bequest from that patient.

In order to consider his transaction a bequest or will in the above meaning, three conditions must be fulfilled:

1. The transaction should be without consideration such as *alms,* gifts and *waqf* or in consideration of a thing which is less than fair price or sale at a price which is less than fair price or buying a thing at a price which is more than fair price. Apart from this, other transactions are valid and effective with respect to the creditors and heirs and they have no right to demand their revocation because it will be presumed that the transactions were meant to meet the imperative needs of the sick person.

2. The disposition should be made in material things. If it is made in usufruct such as hire and share-cropping, it will be effective with respect to the creditors and heirs. They will not have right to revoke these contracts.

3. The disposition should be made in the very substance of things, not in the revenue or profit derived from them. Any assignment of profits arising from *Shrikah* or *muḍarabah* will not be affected by this condition.[20]

b) Transactions for Consideration: If his disposition are for consideration and are not in favour to any one as, for instance, it is a sale at a fair price, such disposition will be valid and effective in the lifetime of sick person. The creditor and heirs will have no right to nullify it after his death, because the rights of sick person have priority over their rights. It will be assumed that this disposition is for the imperative needs of sick person like food, drink, and treatment. It is all the same whether the disposition, which involves no favour, is meant for himself or any of his heirs.

---

[20] Ibid., pp. 376, 377.

Abū Ḥanīfah holds that if a disposition is made for any of the heirs, the other heirs have the right to ask for nullification, even if it were at a fair price, because the rights of heirs are attached to the substance of the inheritance not to its value in his opinion. The followers of Abū Ḥanīfah hold that the rights of heirs are like those of creditors attached to the monetary value of the inheritance, not to their substance. If he disposes at a fair price without showing any favour nothing will be missed from the monetary value of the inheritance.[21]

c) Other dispositions of *Marīḍ marad al-Mawt:*

a) Acknowledgement of debt: A person seized with death-illness can make acknowledgement of debt during death-illness. Such acknowledgement is valid and effective with respect to his heirs, irrespective of the fact that it is in favour of heir or a stranger. To Hanfi jurists an acknowledgement of debt in favour of an heir is valid and enforceable only when other heirs ratify it.

b) Marriage during death-illness: The *Marīḍ maraḍ al-mawt* can validly conclude a marriage contract during death-illness, provided the dower money paid by him does not exceed the amount of fair dower (*mahr mithl*) In case it exceeds the amount of fair dower, it will be treated as donation in the meaning of will which will be enforced by the permission of heirs within the limit of one-third of his estate.

c) The divorce of *marīḍ maraḍ al-mawt* is valid, and will be enforced. If the husband dies before the expiry of her '*iddat.* She is entitled to inherit from him. The reason given being that repudiation by a man in his last illness is nothing but a device to defeat the wife's right of inheritance. But the husband is not entitled to inherit from his wife. If she dies before the expiry of the '*iddat* for he, and not she was responsible for the rupture of conjugal rights.

d) *Mushārakah* and *Muḍārbah* contracts: A sick man on deathbed can enter the contracts of *mushārakah* and *muḍārbah*, because they relate to profit not to capital or substance of things. The profit in partnership contract is similar to usufruct in hiring and crop-sharing contracts that are permissible for *marīḍ maraḍ al-mawt*. It is pertinent to note here that the rights of heirs are attached with *a'yān*

---

[21] Ḥassān, *al-Madkhal*, p.350.

(substance or thing) not with its usufructs or profit. Moreover, the partnership comes to an end with the death of this person, so it is in no way harmful for the heirs.

6. **Intoxication:** Intoxication is a condition, which overtakes a man on account of taking an intoxicant, and along with it his intelligence remains suspended, being neither lost nor diminished.[22]

The drunken person is one who is in a state of intoxication due to the consumption of liquor and does not know what he is saying. The Majority is of the opinion that a contract is established by the statement of a drunken person and gives rise to all kinds of rights and obligations of the contract. They argue (i) that he became intoxicated out of his own choice, (ii) that he knew that drinking was prohibited and a crime should not absolve a person of the duties acquired by him.

The Ḥanbalī jurists are of the opinion that the statement of an intoxicated person is not to be taken into account at all as he does not intend what he is saying. He is just like an insane person or one under duress. Some other jurists try to distinguish between intoxication caused by illegal means and that caused by lawful means. Intoxication is caused by lawful means in the following cases:

i)   when a person drinks intoxicating liquor without knowing that it is forbidden liquor;

ii) when he is forced to do so under duress;

iii) when he is about to die of thirst and no other drink is available; and

iv) when intoxicant is caused by drugs taken medicinally.

Those who prefer the stand of the Hanablīs give the following arguments:

i)   The intoxicated person doesn't intend what he says and thus takes the *ḥukm* of one who is insane.

ii) It is not necessary that the intoxicated person is making a bad bargain and in fact he may suffer if the contract is declared invalid.

---

[22] Ḥassān, *al-Ḥukm al-Shar'ī*, p.204.

7. Taflīs **(Bankruptcy):** A person is considered bankrupt when his debts exceed his assets, and court on the demand of his creditors passes a prohibitory order restraining all alienation by him, and directs the sale of his property for the benefit of his creditors. The purpose of this *al-ḥajr* (interdiction), i.e., to restrict *al-muflis* (bankrupt) in the right of disposal of his property is to safeguard and protect the right of creditors and to prevent him from carrying out transactions detrimental to his creditors. The precedent for such regulation was set by the Prophet (s.a.w.s). It is narrated that Mu'ādh ibn Jabal was a generous man and always gave his possessions away. He was always in debt. His debts were more than his property. So, he came to the Prophet (s.a.w.s) and requested him to ask his creditors to withdraw their claims on the debts. They, however, refused. The Prophet (s.a.w.s), later, sold all Mu'ādh's property to pay the debts, to the extent that he had nothing left.

8. **Coercion:** Coercion is to compel a person without having such a right, to do a thing without his consent or through fear. It is also defined as an action directed against a person, who suppresses his true consent".[23] The contracts and dispositions made under coercion are not valid according to the majority of Muslim jurist. Hanfīs, however, maintain the contract of the person coerced is valid but is suspended, on the extinction of coercion. The *mukrah* (coerced person) has right to ratify it or revoke it. They also hold that the contracts of marriage, divorce, manumission are valid even with coercion.

CHAPTER -6

DELEGATED AUTHORITY

A person sometimes makes transactions on behalf of other people. In such a case he is required to have, besides legal capacity, proper authority to make a transaction. He derives authority either from the person on whose behalf he enters into a contract or from the Lawgiver. The authority in the former case is called agency while in the latter case it is termed as guardianship.

The nature and scope of both the authorities, i.e., agency and guardianship will be discussed in this chapter.

1-CONTRACT OF AGENCY (WAKĀLAH):

Wakalah is to substitute an agent for the principal to perform on behalf of that principal an act, which admits of representation. It creates a fiduciary relationship that exists between two persons, one of whom expressly or impliedly consents that another should act on his behalf. The one on whose behalf the act is done is called the principal *(aṣīl)* and the one who is to act is called agent *(wakīl)*.[1]

A number of legal texts provide justification for the contract of agency. Some of them are produced below:

1. Ḥaḍrat 'Alī (r.a.t.a) narrates that once the Holy Prophet (s.a.w.s) ordered him to distribute the saddles and skins of animals he had slaughtered.[2]

---

[1] Zaydān, *al-Madkhal li Dirāsāt al-Shari'ah al-Islāmiyyah*, p.338; Muḥammad Muṣṭafā, Shalabī, *al-Madkhal li Dirāsat al-Fiqh al-Islāmī*, Beriut: Dār al-Jami'at, *1985*, p.339.

[2] Aḥmad ibn Ḥanbal, *Musnad Aḥmad*, Cairo:Dār al-Ma'ārif, vol. 1, pp.79, 143, 154, 112.

2. 'Uqbah ibn 'Āmir narrates that the Prophet (s.a.w.s.) gave him some sheep to distribute among his companions and a male kid was left after distribution. He informed Holy Prophet (s.a.w.s) about it, and he said "Sacrifice it on my behalf".[3]

3. 'Urwah al-Bariqī (r.a.t.a.) narrated that the Holy Prophet (s.a.w.s.) gave him a dīnār to buy a sheep for him. He bought two sheep by it and sold one of them for one dīnār on the way. He said: When I brought a dīnār and a sheep to the Holy Prophet (s.a.w.s.), he said to me, "May Allah bless the bargain of your right hand".[4]

These traditions prove that a person can delegate his business to an agent to perform it on his behalf. Ḥaḍrat 'Alī is reported to have appointed 'Aqīl for management of his lawsuits; and when 'Aqīl became old, he was replaced by another agent 'Abd Allāh ibn Ja'far.

CONDITIONS OF AGENCY

I. Conditions relating to the principal (muwakkil/aṣīl):

The conditions of the Principal are that he should have full authority of disposing of a matter, which he has entrusted to another person to perform it on his behalf. He, therefore, should be competent to undertake task himself for which he has appointed an agent. Thus, an insane, a minor, and the one placed under interdiction cannot enter into a contract of agency. They cannot make other peoples their agents for the performance of work on their behalf. A discerning minor (*ṣabī mumayyaz*) may, however, appoint agent for the performance of acts which are beneficial for the minor, but he is not allowed to appoint agent for transactions which entail loss for that minor.

II. Conditions relating to the agent (*wakīl*):

The condition of agent is that he should possess the capacity of execution that requires sanity and ability of understanding and discrimination in the agent. Thus, it is not requirement that the agent must necessarily be of age. A person having deficient capacity of execution can act as agent for another person. Ḥanbalī and Shāf'ī

---

[3] Bukhari, *Sahīh,* Kitāb al-Wakālah, No.230; Kitāb al-Daḥāya, no.5555.

[4] Abū Daw'ūd, *Sunan* quoted from , Muḥammad ibn Muḥammad, Fāsī, *Jam'al-Fawā'id,* Lahore:al-Maktabah al- Islāmiyyah, Ḥadīth no.4854.

Jurists, however, postulate complete legal capacity for an agent. To them the general rule to be followed in this regard is that one, who does not have authority to dispose of a thing for him, is ineligible to be agent for disposition of that thing for others.[5] As such, *ṣabī mumayyaz* is not eligible to act as agent for others.

III. Conditions relating to Subject-matter (Muwakkal bihī):

The subject matter of agency is the act for the performance of which the agent is appointed. Agency is permissible in each known disposition recognised by *Sharī'ah*. Some important conditions of the subject matter of agency are as follows:

1. It should be known to the agent to the extent that its performance is possible for him. Thus, if the agency is for the purchase of a thing, the genus, kind, quality and other necessary attributes of the commodity to be bought should be mentioned. The agency will be invalid where a person appoints another person as his agent to sell his property without defining and identifying that property.

2. It should be a lawful and permissible disposition. The agency is not permissible in acts of disobedience such as murder, theft, usurpation of property, and slander.

3. The disposition should be something that admits of representation. Hence, appointment of an agent for the act such as prayer, fasting, giving evidence, or for taking an oath is not permissible because these acts are to be performed by the principal himself. An eyewitness to an incident is required to give testimony himself. He is not allowed to delegate this task to another person. Similarly, an oath can be accepted only from the person concerned, not from his agent.[6]

SUBJECT-MATTER OF AN AGENCY

Some of the acts and dispositions for which agency is permissible are as follows:

---

[5] Ibn Qudāmah *al-Mughnī*. vol. 5, pp. 79-80.

[6] Zuhaylī. *al-Fiqh al-Islāmī wa Adillahtu hū*, vol. 4, p.

1. Sale and purchase
2. Letting and hiring
3. Borrowing and lending
4. Bailment
5. Making gifts
6. Pledge
7. Assignment of debts
8. Suretyship and guarantee
9. Deposits
10. Litigation
11. Marriage contracts
12. Divorce
13. Relinquishment of rights
14. Admissions and acknowledgement of rights

Agent's duty towards his principal

The duties of an agent towards principal are:

1. To perform the undertaking according to instructions, i.e., to observe all the conditions and restrictions laid down by the principal.

2. To exercise due care and skill.

3. To carry out instructions personally, i.e., he is not allowed to appoint another person to do an act delegated to him.

4. Not to permit a conflict of interest to arise, i.e., he is not allowed to purchase for himself property, which he is engaged to sell. The corollary to this case is that he must not sell his own property to the principal without fully disclosing the facts.

5. Not to make secret profit or misuse confidential information.

The effects and rights of the contract of wakālah

Muslim jurists are unanimous on the point that effects of a contract of agency revert to the principal because the agent only enforces orders and instructions of his principal. He derives authority from the principal. Hence, effects should revert to the principal, regardless of whether the agent attributed transaction to himself or to his principal. These jurists, however, differ among themselves regarding the mode of establishment of these effects. Hanafī jurists maintain that the *hukm* or effect is established first for agent and from him it passes on to the principal. The Shāfi'ī and Hanbalī jurists, on the other hand, hold that the effects of a contract revert directly to the principal.[7] The author of *al-Mughnī* says in this regard:

> "If an agent bought some thing for the principal with
> his permission, the ownership will stand transferred
> from the seller to the principal, without first entering
> into the ownership of agent".[8]

As regards secondary liabilities and rights with respect to a disposition, the Hanafī jurists maintain that these are attributable to the agent. For example, the effect of a contract of sale is the transfer of ownership in goods from seller to purchaser, whereas the liabilities and rights of contract are the delivery of the subject matter; claiming the price, exercise of the right of option of defect or inspection and returning goods in case of reclaiming. All these rights and liabilities are to be attributed to the agent not to the principal. This means that the agent is responsible for receiving goods from seller, handing over price to him, returning goods in case of defect to the seller. All these rights belong to the agent not to the principal. He alone will be sued for the price and not the principal.

This principle is applied to all such transactions and dispositions, which do not require attribution explicitly to the principal such as sale and purchase. In all such transactions the rights and liabilities are traceable to the agent. For example, in a contract of sale,

---

[7] Mansūr ibn Yūnus, Bahūtī, *Kashshāf al-Qinā*, Cairo: Matba'ah Anṣār
al-Sunnah al- Muhammadiyyah, 1366/1948 vol.2, p.228.
[8] Ibn Qudāmah, *Al-Mughnī*, vol. 5, p.130.

it is agent alone who can demand price from purchaser. If the principal directs this claim against purchaser, he (purchaser) cannot be forced to make payment to him.

There are, however, certain other contracts, which must be attributed explicitly to the principal such as marriage, divorce, and settlement for murder. The rights in all these cases are traceable to the principal because the agent in these cases is merely an emissary carrying the consent of the principal to other party. Thus, if the agent concludes a marriage contract on behalf of husband, he (agent) will not be demanded to pay dower money. Similarly, the agent of wife cannot demand dower money from the husband. The Hanbalī jurists do not differentiate between the contract of sale and contract of marriage for this purpose. To them the effects as well as rights and liabilities in all the contracts are attributed to the principal.

Termination of agency

Contract of agency is terminated under the following circumstances.

1. Mutual agreement of the parties to terminate the agency.

2. Unilateral termination by any of the two parties. Because of the consensual nature of principal/agent relationship, it is possible for either party to bring it to an end simply by giving notice of termination of agreement. All the acts and disposition of agent before receipts of notice will be considered valid and effective with respect to principal.

3. Discharge of obligation by the agent. When the agent performs the act with which he was entrusted through the contract of agency, the agency comes to an end.

4. Destruction of the subject matter. When the object of the agency becomes non-existent, the agency comes to an end. If the principal, for example, settled a disposition in which he appointed an agent, or its object perished, the agency will stand terminated.

5. Death or loss of legal capacity. When party ceases to possess legal capacity, i.e.. he becomes insane or the court prohibits him from dispositions, the agency will be terminated.

6. Agency cannot be terminated when the right of a third party is attached to the contract. Thus, if a mortgager (debtor) appoints

the mortgagee (creditor) as his agent for the sale of mortgaged property in order that the debt is cleared, then such agency cannot be terminated till the sale is affected.[9]

2- Acts of the Unauthorized Agent (fuḍūlī)

The word *fuḍūlī* is derived from *fuḍulī,* which means meddling or the undertaking of affairs by a person that are not of his concern and *fuḍulī* is one who intervenes in matter that does not concern him. Hence, *fuḍulī* is a person who concludes a contract on behalf of another without proper authority. One who sells the goods of another or purchases something for him when he is neither the *walī* (guardian) of such person nor his duly appointed agent, he is acting as a *fuḍulī* [10]

Legal Status of the acts of a fuḍūlī

There are two opinions of the Muslim jurists regarding the acts of the *fuḍulī.* The first suggests that such acts are *bāṭil* and without any legal effects. According to the second opinion the acts by *fuḍulī* are valid subject to ratification by the person on whose behalf the act has been undertaken.

Opinion No.1: Acts of the fuḍūlī are bāṭil having no legal effects:

The Shāfi'īs and Ḥanbalīs are of the opinion that the contracts concluded on behalf of another are void and have no legal effects. The contracts are *bāṭil* (void) even if they are ratified by the person on whose behalf they are concluded, because a contract, which is bātil, cannot become *ṣaḥīḥ* on the basis of such permission. These jurists have based their opinion on the fact that the basic condition for undertaking such transaction is the proper authority and the *fuḍulī* does not possess such authority. He is neither the owner of the goods nor does he possess the requisite authority and his acts are, therefore ,without legal validity. The jurists holding this opinion rely on the tradition; "Do˙not sell that which is not with you". This is interpreted here to mean, "Don.'t sell what you do not own". The command here was issued by the Prophet (s.a.w.s) in the case of a Companion who used to conclude a sale first and then buy the goods and deliver them later on. These jurists also maintain that a *fuḍulī* does

[9] Zaydān, *al-Madkhal* p.348.
[10] Ḥassān, *al-Madkhal li Dirāsāt al-Islāmī,*p.393.

not have the capacity to deliver at the time of making a contract the thing, which he is selling. As such it resembles the sale of a bird in the air or fish in water, which is *bāṭil*.[11]

Opinion No.2: The acts of the fuḍūlī are Mawqūf (suspended) till ratification:

The Ḥanafīs and Mālikīs are of the opinion that acts of a *fuḍūlī* are valid (*ṣaḥīḥ*) but can be assigned legal effects only when ratified by proper authority. If such ratification is awarded, such acts become valid taking their legal effects. If the ratification is refused the acts are void *ab initio*.[12]

These jurists rely for their opinion on the tradition that the Holy Property (s.a.w.s) ratified the purchase and subsequent sale of a goat on his behalf by one of the Companions. As regards the tradition prohibiting the sale of that which one does not possess, it is maintained by these jurists that it applies to sale on one's own behalf and not on behalf of another. It goes without saying that *fuḍūlī* acts on behalf of other people.

We may now distinguish between the legal effects assigned to a suspended contracts by a *fuḍūlī* in cases ratification is assigned and in cases where ratification is refused.. The Ḥanafīs consider sale and purchase separately for this purpose and we follow their method in this discussion.

a) Sale by a *fuḍūlī:* As already mentioned that Ḥanafīs and Mālikīs consider the sale of a *fuḍūlī* as valid but subject to ratification by the owner of the goods.

The suspension of the contracts concluded by a *fuḍūlī* implies that such contracts may be revoked by the purchaser or by the *fuḍūlī* before ratification. The result of this would be that even if the original owner or the person on whose behalf the *fuḍūlī* acted were to ratify the contract, it could still to be revoked. The reason is that in such a case the interest of the *fuḍūlī* would have priority. This is because the *fuḍūlī* becomes an agent hence all the rights of the contract revert to him. It is

---

[11] Ibn Qudāmah, *al-Mughnī*, vol. 4, p.155.

[12] Ḥassān, *al-Madkhal li Dirāsāt al-Islāmī*, p.396.

he who has to deliver the goods or price and exercise various options
All this may be injurious to him.[13]

The Mālikī jurists do not allow a *fuḍūlī* or a purchaser the
right of revocation. This right belongs only to the owner who may
revoke or ratify the contract, as he likes. If a *fuḍūlī* becomes the owner
of the goods (through inheritance or gift etc.) that he sold without
authority, such sale becomes void according to the Ḥanafīs and he
would have to transact a new sale. Ratification by the *fuḍūlī* in such a
case is not possible. The rule according to the Ḥanafīs is that the cause
of ownership must precede the sale and in this case the cause has come
into existence after the sale.

The Mālikīs allow the *fuḍūlī* in such a case to revoke the sale
if he inherits the property, as according to them, he inherits the right of
ratification with it. If he becomes the owner due to other causes like
purchase and charity, he has no right to revoke the contract and the
sale will be implemented.[14]

b) Purchase by a *fuḍūlī:* The Mālikī jurists do not distinguish between
sale and purchase by a *fuḍūlī*. According to them both are dependent
on ratification by the person on whose behalf such a transaction was
made. The same rule applies to a situation where a *fuḍūlī* attributes the
contracts to himself or to the person on whose behalf he is acting.
Hence, purchase by a *fuḍūlī* on behalf of another is valid but
suspended till ratification. The seller does not have the right to revoke
such a contract. If ratification is accorded, the *fuḍūlī* is considered as
an agent but if ratification is denied, the *fuḍūlī* becomes the buyer.[15]

The Ḥanafī jurists distinguish between purchase and sale and
also whether the *fuḍūlī* is attributing the sale to himself or to the
person on whose behalf he is acting. Thus, if a *fuḍūlī* purchases on
behalf of another but attributes the contract to himself then such a
contract will be valid against him. It will not require buyer's

---

[13] Kāsānī, *Badā'i' al-Ṣanā'i'*, vol. 2, p.233.

[14] Kāsānī, *Kharashī*, vol. 5, p.18; *al-Sharḥ al-Kabīr*, vol. 3, p.12. Cf.
Ḥassān, *al-Madkhal li Dirāsat al-Islāmī,* p 400.

[15] Kāsānī. *Kharashī,* vol. 5, p.18 Cf. Ḥassān, *al-Madkhal.* p.402.

ratification and ownership is transferred to him. Consequently he will be obliged to pay the price. When *fuḍūlī* attributes the purchase to the person on whose behalf he is acting the sale is valid (*ṣaḥīḥ*) but is subject to ratification by such person.[16]

A necessary condition in cases of ratification is that the person on whose behalf he is acting must have legal capacity failing which it should be ratified by the *walī*.

Conditions of Ratification: There are certain conditions that have to be fully complied with before the principal can effectively adopt the contract. These are:

a. The subject matter of the contract must be in existence:

Ratification is futile if the subject matter was destroyed before it was accorded. If the subject matter is destroyed in the hands of the *fuḍūlī* he is liable for its destruction. If it is destroyed at the hands of the buyer the real owner is at liberty either to claim compensation from *fuḍūlī* or from the buyer.

b. All three parties must be alive at the time of ratification:

If ratification is accorded after the death of one of the parties, it shall have no legal effects.

c. Concerned parties must possess legal capacity at the time of the contract:
If a *fuḍūlī* acts on behalf of a minor who accords ratification after attaining puberty, such ratification is without effect.[17]

Mode of Ratification: Ratification is either expressed or implied. Expressed ratification is by words or by way of delivery (of goods or price). Implied ratification is by way of *qarā'in* (context) like the owner of goods gifting away the price of the goods sold by the *fuḍūlī*. The Ḥanafīs maintain that mere silence

---

[16] Zayn al-'Ābidīn, Ibn Nujaym, *al-Bahr al-Rā'iq,* Cairo: 1893,

vol. 6, p.149. Cf. Ḥassān, *al-Madkhal.* p.403.

[17] 'Imrān Nyāzee, *Outlines of Islamic Jurisprudence,* Islamabad: ALSI p. 140.

on the part of the owner when knowledge of the sale has reached him, does not amount to ratification on his part.

Effects of Ratification: If ratification is accorded in conformity with the conditions listed above, the *fuḍūlī* becomes the agent (*wakīl*) of owner. Such agency has retrospective effects from time of the act of the *fuḍūlī*.Thus, the *ḥukm* of the contract will pass to the owner while the *ḥuqūq* shall remain with the *fuḍūlī* who is now the agent.

Denial of Ratification: If in case ratification is denied, the acts of the *fuḍūlī* become null and void having no existence. If ratification is denied when delivery of the goods sold has already been made to the buyer, the owner has the right to demand the return of such goods. If such property is destroyed in the hands of the *fuḍūlī* he alone is responsible, but after delivery both the *fuḍūlī* and the buyer are liable.

In case there is silence on part of the owner the Ḥanafīs keep the contract suspended without any limit of time. Mālikī jurists on the other hand limit it to a period of one year from the time when knowledge of the sale reached the owner after which performance of the contract becomes necessary. It is important to note here that through this opinion the Mālikīs have introduced the concept of limitation into Islamic Law.[18]

3. GUARDIANSHIP (WilāYab) :

Definition

It is an authority granted by the Sharī'ah to a person over the person and property of another person by virtue of which his dispositions in respect of such persons are assigned legal effects.[19] The legitimacy of guardianship has been established by the Qur'ān and the Sunnah. Verses 282 of Sūrat al-Baqarah provides that: "If the party liable is mentally deficient or unable

---

[18] Ḥassān, *al-Madkhal*, pp. 405,406.

[19] Zuhaylī, *al-Fiqh al-Islāmī wa Adillatuhū*, vol. 4, p.139.

himself to dictate, let his guardian dictate faithfully".[20] This shows that a minor has to be subjected to guardianship.

Kinds of Guardianship

There are two kinds of guardianship;

    1. guardianship over the person, and

    2. guardianship over the property.

The first kind implies the protection of the minor, the undertaking of his education and general bringing up. It also includes his marriage. The second kind implies safeguarding of the property of the minor, the lunatic and the insane.

Guardians and grades of guardianship

The following persons are entitled to be guardians of the property in Islamic Law:

    1. the father,

    2. the executor appointed by the father's will,

    3. the father's father,

    4. the executor appointed by the will of father's father,

    5. the judge, and

    6. the executor appointed by the judge.

In default of the first four categories, the court may appoint a guardian from the following persons in the order of priority herein:

    1. full brother,

    2. consanguine brothers,

    3. full brother's son,

    4. consanguine brother's son,

    5. full paternal uncle,

    6. consanguine paternal uncle,

---

[20] Qur'ān 2: 282.

7. full paternal uncle's son, and

8. consanguine paternal uncle's son.

The jurists are unanimous on the point that guardianship of a minor is established for the father. But they differ among themselves regarding the one who follows the father in guardianships and comes next to him. According to Ḥanafī jurists executor appointed by father follows him. And if the father has not appointed executor in his life, it will shift to grandfather and from him to the executor appointed by grandfather. Thus, the executor appointed by the father will be given priority over grandfather.[21] The Mālikī and Ḥanbalī jurists acknowledge guardianship of minor for father and his executor first and then for judge or his nominee.

The grandfather in their view is not entitled to guardianship of property because he is not like the father. He is more distant than him in degree and has less concern for minor's interest.[22]

The Shāfiʿī jurists give grandfather precedence over the executor. He is nearer to minor than executor appointed by father. In the absence of the father and grandfather, guardianship belongs to an executor to be appointed by any of them who died later. And after him it will be transferred to the judge or his nominee.[23]

Conditions of guardian: The jurists have laid down following three conditions for a person who assumes the position of guardian:

1.He should be adult and sane,

2.He must follow the sane religion as followed by his ward,and

3.He should be capable of performing dispositions required by the guardianship.[24]

Rights and duties of guardian: It is a basic requirement of guardianship that all the actions and dispositions of the guardian

---

[21] Zuhaylī, *al-Fiqh al-Islāmī*, vol.4, p.142.

[22] Ibid.

[23] Zaydān *al-Madkhal*, p.336.

[24] Ibid. pp 337-338.

should be directed towards realisation of the interest of the ward. Thus, he is allowed to make any disposition, which may benefit him and augment his wealth. The Qur'ān says:

> "Come not nigh to the orphan's property except to improve it until he attains the age."[25]

This verse makes it imperative for the guardian of the orphan not to touch his property except for the purpose of improving it and the guardian should not take a personal advantage in the bargain made for the ward.

1. It is not permissible for guardian to enter into any contract for ward, which may cause damage to him. Thus, he is not allowed to use his property for granting loans and giving gifts to people.

2. A legal guardian of the property of a minor has power to sell or pledge the goods and chattels of the minor for the minor's imperative necessities suited to his life such as food, clothing, and medication.

3. A legal guardian may enter into a transaction of exchange in respect of minor's property, if it has the effect of conserving it.

4. He can also sell it if the property has been usurped, and the guardian has reason to fear that there is no chance of fair restitution.

5. A guardian of the property of a minor appointed by the court is bound to deal with moveable property belonging to the minor as carefully as a man of ordinary prudence would deal in his own case.

6. Where a minor upon attaining his majority claims to be fit to manage his financial affairs and the executor disputes such fitness, the latter cannot be compelled to deliver the minor's property until the minor has been declared by the judge to be capable of such management.

7. If the executor refuses to deliver the property to the minor after the latter has been declared competent by the judge to administer his own property, and after the minor has duly called upon executor to make such delivery, the latter will be held liable for any loss associated to the property while it is in his hand.

---

[25] Qur'ān, 17:34.

Conclusion

1. Delegated authority refers to the authority of the agent and the guardian.

2. A contract of agency has three elements namely; principal, agent and Subject matter.

3. The subject matter of agency is the act for the performance of which agent is appointed.

4. The subject-matter of agency should fulfil the following conditions:

    a- It should be known to the agent;

    b- It should be lawful; and

    c- It should admit of representation.

5. The agent is required to perform the undertaking according to the instructions of the principal and exercise due care and skill.

6. Agency comes to an end by a number of circumstances such as mutual agreement, unilateral termination, discharge of obligation, destruction of the subject matter and the death or loss of legal capacity.

7. The dispositions of the *fuḍūlī* (self imposed agent) are lawful subject to ratification by the principal in the opinion of Ḥanafī and Mālikī jurists.

8. Guardianship is an authority granted by the Sharī‘ah to a person over the person and property of another person by virtue of which his dispositions in respect of such persons are assigned legal effect.

9. Islamic Law acknowledges guardianship for the father, the executor appointed by him, the father's father, the executor appointed by him and judge.

10. It is a basic requirement of guardianship that all actions and dispositions of the guardian should be directed towards realisation of the interest of the ward.

CHAPTER -7

ṢAḤIḤ, FĀSID AND BĀṬIL CONTRACTS

The Muslim jurists classify contracts into *ṣaḥīḥ* (valid), *bāṭil* (void) and *fāsid* (voidable or irregular) contracts with regard to their legal validity. A *ṣaḥīḥ* contract is that whose *aṣl* (nature and essence) and *wasf* (accessory circumstances or attributes) are in accordance with law. Thus, a contract will be deemed valid when:

i)   its elements are complete;

ii) conditions relating to elements have been met; and

iii) it is free from external prohibited attributes.

Thus, if any of the elements is missing or a condition is not met or the Lawgiver has prohibited it due to some attribute attached to it, the contract is *bāṭil* or *fāsid*.

A contract will, therefore, be *bāṭil* or *fāsid* if the acceptance is missing or it does not correspond with the offer or one of the parties does not possess legal capacity or the subject matter is non-existent or it cannot be delivered or the contract contains an element of *ribā* (interest) or *gharar* (indeterminacy). Thus, the contract is *bāṭil* as an element is missing or a condition has not been fulfilled or an attribute opposes the command of the Lawgiver and each of these results in the same effect according to the majority, i.e., the contract is *bāṭil*.[1]

The Ḥanafīs divided contracts into three kinds: *ṣaḥīḥ, fāsid* and *bāṭil*.

Valid or ṣaḥīḥ contract

The *ṣaḥīḥ* contract is said to be concluded when all its element are found, the conditions of each element have been met and it also possesses such attributes of extrinsic nature which the law takes notice

---

[1] Ḥassān, *al-Madkhal li Dirāsāt al-Fiqh al-Islāmī*, pp.439-430.

of. There is no disagreement among the Ḥanafīs and other jurists regarding this meaning of the *ṣaḥīḥ* contract.[2]

It has been mentioned earlier that according to majority there are three elements of contract namely, the *Sīghah* (form) offer and acceptance; the subject-matter and contracting parties. The Lawgiver has assigned further conditions to these elements. The *sīghah* requires conformity between offer and acceptance, their issuance in the same session, existence of the *ījāb* till the issuance of *qabūl*. It also requires that a party to the contract must be sane, pubert. And that the subject - matter must be legal, in existence, deliverable and known.

If the elements are present and the conditions are met the contract comes into existence in the eyes of the Lawgiver. However, it cannot be called *ṣaḥīḥ* or which is legally enforceable (*mun'aqid*) unless it is free from external prohibited attributes like *ribā*, and *gharar*. If a contract contains any such attributes the Ḥanafīs consider such a contract as *fāsid*. The Ḥanafīs define the *ṣaḥīḥ* contract as that which is legal in its *aṣl* as well as *wasf*. The *aṣl* here stands for the elements and conditions and the *wasf* for the external attributes, or accessory circumstances or non-essential quality of contract. According to Ḥanafī jurists a contract, which contains the condition of *ribā*, is not a void contract because *ribā* occurs either in a loan contract or in a sale transaction, which are basically permissible. It is the vitiating condition of *ribā*, which invalidates such a contract. Thus, it is valid by virtue of the validity of loan or sale, but not by virtue of invalidating accessory attribute of *ribā*. Such a contract, according to Ḥanafī jurists will not be declared void; instead it is an irregular contract that can be made lawful by removing the invalidating condition of *ribā*.[3]

Similarly, a contract that contains an element of uncertainty, indeterminacy or want of knowledge is not a void contract. The example of indeterminacy is where a seller tells a buyer, "I sell you one sheep out of these three sheep", or where a sale takes place without fixing the price of object. In both the cases the sale is *fāsid*,

---

[2] Madkūr, , *al-Madkhal li al-Fiqh al-Isālmī*,Cairo: Dār al-Nahdah al-'Arabiyyah,1380/1960, p.601.
[3] See Sanhūrī, *Maṣādir al-Ḥaqq*, vol. 2, pp. 147, 151.

i.e., irregular according to Ḥanafī jurists, which can be regularised by removing the cause of irregularity, i.e., by identifying the sheep and fixing the price.[4]

The ḥukm of ṣaḥīḥ contract

A *ṣaḥīḥ* contract is assigned all its effects that Lawgiver has determined for it. These effects come into being on conclusion of the contract if it is enforced (*nāfidh)* and after the removal of the cause of suspension if it is *mawqūf* or suspended contract.[5]

Kinds of Valid Contract

A *ṣaḥīḥ* contract. as we have said. is one. which is legal both as regards its *aṣl* and the *waṣf.* Such a contract must give rise to the effects assigned to it by the Lawgiver. Some jurists maintain. however. that there are *ṣaḥīḥ* contracts the effects of which can be delayed till the happening of a future event. Such contracts are called *mawqūf* contracts, i e., held up in suspense. This is the opinion of the Ḥanafīs. Mālikīs. and some Ḥanbalīs The Shāfiʿīs and some Ḥanbalīs do not admit delay in the effects of the contracts. According to them a *ṣaḥīḥ* contract must give rise to its effects immediately, i.e.. it must be *nāfidh* (operative). *Mawqūf* or suspended contracts thus have no existence according to these jurists. Thus. a *mawqūf* contract is a kind of valid contract. It is a contract, which is not immediately enforceable. Dr. Sanhūrī regards it a voidable contract.[6]

i- The *nāfidh* (operative or immediate contract):

The *nāfidh* contract is that in which:

a)   the elements are found;

b)   the conditions are met;

c)   the external attributes are legal; and

d)   the contract is not dependent upon ratification.

ii-The *Mawqūf* contract is that in which

---

[1] Ḥassān. *al-Madkhal li Dirāsāt al-Fiqh al-Islāmī* p. 432.

[5] Ibid. p. 431.

[6] Sanhūrī. *Maṣādir al-Ḥaqq*, p.276.

a)   the elements are found;

b)   conditions are met;

c)   *waṣf* is legal; but

d)   the effects are dependent upon ratification

This contract. as we have noted. is not acceptable to the Shāfi'īs and some Ḥanbalīs

Causes of suspension

The cause due to which the effects of a *ṣaḥīḥ* contract are suspended may be summarized as under:

a) **Defective capacity:** Contracts of minor possessed with discretion (*ṣabī mumayyaz)* or the one under interdiction (*ḥajr)* due to *safah* (weakness of intellect) or *'atah* (lunacy or partial insanity)

b) **Lack of proper authority:**Contracts in which a person acts on behalf of another without proper authority are suspended. These are the contracts of a *fuḍūlī*. i.e., one who is neither guardian nor agent nor the owner or contracts of an agent who transgresses the limits prescribed by the principal

c) **Right of third party:**If the owner sells the mortgaged property. it will be subject to the ratification of the mortgagee.

The cases of *maraḍ al mawt* (death illness) and *ghaṣb* (usurpation) are also treated the same way We may analyse the above causes in little more detail.

a) **Contracts suspended due to defective capacity:** The *ṣabī mumayyaz* can be permitted to undertake certain kinds of transactions Those. which are purely harmful. cannot be permitted. Those. which result in benefit only. are allowed. However. a transaction by such a minor in which there is a likelihood of both benefit and harm are valid subject to ratification. The ratification may be accorded by the guardian after the transaction and before the minor attains puberty or by the minor himself after majority in case the guardian did not reject the contract before attaining majority.

The *ḥukm* of such a contract is that before ratification there are no effects and ownership is not transferred in goods or price. Once ratification is granted it acts retrospectively and the effects come into operation from the date of the contract. In case ratification is refused the contract becomes void.

b) **Suspension due to lack of proper authority:** The rules relating to the *fuḍūlī* have already been studied and are applicable here. The contracts of the *fuḍūlī* are *ṣaḥīḥ* but *mawqūf*. If such contracts are ratified by one who possesses the authority then the effects come into operation. Refusal to ratify shall make the contracts of the *fuḍūlī* void. In case the *fuḍūlī* has delivered the property, the *aḥkām* of *ghāṣb* (usurpation) shall operate against him, i.e., he shall return the property or become liable for compensation. Ratification ofcourse shall operate from the time of the contract.

c) **Suspension due to right of third parties:** There are cases where a person has the capacity and authority to act, i.e., he is the owner of the subject matter, but the rights of third parties are linked to it. The contract thus, is suspended and needs to be ratified by such third party.[7]

Thus, if A, a mortgager decides to sell his property mortgaged with B from whom he has borrowed money, the right of B is likely to be endangered. B can claim that his loan be repaid first. This contract shall, therefore be suspended. In case B decided to forgo his claim upon the property he may ratify the contract, which shall be declared. In case he refuses to do so the contract shall become *bāṭil*. It may be mentioned here that before ratification by B, the buyer has a right to revoke the

---

See Sanhūrī, *Maṣādir al-Ḥaqq*, pp. 128-130; Ḥassān, *al-Madkhal*, pp. 449,450; Zuhaylī, *al-Fiqh al-Islāmī wa adillatuhū*, vol. 4, pp. 229-230

Contract but A the mortgager/seller has no right to revoke the contact of sale made by him.

In the case of *maraḍ al mawt* (death illness) we know that any transaction, which is not at market value, will take the *ḥukm* of bequest and shall be valid up to one-third of the property. Beyond one-third of the property ratification shall be required from persons whose rights are affected namely the creditors and heirs.

The Lāzim (binding) and Jā'iz (Non-binding) Contract

A contract, which is *ṣaḥīḥ* and *nāfidh* is divisible into *lāzim* (binding) and *ghayr lāzim* also known as *Jā'iz*. (non-binding or terminable).

The Lāzim Contract

The *lāzim* contract is that in which none of the parties has a right to revoke the contract without the consent of the other, unless options have been granted to a party by virtue of which the right to revoke can be exercised.

The *Jā'iz* or *ghayr lāzim* Contract

It is that contract in which the right to revoke can be exercised by either party without the consent of the other party. The reason for a contract being *ghayr lāzim* or revocable are two:

a) The nature of the contract, which allows independence to both parties as in *wakālah* (agency), *sharikah* (partnership), *wadī'ah* (deposit), *kafālah* (suretyship), and *āriyah* (commodate loans). These contracts are *jā'iz* (terminable) or *ghayr lāzim* (non-binding) with respect to either party or one of them.

b) An option is stipulated in the contract that prevents it from becoming *lāzim* Thus, the party possessing the option can revoke the contract without the consent of the other party within the period of the option[x] (options have been discussed in detail under the title "Islamic Law of Options").

---

[x] See Ḥassān. *al-Madkhal*, pp. 452.453.

Fāsid (Irregular Contract)

The *fāsid* (irregular) contract is that whose elements are present (i.e., offer and acceptance) and all the essential conditions are complete, but an external attribute attached to the contract has been prohibited by the Lawgiver. The contract is legal as regards its *aṣl* but it is not proper as the *waṣf* is prohibited.[9]

Causes of Irregularity in Fāsid contracts:

Some important causes, which render a contract *fāsid are as follows:*

    i)   defective consent, i.e., a consent obtained through coercion;

    ii)   want of knowledge leading to dispute (*gharar* and *jahl*);

    iii)   invalid condition or an ancillary condition not being collateral to the contract and not admitted by commercial usage and being one, which gives advantage to one of the contracting parties at the cost of the other; and

    iv)   ribā (usury) or undue enrichment.[10]

Discussion of the cause of irregularity in detail:

1. Defective consent due to coercion:

The Majority of the Muslim jurists hold the view that a contract made under coercion is a void contract. The Ḥanafī jurists, on the other hand, view it as an irregular contract. To them such contract must be dissolved. However, if the coerced party after the removal of coercion ratifies the contract, it will become a valid contract. Thus, it can be regularised by ratification. According to Imām Zufar, a Ḥanafī jurist, it is a valid contract, however, it is suspended one, which is subject to ratification.[11] To him coercion is an impediment to enforcement of contract not to its validity. The ratification of irregular contract is possible before possession as well as after it.

---

[9] Zaydān. *al-Madkhal li dirāsāt al-Sharī'ah al-Islāmiyyah.* p. 366

[10] Sanhūrī. *Maṣādir al-Ḥaqq* vol. 2. p. 127.

[11] Zuhaylī. *al-Fiqh al-Islāmī wa adillatuhū.* vol. 4. p. 380.

II.Want of knowledge:

Want of knowledge that invalidates contracts is the one that is likely to lead to dispute among the parties. For example, a person sold an unidentified sheep out of herd of sheep. This will certainly give rise to a dispute between the contracting parties because the buyer would naturally ask for the best sheep in the flock, whereas the seller would like to give the worst. It is, however, permissible to sell one item out of few identified items with the option of determination in favour of the purchaser.

Want of knowledge affecting the validity of contract is of the following types:

1. want of knowledge relating to the subject-matter such as indeterminate object in a sale contract, or unidentified property in leasing contract;

2. want of knowledge relating to consideration. It is where price of the sold article has not been fixed, and is left unspecified;

3. want of knowledge relating to the time of performance. For example. A rented his house to B without fixing the hiring period, or A sold an object to B on credit without specifying the time of payment of price. Indeterminacy of period in a partnership contract does not invalidate it because partnership is a non-binding contract in Ḥanafī jurisprudence. It can be terminated at any time.

4. Want of knowledge relating to means of suretyship. Thus, if seller asked the purchaser to provide a guarantor or pledge some property as security for the deferred price of sale, it is necessary that the guarantor or pledged property be identified and made known to the creditor, otherwise the contract will be irregular on account of want of knowledge relating to means of suretyship.[12]

Gharar or uncertainty relating to necessary characteristics of a commodity also renders a contract irregular in the following manner:

a) In sale contract: If a person sold a cow believing that it gives a particular quantity of milk, it will be an irregular sale

---

[12] Ibid, pp. 379-380

because of uncertainty of milk yield or if he sold a cow believing that it bears in its womb a calf, again the sale is irregular on account of uncertainty.

b). In partnership contracts: If the contracting parties agreed on particular amount of profit for one party, the contract is irregular because it is possible that partnership earns only that much profit which has been stipulated for one party or it does not earn anything. A contract of partnership with such a stipulation is regarded irregular.[13]

III- Invalid condition or an ancillary condition not being collateral to the contract:

Irregularity can also arise from the stipulation of an irregular condition. In Ḥanafī jurisprudence a condition is deemed to be irregular in the following cases:[14]

i) When it is repugnant to the requisite of the contract such as to stipulate that the buyer will not sell the object he has purchased; or he will not rent it out, or to stipulate in a marriage contract that husband will not establish matrimonial relationship with his wife.

ii) When it is expressly prohibited by the Lawgiver, like selling an article on the condition that the purchaser will sell something else to the buyer or lend him some money or make him a gift. Such conditions are prohibited because Islamic Law expressly prohibits combination of two mutually inconsistent contracts and a loan and a sale.

iii) When it is against the commercial usage such as condition by the purchaser of corn that the seller will grind it, or a condition by a buyer of a piece of cloth that the seller will sew it.

iv) When it is advantageous to one party at the cost of other party. For example, where the seller reserves for himself an advantage from the sale such as the condition that he shall reside in the house sold for a period of two months after sale, or he will lend him some money.

---

[13]Muṣṭafā Aḥmad Zarqā, *al-Madkhal al-Fiqhī,*
   al-'Āmm, Demascus:Maṭba 'ah Tarbīn,1387/1968, vol. 2, pp.699,700.
[14] Zuhaylī, *al-Fiqh al-Islāmī wa adillatuhū.*, vol. 4, pp. 381,382.

Examples of such irregular conditions in a marriage contract is a stipulations by a wife that husband will not marry another woman, or he will never divorce her, or he will divorce the existing wife. All such conditions render a contract irregular. It is pertinent to note here that these irregular conditions affect only the commutative contracts such as contract of sale, hiring, and cultivation, and do not affect gratuitous contracts such as gift, donation, *waqf* or the contracts of suretyship such as *kafālah*, mortgage, and *hawālah* (assignment of debt), or the contract of marriage. Irregular conditions in the aforesaid contracts do not invalidate them. Only the invalid condition is abrogated. The other part of the contract remains valid and effective. (Extrinsic conditions have been dealt with in detail in chapter 11, entitled "Extrinsic Conditions and their Effect on Contract".)

IV. Ribā:

Ribā occurs either in a loan transaction or in a barter contract. *Ribā* in a loan transaction means to stipulate excess over and above the principal sum to be paid by the debtor. It also takes place in a barter transaction. It is where a person exchanges two commodities of the same kind with excess such as two parties exchange 5 k.g. of wheat for 7 k.g. of wheat.

According to Hanafi jurists a contract containing an element of *ribā* is an irregular contract. It can be made valid by removing the cause of irregularity. Thus, if the party, which has stipulated excess in its favour, annuls the condition of excess in the session of contract, the contract will become a valid contract. The issue of *ribā* has been discussed in detail in chapter 9 under the title " Extrinsic Causes of Invalidity:Ribā (Usury)"

The ḥukm of an irregular contract

Before Possession:

Legal effects are only assigned to the *ṣaḥīḥ* contract and not to an irregular contract. This rule has been applied by the Hanafīs to an irregular contract in which possession of the property has not been delivered. Such a contract must be revoked without the consent of either party. Thus, ownership in the property is not transferred and no rights and obligations have arisen. The seller cannot demand the price nor can the buyer force the seller to deliver the goods. The parties to such a contract have no option to permit an irregular contract or to relinquish the right of revocation. Each one of the parties can revoke the contract without the consent of the other.

The only way in which an irregular contract can become a valid or *ṣaḥīḥ* contract is by the removal of the cause of irregularity, i.e, the removal of the prohibited *waṣf*. Thus, if a contract declared irregular because of *ribā*, which is stipulated in the contract such irregularity can be removed if the party in whose favour *ribā* has been stipulated, decides to forgo it.

After Possession:

If the parties to the contract decide to implement it, e.g., the delivery of the goods by the seller to the buyer and delivery of the price to him by the buyer, then this contract, is strengthened somewhat as compared to the position before delivery. The result of this is that the right to revocation, which rested with, either party without the consent of the other now will rest with the party who had the benefit of the condition. This is so in cases like sale for an undetermined period or with the condition of extending credit to the seller. As regards cases like *ribā* or where the price is in form of wine, the right of revocation still rests with both parties.

When the buyer takes possession of property with the consent of the seller, then he can use it as the ownership passes to him by possession. In such a case, his obligation is to pay the value or market price of the goods purchased to the seller and not the price that was fixed in the agreement. Article 371 of the Majallah points to this fact. It reads: "In *bay' fāsid*, where the buyer has received a thing sold with the permission of the seller, he becomes the owner ".[15]

However, the parties can still revoke it if the buyer has not disposed of it. In such a case, if the seller wishes to resume the object, he must first pay the purchase-money to the buyer.[16] Until such

---

[15] *Majallat al-Aḥkām al-'Adliyyah*, Art. 371.
[16] Ibid, Art. 373.

restitution the goods are held by the purchaser as a pledge.[17] But if the buyer disposed of the property by resale or donation or added or subtracted from it, or changed it in such a way that it can no longer be regarded as the same object, then there is no right for either party to annul the contract.[18] Thus, where the buyer has sold the property, this second sale is valid and legally enforceable, it cannot be obstructed in Islamic Law by the fact that first sale was irregular.

Difference Between Valid and Irregular Contracts

Some differences between valid contract and irregular contracts are as follows:

1. Ownership in a valid contract is transferred from the seller to the purchaser by mere offer and acceptance, whereas in irregular contract it is transferred to him by possession taken with the consent of the seller.

2. In an irregular sale the value of the thing, i.e., its market price, is admissible whereas in a valid contract agreed price is paid. In an irregular hiring contract the lesser is entitled to equitable and proper rent (according to market rate) and not to the specified rent. Similarly, in an irregular partnership, each partner gets the profit in proportion to his capital and not according to the agreement.

Revocation of Irregular Contract

Islamic Law does not approve of an irregular contract. Therefore, its revocation is necessary regardless of whether delivery has been made or not. However, it cannot be revoked if the subject-matter has changed shape or is destroyed or has been disposed of by the buyer through sale or donation, and the second purchaser has sold it further. In all these cases the contract cannot be revoked.[19]

Some forms of Irregular Contract

Some important forms of irregular transactions according to Hanafī jurists are as follows:

---

[17] Marghīnānī. *Hedāyah*, tr. Charls Hamilton,Sweedon,1891, p. 276.
[18] *Majallah*, Article 372.
[19] Zarqā, *al-Madkhal al-Fiqhī al-'Āmm*, vol. 2, p. 703.

1. Bay' al-Majhūl: It refers to a sale in which the object of sale or its price or the time of its payment remains unknown and unspecified.

2. Contingent contract: It is a contract that is contingent upon an uncertain event. For example says to B, "I sell you my house if X sold me his house".

3. Sale contract effective from future date: It is a contract that comes into effect from future date:

4. Bay al ghā'ib : It is a sale of what is not visible at the meeting of the parties. The seller in *bay al-ghā'ib* has title over the subject matter but it is not available at the parties' meeting because it is elsewhere.

5. Sale contract with unlawful consideration: It refers to a sale whose consideration or price is something prohibited by Islamic law such as wine or pork.

6 .Bay'al-'Īnah: It is to sell a property on credit for a certain price and then to buy it back at a price less than the sale price on prompt payment, both transactions taking place simultaneously in the same session of the contract. According to Imām Abū Yūsuf, a Ḥanafī jurist, such sale is valid.

7. Two sales in one: Where a single contract relates to two sales. Such as to sell one commodity for two prices, one being cash and the other credit price, making contract binding against one of the two prices.[20]

The bāṭil Contract

A *bāṭil* contract is defined by the Ḥanafīs as that which is illegal in its *aṣl* as well as its *waṣf*.[21] The word *aṣl* refers to elements and essential conditions pertaining thereto while the *waṣf* is the external attribute. The Ḥanafī say that there is only one element, i.e., *ṣīghah* (form). The *ṣīghah* has conditions that relate to *ījāb* and *qabūl* like conformity between them, their issuance in the same *majlis*, existence of the *ījāb* till the issuance of the *qabūl* or those, which relate to the capacity of

---

[20] See, Zuhaylī, *al-Fiqh al-Islāmī wa adillatuhū*, vol.4, pp.454-472.
[21] Zaydān, *al-Madkhal*, p. 366.

the parties or the subject-matter. If any of these conditions is not fulfilled the contract becomes *bāṭil*. All this relates to the *aṣl*. As regards the *waṣf* they maintain that it is an external attribute introduced into the contract by the parties, which is against Islamic Law.

The *bāṭil* contract does not give rise to any effect. Thus, no ownership is transferred nor is any kind of obligation found. The reason is that the contract in itself is prohibited and what is prohibited cannot give rise to rights. Performance of the contract is, therefore, not possible and none of the parties can enforce it.[22] If delivery of the goods has already been made then the property must be returned to the other party regardless of whether such illegality was known to the parties. If the buyer sells the goods to a third party after taking delivery, the original seller cannot be prevented from claiming the goods. The reason is that ownership cannot be transferred through a contract that is *bāṭil*. This *ḥukm* is clearly different from that of a *fāsid* contract.

Ratification also has no role to play in a *bāṭil* contract. In case a *bāṭil* contract is concluded by a person suffering from death illness then the creditors or heirs have a right to claim restitution of property.

Causes of Invalidity

The causes which render a contract invalid, may be divided into two kinds:

a) **Intrinsic causes:** These are the causes, which relate to *aṣl* or elements of contract such as the unlawfulness of subject-matter, non-existence of subject-matter, the absence of contractual capacity.

b) **Extrinsic causes:** Extrinsic causes are the causes, that relate to *waṣf*, i.e., external attribute such as the contract contains element of *ribā* or *gharar*. It is pertinent to note that *ribā* and *gharar* are causes of irregularity of contract in Ḥanafī Law while in other schools they are causes of invalidity of contract. We will discuss here causes, which relate to first kind. (*ribā* and *gharar* have been discussed in the following chapters).

---

[22]Zuhaylī, *al-Fiqh al-Islāmī wa adillatuhū,* vol. 4, p. 237.

1. Unlawful Object :

It is a condition for the validity of a contract that the object of the
contract be legal and lawful. It means that the object should be a thing
in which transactions are permissible in the *Sharī'ah*. It should be
ritually and legally clean. Any substance which is religiously and
legally unclean, and the disposal of which have been restricted, cannot
be a valid object of sale; e.g., wine, pig, intoxicants, blood and
carcasses. The Ḥanafī jurists do not consider bones of dead animals,
hair, skin. filth, so they allow their sale.[23] The rule to them is that
anything not prone to death and decay is pure.

The legality of the object further requires that the purpose of
the contract and its underlying cause should be recognized by the
Sharī'ah. It should not be contrary to the objectives of the *Sharī'ah*.
Therefore, a contract to run a brothel or a gambling house is void,
because in the former case the contract is contrary to the preservation
of the family unit, progeny and offspring which is an objective of the
Sharī'ah and, in the letter case, the object is opposed to the
preservation of property and amounts to devouring another person's
properties wrongfully.[24]

The legality of the object also means that the act or service
which is the subject-matter of contract must not be harmful for the
contracting parties or the general public, e.g., hoarding commodities,
growing of opium, a contract to kill a person, to usurp the property, or
deprive a person of his property without compensation. [25]

Furthermore, if the object does not fulfill the intended
objectives, again it will be held to be a void contract. Thus vegetables
cannot be made the object of a pledge, because the purpose of a pledge
is to retain pledged prope ty and to sell it for satisfaction of the claim
whereas vegetables are easily perishable. They, therefore, do not serve
the intended purpose. Likewise public roads and public parks cannot

---

[23]See Kāsānī , *Badā'i' al-Ṣanā'i'*, vol. 5, p.140; *Mughnī al-Muḥtāj,*
    vol.2, p.11; Ibn Qudāmah , *al-Mughnī*, vol. 4, p.260.
[24] See Zuhaylī, *al-Fiqh al-Islāmī*, vol. 4, pp.185-186.
[25]Mushtaq Aḥmad, *Business Ethics in Islām*,Islamabad,International
    Institute of Islamic Thought and International Institute of Islamic
    Economics,1995, p.95.

be made the objects of sale, because they are meant for the benefit of the public not for the benefit of an individual or a specific group of people.[26]

2. Absence of Contractual Capacity:

As mentioned earlier, it is a requirement for a valid contract that the contracting parties be competent to conclude a contract. This means that they should be major and sane, and not prevented from transactions. Thus a contract will be deemed void if it is entered into:

i)   by an insane person.

ii)   by a minor not possessed with discretion. (*ṣabī ghayr mumayyaz*).

iii) by a minor possessed with discretion if he made a transaction which is harmful to him or a transaction which may equally result in benefit and loss without permission of his guardian.

iv)   by a *ma'tūh* (partially insane) if it is a harmful contract for him.

v)   by a *safīh* (weak of intellect) after he has been put under interdiction by the court.

vi)   by a *muflis* (bankrupt) whose debt exceed his earnings and the court, on the demand of his creditors has passed prohibitory orders. The disposal of property by such a person would be invalid and will produce no effects after such interdiction by the court.

vii) by a *fuḍūlī* (unauthorized agent) whose action has not been subsequently ratified by the principal.

3. Non-existence of the subject- matter :

Non-existence of the subject-matter is generally considered a cause of invalidity of contract. This principle applies to both commutative and gratuitous contracts. Mālikī jurists, however, allow

---

[26]Zaydān, *al-Madkhal li Dirāsāt al-Sharī'ah al-Islāmiyyah*, p.308.

donation or gift of a non-existent object.[27] Hence it is permissible in their opinion to donate fruit a palm tree will produce next year. According to other jurists the object of contract should exist at the time of contract regardless of whether the contract is commutative or gratuitous. Examples of non-existent objects are:

a)   sale of fruits before they have made appearance;

b)   sale of unborn animal;and

c)   sale of milk in the udders.

Contracts of *salam* and *istiṣnā'* are approved by way of *'Istiḥsān* (juristic preference) despite absence of the object of contract.

4. Illegal purpose:

It is a requirement of valid contract that its object and motivating cause should be lawful. Thus, any contract contrary to the intention of the Lawgiver and against the objectives of the *Sharī'ah* is considered invalid in Islamic Law. Therefore, selling a weapon to a person who will use it to kill an innocent person, to enter a marriage contract in order to facilitate re-marriage between the divorced couple are invalid contracts.

In conclusion, we may say that a contract is valid according to the requirements of the *Sharī'ah* with regard to its essence and external attributes while a void contract is contrary to Islamic Law both in its essence as well as external attributes; it does not give rise to any effect.

Conclusion

The above discussion may be summarized as follows:

1.   A *ṣaḥīḥ* (valid) contract is that whose basic elements, conditions and external attributes are in accordance with Islamic Law.

---

[27] See Ibn Rushd, *Bidāyat al-Mujtahid* vol.2, p.331, Qarāfi, *al-Furūq*, Beriut: al-Kutub al-'Ilmiyyah,1986, vol.1, p.150; Ibn Juzy, *al-Qawanīn al-Fiqhiyyah*,Beriut:Dār al-'Ilm li al-Malāyīn,1973, p.352.

2. A *bāṭil* (void) contract is contrary to Islamic Law both in its essence and external attributes. It does not give rise to any effect

3. A *fāsid* (irregular) contract is one whose elements and essential conditions are valid according to the *Sharī'ah*, but an external attribute attached to the contract has been prohibited by Islamic Law.

4. Important causes of irregularity are defective consent, want of knowledge, invalid condition and element of *ribā,*.

5. An irregular contract can become a valid contract by the removal of the cause of irregularity.

6. Ownership in an irregular contract is transferred to the buyer by the possession taken with the consent of seller, not merely by the contract.

7. In an irregular sale contract the value or the market price of the thing and not the agreed price is paid to the seller.

CHAPTER- 8

EXTRINSIC CAUSES OF INVALIDITY: GHARAR (UNCERTAINTY)

Gharar is one of the major causes of the Invalidity of a contract. It is an external prohibited attribute that invalidates the contracts. Literally, *gharar* means risk or hazard. *Taghrīr* being the verbal noun of *gharar* is to unknowingly expose oneself or one's property to jeopardy.[1] It includes such elements as doubt, suspicion, uncertain conditions, the absolute lack of knowledge about and in determinability of the basic elements of the subject-matter.

Definitions of Gharar

1. According to Sarakhsī: *Gharar* takes place where the consequences (of a transaction) remain unknown.[2]

2. According to Ibn-Ḥazm: *Gharar* in sales occurd where the purchaser does not know what he has bought and the seller does not know what he has sold.[3]

3. Ibn 'Ābidīn defines *gharar* in the following words: *Gharar* is uncertainty about the existence of the subject-matter of sale.[4]

4. Ibn al-Qayyim has described *gharar* as being the subject matter, the vendor is not in position to hand over to the buyer whether the subject matter exists or not.[5]

---

[1] Moḥammad Siddīq Darīr, *al-Gharar fī al-'Uqūd wa Āthāruhu fī al-Tatbīqāt al-Mu'āṣirah*, p.10.

[2] Sarakhsī, Abū Bakr Muḥammad Ibn Aḥmad, *al-Mabsūt*, Beriut:Dār al-Ma'rif,1978,vol.13, p.194.

[3] Ibn Ḥazm, *al-Muḥallah*, Dār al- Āfāq al-Jadīdah,vol. 8, pp. 343-389.

[4] Ibn 'Ābidīn, *Radd al-Muḥtār*, vol. 4, p.147.

[5] Ibn al-Qayyim, *I'lām al-Mu'qqi'īn*, vol. 1, p.357.

5. According to Ibn Rushd, *gharar* is to be found in contracts of sale when the seller suffers a disadvantage as a result of his ignorance, with regard to price of the article · or the indispensable criteria relating to the contract or its object or quality or time of delivery.[6]

6. Sanhūrī, an eminent modern jurist is of the view that lack of knowledge about the material terms of contract is the distinct feature of a *gharar* contract. He says that *gharar* takes place in the following circumstances:

   a) when it is not known whether the subject-matter exists;

   b) if it exists at all, whether it can be handed over to the buyer;

   c) when want of knowledge affects the identification of the genus or species of subject matter;

   d) when it affects its quantum, identity or necessary conditions;and

   e) when it relates to the date of a future performance.[7]

Forms of gharar according to Ibn Juzy

Ibn Juzay, a Mālikī jurist, has given a list of ten cases, which constitute in his view, a forbidden *gharar*:

i) Difficulty in putting the buyer in possession of subject-matter, such as sale of a stray animal or the unborn offspring when the mother is not part of the sale.

ii) Want of knowledge with regard to the price or the subject matter, such as the vendor saying to buyer, "I sell you what is under my sleeve".

iii) Want of knowledge with regard to the characteristics of the subject-matter such as the vendor saying to the potential

---

[6] Ibn Rush, *Bidāyat al-Mujtahid*, vol. 2, p.156.
[7] Sanhūrī, *Maṣādir al-Ḥaqq*, vol. 3, pp.31-41.

buyer: "I sell you a piece of cloth which is in my home". Another example is the sale of an article without the buyer inspecting or the seller describing it.

iv) Want of knowledge with regard to the quantum or the price or the quantity of the subject matter, such as an offer to sell "at today's price" or "at the market price".

v) Want of knowledge regarding the date of future performance, such as an offer to sell when a particular person enters the room or when a particular person dies.

vi) Two sales in one transaction, such as selling one article at two different prices, one for cash and the other for credit; or selling two different articles at one price: one for immediate remittance and the other for a deferred payment.

vii) Sale of what is not expected to revive such as the sale of a sick animal.

viii) *Bay' al-ḥasāt*, which is a type of sale whose outcome is determined by throw of a stone.

ix) *Bay' al-munābadhah:* a sale performed by the vendor throwing a cloth at the buyer and achieving the sale transaction without giving the buyer the opportunity for properly examining the object of sale.

x) *Bay' al-mulāmasah*, where the bargain is struck by touching the object of the sale without examining it.[8]

Forms of gharar transactions according to Siddīq al-Darīr

Siddīq al-Darīr an eminent modern scholar of *Sharī'ah* has given a detailed list of transactions that involve element of *gharar*. *Gharar*, in his view, sometimes relates to the form of contract and sometimes to its subject matter.[9]

---

[8] Ibn Juzy, *Qawanīn al-Aḥkām al-Sharʿiyyah*, pp. 282,283.
[9] Darīr, *al-Gharar fī al-ʿUqūd*, pp. 13-30.

I- Gharar or uncertainty relating to ṣīghah (form) of contract:

The transactions belonging to this category are as follows:

1.Two Sales in one: Two sales in one means that a single contract relates to two sales. It is where a seller says to a buyer: "I sell you this commodity for hundred (Rupees) on cash and hundred and fifty on credit", and the buyer accepts it without specifying the price at which he will buy the commodity. The *gharar* inherent in this contract is indeterminacy of the price. Thus the seller does not know at which price the buyer will buy the object.

2. Earnest money ('Arbūn) sale: It is a sale in which a person buys an item and pays a certain amount of money in advance to the seller on condition that if the transaction is completed the advance will be adjusted and if the bargain is cancelled the seller will not return the advance.

The majority of Muslim Jurists except Imām Aḥmad, hold that earnest money sale is invalid[10] because it amounts to taking of other's money without any compensation and also because it involves uncertainty regarding the completion of transaction. Darīr is inclined to majority's view of invalidity.[11]

In our view earnest money is in the nature of an option contract. The money is being paid as a consideration to gain time from the selling party. The selling party is reciprocating by restraining himself in exercise of his legal right in respect of his property. However, the earnest money cannot be forfeited if the transaction cannot be completed because of the fault of selling party.

3. Contingent Sale: It is a contract that is contingent upon a condition e.g. "I sell you my house if A sold his house to me". The *gharar* at work behind this contract is that it is contingent upon the

---

[10] See *Bidāyat al-Mujtahid*, vol.2, p.161, Ibn Qudāmah, *al-Sharḥ*

al-Kabīr, vol3, p.63; Ibn 'uzy, *al-Qawānīn al-fiqhiyyah*, p.258; Shirbīnī, *Mughnī al-Muḥtāj*, vol.2, p.39.

[11] See Darīr, *al-Gharar fī al- 'uqūd* , p.14.

happening of an uncertain future event. Such sale is void in the opinion of the majority of Muslim Jurists. Imām Ibn Taymiyyah regards it valid.[12]

4. Contract effective from future date: It is a contract, which comes into effect at some future date e.g. the contract, shall be effective from such and such date. The *gharar* contained in such sale according to Darīr is the possible change in price or other circumstances of the sale, which may affect real consent of the contracting parties when the time of performance approaches. But the fact is that there is no *gharar* in such sale. This sale is also valid in the opinion of Imām Ibn Taymiyyah.[13]

II. Gharar or uncertainty relating to subject- matter:

This is of the following eight types:

1. Uncertainty regarding the genus of the object: It is where a person says to another. "I sell you an item for ten", and does not specify the object of sale.

2. Uncertainty regarding the kind of the object: Uncertainty and indeterminacy pertains to kind if the seller tells the buyer: "I sell you an animal at such and such price", without indicating the kind of animal.

3. Uncertainty regarding attributes of object: It is where the necessary attributes of the object of the sale are not described.

The opinion of Muslim Jurists is divided regarding the requirement of describing the subject-matter. Ḥanafī Jurists are of the view that the description of subject-matter is not necessary as long as it is present and visible for the buyer. But if the subject-matter is not visible, its description is necessary. Some Ḥanafī jurists disagree with this view and hold that description is not necessary as long as the right of inspection is established for the buyer. By exercising this right he can reject the object if it does not correspond with description. But the proponents of description do not accept this argument. They say that

[12] Ibid: p.16.
[13] Ibid: p.17.

right of inspection is given to buyer only to remove light uncertainty not the excessive one resulting from leaving a thing undescribed. An invisible object, therefore, should be described at the time of contract, and if some uncertainty still remains, it may be removed by exercise of right of inspection.[14]

Mālikī jurists regard description of subject-matter obligatory irrespective of the fact that it is present or absent, visible or invisible.[15]

Three opinions are attributed to Shāfi'ī jurists: **First**, sale is not valid until detailed description is given as in *salam* sale. **Second**, sale is not valid until relevant attributes are mentioned. **Third**, sale is valid even without mentioning attributes of object as long as the buyer has right of inspection.[16]

The Ḥanbalī jurists maintain that sale of an object with unknown attributes is not permissible.[17]

Some sales prohibited explicitly by the text due to uncertainty of the attributes are:

i)   sale of unborn calf without its mother;

ii) sale of embryos; and

iii) sale of bull's sperm etc.

As regard selling what is hidden in the ground such as carrot, onions, garlic, it is allowed by Ḥanafī jurists provided the buyer exercises the right of inspection when he uproots them. The sale of above mentioned things is invalid according to Imām Shāfi'ī and Imām Aḥmad as long as they are hidden in the ground.

To Imām Mālik it is permissible only when the buyer acquires complete knowledge about the object of sale.

---

[14] Ibn 'Ābdīn *al-Durr al-Muḥtār*, vol. 4, p.29.
[15] Ibn Rushd, *Bidāyat al-Mujtahid*, vol. 2, p.148.
[16] Abū Zakariyyā Nawawī, *al-majmū'* Cairo: Maktabah al-'Āṣimah,1966, vol.9, p.288.
[17] Abū Isḥāq Shirāzī, *al-Muhaddab*, Cairo: Dār al-Naṣr vol.4, p.109.

4. Uncertainty regarding the quantity of the object: The knowledge of the quantity of object is necessary for validity of sale. Thus, to sell a heap of grain haphazardly without reference to its quantity is impermissible.

A traditional example of uncertainty regarding the quantity of object is *muzābanah*. It has been explained as sale of fresh dates on the palms against harvested dried dates. It implies buying something whose number, weight and measure is not known.

5. Uncertainty regarding specification of object: *Gharar* relates to specification when things of different entities are sold without specifying one of them in particular such as in the sale of a piece of cloth out of bulk or a sheep out of a herd. Such sale is invalid according to Shāfiʿī and Hanbalī jurists on account of non-specification of object.[18] Hanafī jurists allow it to the extent of three items.[19] For example, the seller tells the buyer: "I sell you one sheep out of these three sheep." This sale is valid provided the buyer has the right to select one out of three later on. Mālikī jurists allow such sale with option of determination for the buyer, without fixing any number. Thus, it can be affected on small number as well as on large number.

6. Uncertainty regarding the time of performance: If the sale is on credit i.e. on deferred payment basis, the time of payment should be made known to the seller.

7. Uncertainty regarding the existence of object: This is another form of *gharar*, which relates to non-existent commodity such as sale of what this animal will produce.

Some jurists have reported *ijmāʿ* (consensus of opinion) of Muslim jurists on declaring sale of non-existent object invalid. They cite in support of this view a *hadīth* narrated by Abū Hurairah (r.a.t.a) that Holy Prophet (s.a.w.s.) prohibited *gharar*

---

[18] Ibid; vol.1, p.863; Ibn Qudāmah, *al-Mughnī*, vol.4, p.131.
[19] Kāsānī, *Badāʾiʿ al-Ṣanāʾiʿ*, vol.5, p.158.

sale.[20] *Gharar* refers to a thing which is not known and whose outcome is concealed.

The fact is that the *ḥadīth* prevents only that non-existent which involves *gharar* such as sale of unborn calf but the things, whose existence is certain in future, are permissible objects of sale because they do not involve any *gharar*, which may lead to dispute and litigation among the parties. An example of this case is *salam* ((sale of future goods with advance) and *istiṣnāʿ* (contract of manufacturing). Both are permissible in the *Sharīʿah* although the subject-matter does not exist at the time of contract.

8. Uncertainty regarding delivery of object: Inability of seller to deliver the object of sale to the buyer also forms *gharar*, which invalidates the contract.

Examples:

i)   Sale of stray animal whose whereabouts are not known to the owner.

ii)   Sale of a car which has been stolen by somebody and the vendor does not know where is it,

iii) Sale of goods yet to be acquired by the seller.

Effect of gharar on contracts

Gharar primarily affects commutative contracts meant for alienation of property for consideration such as sale and hire. The effect of *gharar* on hire is the same as on sale contract. Some points of similarity between the two contracts with regard to the effects of *gharar* are as follows:

i)   ʿArbūn (earnest money) is impermissible in hire as it is unlawful in a sale contract.

ii)   Both the sale and hiring contracts are not allowed to be made contingent upon some uncertain future event.

---

[20] Qarāfī, *al-Furūq*, vol.1, p.150; Ibn Rushd, *Bidāyat al-Mujtahid*, vol.2, p.331.

The rent and rented utility in a hiring contract should be known and specified in the same way as price and commodity should be known in sale contract.

iii) It is a condition of valid sale that its subject-matter should be deliverable. The same rule applies to hiring contract. As such, the *ijārah* of stray animal is not permissible.

iv) The time of *ijārah* should be fixed. In a deferred payment sale the time of payment of price should also be fixed.

The Muslim jurists differ on the effects of *gharar* on gratuitous contracts. To Mālikī jurists, *gharar* has no effect on donations.[21] Thus, it is valid to donate escaped animal, fruits before they ripen. But according to Shāfi'ī, Ḥanafī and Ḥanbalī jurists, the subject matter of donation should be known and determined. They do not allow the donation of an unborn animal or milk in the udders.[22]

As regards will, all the jurists are unanimous that it is valid even if the subject matter is non-existent, undetermined and outside the control of testator or beneficiary. It is, therefore, permissible to make bequest of what an animal or a tree will produce. It is also valid to make bequest of an undetermined portion of property. This testament is treated valid and it is the duty of the heirs to specify that portion.

Insurance: A modern contract of gharar

Definition

> "A contract of Insurance is one whereby one party, i.e., Insurer promises in return for a money consideration, i.e., the premium to pay to the other party, i.e., the insured, a sum of money or provide him with some corresponding benefit, upon the occurrence of an event specified in the contract".[23]

---

[21] Shirāzī, *al-Muhaddab* vol. 1, p.453.

[22] Kāsānī, *Badā'i' al-Ṣanā'i'*, vol.6, p.188.

[23] *Parkington and Anthony On Insurance Law*, London: O'Dowd Sweet & Maxwell 17th Edition, 1981, p.3.

The premium is a price of an insurance policy. "It is the price at which the insurer i.e. the company is prepared to take risks and bear the burden of the probable loss involved in the contract of insurance. On the basis of law of averages and through experience the insurer finds a reasonable amount sufficient to cover his risk as well as other charges including his profit.[24] An insurance policy aims at providing compensation for potential loss or damages that are specified in the contract. For example when a person insures his car with the insurance company he gets an undertaking from the company that it will undertake repairs of the damage, which is caused to the car of insured as a result of an accident.

A contract of insurance is normally a contract of indemnity because it insures a compensation for loss to the insured. The life insurance and personal accidents insurance, however, are not contracts of indemnity for, in all such cases, the insurer has to pay compensation on the happening of an event without reference to loss.[25]

Types of Insurance

With regard to the subject matter of insurance and the risk covered by it, Insurance is of the following four types:[26]

1. Life Insurance:

This is insurance against the loss of life. The objective of life insurance is to provide financial help to the families of insured persons after their death so that in their absence the families do not become destitute and public charges.

2. Health Insurance:

Health insurance policy covers expenses of medical treatment of insured in case of his illness or bodily injury.

---

[24] Liaquat Ali Khan Niazi, *Islamic Law of Contract*, p. 384.

[25] Ibid, p. 386

[26] See M A Chishti, *Islam and Insurance: Alternative options*, paper presented at Senior Officers Training Programme held in Islamabad on Feb.24-, 1992.

3. Property Insurance:

Property Insurance policy provides compensation to the insured who suffered some loss or damage consequent upon occurrence of a catastrophe or disaster inflicted upon his property, assets and other belongings.

4. Liability insurance:

This is also called third party insurance. It refers to a situation where a person/institution incurs some liability towards a third person. These policies cover a variety of business and professional liability exposures. They protect people and organization against financial loss due to legal liability claim. In liability insurance the insurance company undertakes to compensate the effectee on behalf of insured person/institution.

Sharī 'ah appraisal

A large number of contemporary Muslim jurists regard modern commercial insurance invalid and incompatible with the injunctions of Islamic Law.[27] Islamic Law does not allow *gharar* transactions in which the seller does not know what he has sold and the purchaser does not know what he has purchased. In insurance, the buyer of insurance policy does not know what he has bought by his premium. The time of occurrence of event is also uncertain for the parties. As such, insurance is primarily a *gharar* contract.

Types of gharar in insurance

The element of *gharar* present in the insurance is of the following types:

---

[27] See Muftī Muḥammad Shafī', *Bīmah Zindagī*, Karachi, Dār al-Isha‘at; Abul A‘ lā Mawdūdī, *Ma ‘āshiyāt-e- Islām*,Lahore: Islamic Publications,1988. Hussain Ḥāmid, *Ḥukm al-sharī ‘ah al-Islāmiyyah fī 'uqūd al-Tāmīn,* Cairo:1976; Muḥammad Siddīq Darīr, *al- Gharar wa Atharuhū fi al- 'Uqūd,* Cairo:1967; Zuhaylī, *al-Fiqh al-Islamī wa adillatuhū.* vol.4,p.671;Muṣliḥuddīn , *Insurance and Islamic law*, Lahore: Islamic publications,1978. See *Majallah al-Buḥūth al-Islamiyyah*, Riyadh, vols. 19-20, 1987, Pakistan :Council of Islamic Ideology,Report on Islamic Insurance system,1992.

1. Uncertainty about the payment of insurance amount:

The opponents of insurance assert that there is uncertainty as to whether the insured person will be able to get amount of compensation. In other words there is uncertainty about what the insured personbuys with the premium.

For this purpose one may take the example of car insurance. In this type of insurance the insured person drives car throughout the year. If he does not come across any accident, he can make no claim against the company and thus his premium money is wasted without any material benefit occurring to him. On the other hand, if he comes across a serious accident which causes extensive damage to his car, in that case the company pays him several times greater than the premium he has paid. This shows that the insured does not know at the time of contract what he buys by the amount of premium. This mean that he gets nothing if the accident does not occur. On the other hand, he gets several times greater than the premium he paid, if he comes across serious accident. Both these situations are uncertain for him.

2. Gharar with regard to time of payment:

Another form of *gharar* is uncertainty about the time of occurrence of event, and the time of the payment of compensation. The particular event against which insurance is required, is uncertain in nature. The parties to the contract do not know at the time of contract, whether the event will occur or not. If the event occurs it will bring pecuniary benefits in compensation for the insured and if it does not occur, he will get nothing. Thus, the acquisition of pecuniary benefits depend upon the occurrence of the event specified in the contract.

3. Gharar with regard to quantum :

This means that the insured person does not know at the time of contract how much compensation he will get because it depends upon the magnitude of the unpleasant event which is the subject matter of contract.[28]

View Point of Proponents of Insurance Regarding Gharar

---

[28] Hussain Ḥāmid, *Ḥukm al- Sharī'ah al-Islāmiyyah fī 'uqūd al-Tāmīn,* pp.84-86; Darīr, *al- Gharar wa Atharuhū fī al-'Uqūd,* p.65; *Majallah al-Buḥūth al-Islāmiyyah,* Riyadh, vols. 19-20, 1987.

In opposition to the view as described above, another group of Muslim scholars hold the view that insurance is not contrary to the Shariah. These scholars do not see an element of uncertainty in it. Some scholars of this group admit that there is an element of *gharar* in insurance but it is not too large to call for the invalidity of contract.

Their view point is discussed here in some detail:

I. Insurance does not contain gharar:

This view suggests that there is no uncertainty in the contract of insurance. In insurance what a person buys when he seeks insurance cover, is not the amount of compensation he receives when something happens to him or to his property. What he buys in fact is peace of mind. This is tangible return for the money he pays. This peace of mind is fair return on his investment. If something happens to him or to his property, he is compensated and his loss is redeemed. But if nothing happens he is happier, because he does not have to contend with any misfortune.

This assertain is factually incorrect. The buyer of the policy does not buy the peace or security by the premium he pays, instead, he buys the amount of insurance. This is clearly indicated in the contract. The contract specifies that the premium is price for amount of compensation. It does not refer to peace or security as consideration of premium. This goes without saying that human emotion are not tangible property which is sold or purchased. No one can promise the other that he will provide him pleasure, peace of mind or tranquility. This is an undertaking which the undertaker is unable to fulfill.

II. Gharar in Insurance is of small degree:

This suggests that the *gharar* contained in insurance is of small degree. Therefore, it does not call for the invalidity of contract. The reason is that insurance company can predict the chance of actual occurrence of event. It determines the risk through its past experience and scientific observation of certain incidents. The law of large number helps the company to calculate the number of likely happenings with some accuracy. This law points to the fact that some quantities which are uncertain and changing in individual cases, being different for each one, remain constant for a large group of similar persons. The gap between the probable and actual number of these accidents can also be determined. As such the element of *gharar* is negligible in the contract of insurance. [29]

Mustafā Zarqā asserts that the prohibition of *gharar* is confined to the area of sale contracts when the outcome of a sale is not certain but depends upon chance. Forbidden *gharar* occurs only when uncertainty exceed acceptable limits.[30] An insurer can by the simple use of the law of average know and determine the amount received from and given to the insured person.

If we consider this particular aspect, we find that the assertion that the element of uncertainty in insurance is negligible, is not correct. Insurance by its nature is a contract of uncertainty. *Gharar* and uncertainty always remain distinct features of this contract. But if we suppose for a while that it is not a contract of uncertainty because the company has the ability to predict the event with some accuracy, this remain an undeniable fact that the event is always uncertain for the insured person. He does not know whether it will happen or not. Thus, it is an uncertain contract for him.

Islamic Alternative to insurance business

Takāful or mutual guarantee is generally considered as an Islamic alternative to the modern insurance business. *Takāful* refers to an agreement among group of people called participants to guarantee jointly that, should any of them suffer a catastrophe or disaster, he would receive certain sum of money to meet the loss or damage. Thus, it is a method of mutual help. Since the contributions in *takāful* business are invested on the basis of *muḍārabah,* it is also known as

---

[29] See Mustafā Zarqā , '*Aqd al-Ta 'mīn wa Mawqif al-Shari 'ah Minhu.* Damascus : University Press,1381/1962. Muḥammad Nejatullah Ṣiddīqī, *Insurance in an Islamic Economy*, Leicester: The Islamic Foundation 1984. M.A.Chishtī , *Islam and Insurance Alternative options*, Islamabad: International Institute of Islamic Economics,1992.

[30] See Mustafā Zarqā, *Nizām al-Ta'mīn wa Mawqif al-Sharī'ah Minhu.*Paper presented at first International Conference on Islamic Economics, Makkah, 1976.

solidarity *mudārabah*.[31] In *takāful*, the concept of *waqf* or donation is combined with that of *mudārabah*. A participant, while entering *takāful* business, concludes two contracts, i.e. , (i) Contract of donation or *tabarru'* whereby he undertakes to donate a portion of his contribution in waqf or tabarru' fund established to provide *takāful* benefits to any participant who suffers some material loss or damage; and (ii) Contract of *mudārabah* whereby he undertakes to pay a portion of his contribution to the company for the purpose of business on the basis of *mudārabah*. *Takāful* benefits, i.e., insurance benefits are paid from *waqf* or *tabarru'* (donation) fund. But if the fund proves insufficient, then the deficit is covered from the profits of *mudārabah* business, if any, or from the capital of *mudārabah*. The participants in *takāful* may also be required to make additional contributions for this purpose. Thus, the participants in *takāful* or solidarity *mudārabah* have the right to share the profits generated by such *mudārabah* business, but at the same time they are liable for contributing to amounts in addition to the premiums they have already disbursed, if their initial premiums paid during a particular year are not sufficient to meet all the losses and risks incurred during that year.[32] In other words the sharing of the profit or surplus that may emerge from the operations of *takāful* is made only after the obligations of assisting the fellow participants have been fulfilled.

Under *mudārabah* agreement the participants pay their contribution to the entrepreneur or *mudārib*, i.e., *takāful* company to invest that money in some profitable business in accordance with Islamic modes of investment. The profits are shared by the participants and the *takāful* company (in its capacity as *mudārib*) according to a ratio agreed upon between contracting parties.

There are two types of *takāful* (insurance) business usually managed by *takāful* companies, i.e., life *takāful* (insurance) and general *takāful*. Under life *takāful*, the company provides cover of

---

[31] See Chaudry Muhammad Ṣādiq, *Islamic Insurance (takāful) concept and practice, Encyclopaedia of Islamic Banking and Insurance*, p.198, London: Institute of Islamic Finance and Banking , 1995.

[32] See Nabīl Ṣāliḥ, *Unlawful gain and legitimate profit in Islamic Law*, p.126.

mutual financial aid in the form of *takāful* benefits in case of untimely death of participant.

The general *takāful* provides various policies and schemes to a participant with a view to protect him against material loss or damage arising from catastrophies, or disaster inflicted upon his properties. General *takāful* are generally short-term contracts. Amount of *takāful* contribution varies according to the value of the property to be covered. Installments in general *takāful* are called *tabarru'* (donation). Company Invests the *tabarru'* fund and the profits accrued are allocated between the fund and the management on the basis of *mudārabah.* Indemnity is paid out of *tabarru'* fund. If the *tabarru'* fund generates net surplus, then unlike insurance, surplus is shared between participants and the company[33].

Here we will dilate upon the working of *takāful* business in Malaysia.

Working of the takāful business

Mudārabah and *tabarru',* Involvement of these two Islamic forms of business eliminates the elements of *ribā* and *gharar* from the insurance contract. The operational details of different *takāful* businesses are as follows:

Family takāful (Life Insurance)

Any individual between the ages of 18 to 55 years can participate in the family *takāful* business. Participants are required to pay *sharikah takāful* Malaysia regularly the *takāful* installments that are then credited into a defined fund known as the family *takāful* fund. Each *takāful* installment is divided and credited into two separate accounts namely, the Participant's Account (PA) and the Participant's Special Account (PSA). A substantial proportion of the installments is credited into the PA solely for the purpose of savings and investment. The balance of the installments is credited into the PSA as *tabarru'* for *sharikah takāful* Malaysia to pay the *takāful* benefits to the heirs of any participant who may die before his maturity of the family *takāful* plan. The amount accumulated in the PA is investment in various

---

[33]Muhammad Anwar, *A Comparative Study of Insurance, and takāful,* Islamabad: Pakistan Institute of Development Economics, 1994, p. 14.

types of business carried out according to Islamic financing techniques, and the resultant profits are divided between the *sharikah* and the participants according to a ratio, e.g., 30-70 agreed upon between the parties. The participants' share is calculated according to their individual share in the PA, and credited into their respective accounts i.e. the PA and the PSA. For example if a participant is paying RM 1000 to the *sharikah* as his installment the use of the amount could be shown with the help of the following chart: [34]

Family *Takāful* Fund RM1000	
Participant's Special Account RM2000	Participant's Account RM978.00
All Family *Takāful* Fund RM1000	
	Investment profit (Example: RM70)
70% (Example) Participant (RM49.00)	30%(Example) Company (RM21.00)
Participant's Special Account RM22.00 RM1.08 RM23.08	Participant's Account RM 978.00 RM47.92 RM 1025.92

---

[34] See Chaudry Muḥammad Ṣādiq, *Islamic Insurance (takāful) concept and practice, Encyclopaedia of Islamic Banking and Insurance*, pp.197-208.

In case of occurrence of unhappy event, death or disability, the *sharikah* makes payment to the policy holder or his heirs. The amount desposited in the PA along with the profits plus some amount from the PSA according to a formula is paid by the company. This scheme is explained as under by considering some cases.

Upon the occurrence of certain events the company will arrange *takāful* benefits to the rightful claimant in the following manner:

Case-1

In the event of: untimely death of the participant or permanent and total disability suffered by the participant.

Should the participant die or suffer permanent and total disability in the fifth year of participation, *takāful* benefit will be paid in the following manner:

(i)   From Participant's Account   RM 4,890.00

RM 978 x 5 (i.e. installments paid by

the Participant into his participants

account from the date of entry up to

the date of death or suffering of

permanent and total disability (PTD)

together with profit if any, which

have been earned from investment for

during the same period, say   RM   400.00

(ii) From participants special accounts (i.e. outstanding amount of *takāful* installments that would have been paid should the Participant survive). RM5000.00

Total *takāful* Benefit Payable.   RM 10,290.00

For the PTD cover takaful benefit shall be paid in ten equal installments annually.

Case No 2

If Participant is still alive at maturity: Should the Participant survive until the maturity of his Family *takāful* FTP, payment of *takāful* benefit will be made to him as follows:-

i)   From his Participant's Account =   RM 9,780.00

RM 978 x 10 (i.e. total amount installments credited into his Participant's Account from date of entry to the maturity) together with the profit from investment if any, accumulated during the same   period.

RM 1,800.00

ii)   From Participant's Special Account's, surplus. if any as determined.

(b) By *Sharikah Takāful.*   RM XXX

Total *Takāful* Benefit =   RM
           - 11,580.00 + surplus as determined by *Sharikah Takāful..*

Case No 3

In the event of untimely Death of Participant due to accident:

Based on the above example, should the participant suffered death due to accident, then the total *takāful* benefits payable will be as follows:

(a) If the Participant died in the fifth year of participation. the payment of the benefit will be in the following order:

(i)   From Participant's Account   RM 4.890.00

RM 978 x 5, and profit from Investment if any. accumulated in the Account during the same period. say
RM   400.00

(ii) From Participant's Special Accounts RM   5,000.00 = RM 1000 x 5 (i.e. outstanding or balance of *takāful* installments to be paid by the Participant should he survive until maturity).

(iii) From Group Family *Takāful* Account.

RM   15,000.00 Total *Takāful* Benefit.
RM   25,290.00

(b)   If Participant suffered bodily injury arising from accident, Such as loss of arm or leg (rates of benefit fixed according to scale of disability or injury), then the amount of *takāful* benefits payable will be made from Group Family *Takāful* Account only, as follow: 50% x 15,000.00   RM 7,500.00

Case No 4

In event that the Participant is hospitalized:

Based on the same example, should the Participant be warded into any hospital for a period of 5 days the *takāful* benefit will be made from Group Family *Takāful* Account as follows:-

30 x 5 days.   RM   150.00

General Takāful Business

General *takāful* schemes are basically contracts of joint guarantee, on a short-term basis, based on the principle of *mudārabah* , between a group of participants to provide mutual compensation in the event of a defined loss. The schemes are designed to provide protection to both individuals and corporate bodies against any material loss or damage consequent upon a catastrophe or disaster inflicted upon properties, assets or other belongings of its participants.

In consideration for participating in the various schemes, participants agree or undertake to pay *takāful* contributions as *tabarru'* for the purpose of creating a defined asset as illustrated in the 'General *Takāful* Fund'. It is from this Fund that mutual compensation would be paid to any participant who suffers a defined loss or damage arising from a catastrophe or disaster affecting his property or belonging.

As the *mudārib, Sharikat Takāful* Malaysia invests the Fund. All returns on the investment are pooled back to the fund. In line with the virtues of mutual help, shared responsibility and joint guarantee as embodied in the concept of *takāful,* compensation or indemnity is paid to any participant who suffers a defined loss. Other operational costs for managing the general *takāful* business such as the cost of arranging re-*takāful* program and setting up of reserve is also deducted from the fund.

A participant who wishes to participate in a general *takāful* scheme such as Motor *takāful* to cover his motor vehicle, Fire *takāful* to cover his house from loss or damage against fire or Public liability *takāful* to cover against his third party liability, pays a certain sum of money called *takāful* contributions. The amount of *takāful* contribution varies according to the value of property or asset to be covered under the scheme. If no claims are made or incurred and after deducting all the operational costs, the fund registers a surplus, it is shared between the participants and *sharikat takāful* Malaysia according to an agreed ratio such as 6:4; 5:5. Profits attributable to the participants are paid on expiry of their respective general *takāful* schemes provided they have not received or incurred claims during the period of participation.

The general *takāful* business is different from family *takāful* as all the payments are credited to only *tabarru'* account, and not divided into two separate accounts. After deducting all administrative costs and claims if this account shows some surplus (or profit) it is distributed among the policyholders as well. The problem here is that if the contributions of participants are *tabarru'*, then he should not get any profit on it, and if it is considered as a loan then the surplus amount earned by him, will amount to *ribā*. Therefore, the company should divide the available funds into two separate accounts. If due to short period of policy it is not possible to make investment and earn some profit *tabarru'* and subsequently no return should be given to them. If the surpluses accumulate, then the regulatory body can decide to reduce the amount of premium for next periods. It will indirectly help the policyholders.

Sharī'ah appraisal of takāful business

The *takāful* business of Malaysia is satisfactory from Sharī'ah point of view. It is constructed on the Islamic concepts of *muḍārbah* and *tabarru'*. It is also free from the element of *ribā*, because the participant or the policyholder does not get a fixed return on P.A. (Participant's Account), instead he gets a varied income. His capital is subjected to the principle of profit and loss sharing as enunciated in the tradition of the Holy Prophet (peace be upon him) "profit goes side by side with the risk". The amount accumulated in P.A. is invested in various forms of business strictly in accordance with Islamic techniques of financing and investment.

As regards participants in special account, this is the same fund which has been designated as *waqf* by the 'Ulamā of Indo-Pakistan. Being a contract of donation, any uncertainty about the *takāful* benefits to be earned by any participant, does not affect the validity of contract. A contract of donation with *gharar* and *jahl* is permissible in the Sharī'ah. Thus a participant who dies or suffers from total disability in the fifth year of participation, is entitled to get his capital and profits along with five yearly installments from participants special account i.e. from donation fund. This benefit is lawful and does not form *ribā* because it has been paid as donation to him. The Muslim Jurists are unanimous on the point that *gharar* (uncertainty), invalidates the exchange contracts only and not the contracts of donation. They say that the donation of stray or unidentified animal, or fruit before its benefits are evident, or usurped thing is permissible but their sale is unlawful. From this we may conclude that *takāful* provides an Islamic alternative to the present Insurance business.

Conclusion

The preceding discussion may be summarised as follows:

> 1. *Gharar* refers to lack of knowledge about the material terms of contract.

> 2. *Gharar* takes place when it is not known whether the subject-matter exists or not, or if it exists, whether it can be handed over to the buyer or not.

> 3. Following are some forms of *gharar* contract:

I. Uncertainty regarding the existence of the subject-matter

II. Inability to deliver the object of sale.

III. Lack of knowledge with regard to necessary characteristics of the subject-matter.

IV. Want of knowledge with regard to the time of performance of contract.

4. Some traditional types of *gharar* are:

i)   Two sales in one transaction

ii)   Earnest money sale

iii)   *Bay' al-munabadhah* (Throw Sale)

iv)   *Bay' al-mulāmasah* (Touch Sale)

v)   *Bay' al-ḥaṣāt* (Sale taking place through pebbles)

vi)   Contingent contract.

5. *Gharar* affects commutative contracts, meant for alienation of property for consideration such as sale, hire. It does not affect gratuitous contracts such as waqf, donation, gift.

6. The Modern insurance contract is a contract of *gharar*. The element of uncertainty and lack of knowledge inherent in the insurance relates to the occurrence of the event, i.e.. the subject matter of contract, the acquisition of amount of insurance, its quantity and time of payment.

CHAPTER- 9

EXTRINSIC CAUSES OF INVALIDTY: RIBĀ (USURY)

Ribā also forms a major cause of the invalidity of contracts. It operates mainly in the contracts of loan and *ṣarf* (money barter).

Literal Meaning of Ribā

Ribā literally means increase, addition, and augmentation. The Qurʾān has used the word *ribā* in its literal meaning in *Sūrat al-Rūm*, which says:

وَمَآ ءَاتَيۡتُـم مِّـن رِّبًا لِّـيَرۡبُوٓاْ فِـىٓ أَمۡوَٰلِ ٱلنَّاسِ فَلَا يَرۡبُواْ عِنـدَ ٱللَّـهِ

وَمَآ ءَاتَيۡتُـم مِّـن زَكَوٰةٍ تُرِيـدُونَ وَجۡـهَ ٱللَّـهِ فَأُوْلَـٰٓئِكَ هُـمُ ٱلۡمُضۡعِفُونَ

> "That which you give in usury in order that it may increase on other people's property has no increase with Allah, but that which you give in charity seeking Allah's pleasure, has increase manifold".[1]

Technical Meaning of Ribā

Technically, *ribā* means an increase in the principal, stipulated in loan transaction. So, anything chargeable in addition to the principal amount as a contractual obligation falls under the purview of *ribā* and is, therefore, prohibited.

Abū Bakr Jaṣṣāṣ has defined *ribā* in the following words:

> "It is a loan given for stipulated period with stipulated increase on the principal payable by the loanee.[2]

---

[1] Qurʾān. 30 39

[2] Jaṣṣāṣ, *Aḥkām al-Qurʾān* ; Lahore: Suhail Academy.

The above definition carries the following ingredients:

i) *Ribā* is an increase over and above the principal sum.

ii) It is an excess which is payable as a contractual obligation in a loan contract.

iii) It is excess, which is against a specified period of deferment. It is evident from this explanation that the above definition only covers that *ribā* which occurs in loan transactions, i.e., *ribā al-nasī'ah* or the *ribā al-jahiliyyah* (*ribā* of time of ignorance). It does not touch upon the *ribā*, which occurs in barter transactions dealt with by the *Sunnah* of the Prophet (s.a.w.s.).

An eminent scholar, Muḥammad 'Alā Thānwī, author of *Kashshāf Iṣṭilāhāt al-Funūn*, has defined *ribā* in the following words:

"*Ribā* is an increase without any corresponding consideration which has been stipulated in favour of one of the two parties, in a contract of exchange."[3]

Ingredients of the definition

The following are the ingredients of definition:

1. *ribā* is an increase (actual or constructive);

2. it is without corresponding consideration, i.e., without risk, labour and capital;

3. the increase is stipulated in favour of one party;

4. it is stipulated in an exchange of property for property.

The distinct feature of this definition is that it embraces in its ambit all forms of *ribā* and does not restrict *ribā* to loan transaction referred to in the definition of Abū Bakr al-Jaṣṣāṣ,. It describes *ribā* in a comprehensive sense to include the *ribā* of loan transactions as well as *ribā* of barter transactions. It encompasses every return and all excess arising from exchange of property for property regardless of whether exchange takes the form of loan or sale of money for money

---

Muḥammad 'Alā Thānwī, *Kashshāf Iṣṭilāhāt al-Funūn*, Beirut Sharikat al-Khayyāt le al-Kutub,n.d.,vol.3,p 592.

or barter transaction between two homogeneous articles or transaction
between two different commodities.

Other Meanings and Definitions of Ribā

1. *Ribā* is the stipulated excess without a counter-
   value in sale.[4]

2. *Ribā* is an excess according to a legal standard of
   measurement or weight in one or two homogeneous
   articles opposed to each other in a contract of exchange
   and in which such excess is stipulated as an obligatory
   condition on one party without any return. [5]

3. *Ribā* is an increase in one of the homogeneous
   equivalents exchanged without this increase being
   accompanied by a return.[6]

4. *Ribā* is an illicit profit or gain resulting from
   inequivalence in the counter value of the reciprocal
   benefits during an exchange of two articles of the
   same species and genus governed by the same
   efficient cause.[7]

5. It is undue profit not in the way of legitimate trade
   out of the loan of gold and silver and necessary
   articles of food.[8]

Ribā in the Qur'ān

The Qur'ān has dealt with the issue of *ribā* in the following verses:
These are produced below in order of their revelation.

First Revelation (5 years before Hijrah) Sūrat al-Rūm, verse: 39.

وَمَآ ءَاتَيۡتُم مِّن رِّبًا لِّيَرۡبُوَاْ فِىٓ أَمۡوَٰلِ ٱلنَّاسِ فَلَا يَرۡبُواْ عِندَ ٱللَّهِ

وَمَآ ءَاتَيۡتُم مِّن زَكَوٰةٍ تُرِيدُونَ وَجۡهَ ٱللَّهِ فَأُوْلَٰٓئِكَ هُمُ ٱلۡمُضۡعِفُونَ

[4] Sarakhsī, *al-Mubsūṭ*, vol 12, p. 105
[5] Muḥammad ʿAlā al-Dīn Haṣkāfī, *Tanwīr al-Abṣār*, Cairo: Maṭbaʿah
    al-Wāʿiz, vol. 2, p. 255.
[6] ʿAbd al-Reḥmān, Kitāb al-Fiqh ʿAlā al-Madhāhib al-Arbaʿah, vol. 2, p. 246.
[7] Nabīl Ṣāliḥ, *Unlawful Gain and Legitimate Profit in Islamic Law*, p. 16.
[8] Abdullah Yūsuf ʿAlī, *The Holy Qur'ān, Translation and Commentary*, p 15.

"That which you give in usury in order that it may increase
on other people's property has no increase with Allah: But
that which you give in charity seeking Allah's pleasure, has
increase manifold".

In this verse Allah has expressed His disapproval of *ribā* and
stated that *ribā* does not carry a reward from Allah in the hereafter.
The wealth acquired through *ribā* is deprived of the blessing of Allah.
Charity on the other hand, brings Allah's blessing and favour.

Second Revelation Sūrat al-Nisā Verse, 161 (Early Madīnan Period).

وَأَخْذِهِمُ ٱلرِّبَوٰاْ وَقَدْ نُهُواْ عَنْهُ وَأَكْلِهِمْ أَمْوَٰلَ ٱلنَّاسِ بِٱلْبَٰطِلِ

وَأَعْتَدْنَا لِلْكَٰفِرِينَ مِنْهُمْ عَذَابًا أَلِيمًا

"That they took usury though they were forbidden and that
they devoured man's substance wrongfully, we have
prepared for those among them who reject faith a grievous
punishment".

In this verse the Qur'ān tells us that *ribā* was prohibited for
Jews and that they incurred the wrath of Allah for taking *ribā*.

Third revelation (After Ghazwah Uhḥud) Sūrat Āl - 'Imrān, verse 130.

يَٰٓأَيُّهَا ٱلَّذِينَ ءَامَنُواْ لَا تَأْكُلُواْ ٱلرِّبَوٰاْ أَضْعَٰفًا مُّضَٰعَفَةً

وَٱتَّقُواْ ٱللَّهَ لَعَلَّكُمْ تُفْلِحُونَ

"O Believers' Take not doubled and redoubled interest and
fear God so that you may prosper".

In this verse the Qur'ān has pointed out the heinous practice of
taking double and multiplied interest prevalent amongst Arabs. The
believers have been enjoined to refrain from such act.

Fourth Revelation (shortly after Āl - 'Imrān) Sūrat al-Baqarah verse 275-277.

ٱلَّذِينَ يَأْكُلُونَ ٱلرِّبَوٰاْ لَا يَقُومُونَ إِلَّا كَمَا يَقُومُ ٱلَّذِى يَتَخَبَّطُهُ ٱلشَّيْطَٰنُ

مِنَ ٱلْمَسِّ ذَٰلِكَ بِأَنَّهُمْ قَالُوٓاْ إِنَّمَا ٱلْبَيْعُ مِثْلُ ٱلرِّبَوٰاْ وَأَحَلَّ ٱللَّهُ ٱلْبَيْعَ

وَحَرَّمَ ٱلرِّبَوٰاْ فَمَن جَآءَهُۥ مَوْعِظَةٌ مِّن رَّبِّهِۦ فَٱنتَهَىٰ فَلَهُۥ مَا سَلَفَ وَأَمْرُهُۥٓ

إِلَى ٱللَّهِ وَمَنْ عَادَ فَأُوْلَٰٓئِكَ أَصْحَٰبُ ٱلنَّارِ هُمْ فِيهَا خَٰلِدُونَ ﴿٢٧٥﴾ يَمْحَقُ

ٱللَّهُ ٱلرِّبَوٰاْ وَيُرْبِى ٱلصَّدَقَٰتِ وَٱللَّهُ لَا يُحِبُّ كُلَّ كَفَّارٍ أَثِيمٍ ﴿٢٧٦﴾

ٱلَّذِينَ ءَامَنُواْ وَعَمِلُواْ ٱلصَّٰلِحَٰتِ وَأَقَامُواْ ٱلصَّلَوٰةَ وَءَاتَوُاْ ٱلزَّكَوٰةَ لَهُمْ

أَجْرُهُمْ عِندَ رَبِّهِمْ وَلَا خَوْفٌ عَلَيْهِمْ وَلَا هُمْ يَحْزَنُونَ ﴿٢٧٧﴾

"Those who devour usury will not stand except as stands one whom the Evil one by his touch has driven to madness. That is because they say: "Trade is like usury". But God has permitted trade, and forbidden usury. Those who after receiving direction from their lord, desist shall be pardoned for their past. Their case is for God to judge. But those who repeat (the offence) are the companions of the fire; they will abide there forever. God will deprive usury of all blessings, but will give increase for deeds of charity. For He loves not creatures ungrateful and wicked. Those who believe and do deeds of righteousness and establish regular prayers and regular charity will have their reward with their lord. On them shall be no fear, nor shall they grieve.

The fourth revelation severally censured those who take *ribā* and established clear distinction between trade and *ribā*.

Fifth Revelation (9 or 10 AH before Farewell Pilgrimage) verse 278-280.

يَتأَيُّهَا الَّذِينَ ءَامَنُواْ اتَّقُواْ اللَّهَ وَذَرُواْ مَا بَقِىَ مِنَ الرِّبَوٰاْ

إِن كُنتُم مُّؤْمِنِينَ ۝ فَإِن لَّمْ تَفْعَلُواْ فَأْذَنُواْ بِحَرْبٍ مِّنَ اللَّهِ

وَرَسُولِهِ وَإِن تُبْتُمْ فَلَكُمْ رُءُوسُ أَمْوَٰلِكُمْ لَا تَظْلِمُونَ وَلَا تُظْلَمُونَ

۝ وَإِن كَانَ ذُو عُسْرَةٍ فَنَظِرَةٌ إِلَىٰ مَيْسَرَةٍ وَأَن تَصَدَّقُواْ

خَيْرٌ لَّكُمْ إِن كُنتُمْ تَعْلَمُونَ ۝

"O you who believe! Fear God and give up what remains of your demand for usury, if you are indeed believers. If you do it not, take notice of war from God and His apostle, but if you turn back you shall have your capital sums. Deal not unjustly and you shall not be dealt with unjustly. If the debtor is in difficulty, grant him time, till the time of ease. But if you remit it by way of charity, that is best for you if you only know *(al-Baqarah 278-280)*.

Inferences drawn form these verses:

1. There is a sharp contrast between charity and usury. Usury creates conflict, hatred, jealously and economic warfare among individuals whereas charity promotes harmony, cooperation and collaboration in the society.

2. There is distinct difference between legitimate trade and usury. Not every surplus in transaction is forbidden. The surplus, which is a result of selling and purchasing, is legitimate and lawful. The surplus which one earns without exertion and bearing risk and liability is prohibited.

3. The believers have been asked to give the remaining amount of *riba* and permitted to receive their principal amounts. This gives Quranic definition of *riba*, that is, any addition to the capital in a transaction of loan is *riba*

4. No distinction has been made between an addition in the capital sum of the loan based on simple interest and an addition based on compound interest.

5. No distinction has been made between a loan contracted for the purpose of consumption and that contracted for production.

6. The creditors have right to their capital sums only.

7. To demand excess in the capital is injustice to the debtor and to deny the creditor his principal amount is an injustice to him.

8. Continuing any further dealings in *riba* will amount to inviting war from Allah and His Messenger.

9. Creditors have been asked to give time to debtors for repayment of capital, if necessary.

10. To write off a debt altogether is an act of charity.

Forms of Ribā al-Qur'ān ,i.e., Ribā al-Jahiliyyah

The *riba* mentioned in the Qur'ān was practiced by the Arabs in the pre-Islamic period in the following three forms.

1. They advanced loan by stipulating excess over and above the principal sum of loan contract. Thus, the increase was stipulated in the beginning of the contract i.e. at the time of advancing a loan. Abū Bakr al- Jaṣṣāṣ,. writes in *Aḥkam al-Qur'ān*:

> "The *riba* which was known to and practiced by the Arabs was that they used to advance loan in the form of *dirham* and *dīnār* for a fixed term with an agreed excess over and above the amount of loan."[9]

2. They used to advance loan on the condition that they would take a fixed amount each month, while the principal amount still remained. Thereafter, when it was time for the repayment of the debt, they demanded the principal from the

---

[9] Abū Bakr al- Jaṣṣāṣ,. *Aḥkām ul- Qur'ān*, Beriut: Dār al-Kitāb al-'Arabī, vol. 1, p.465.

debtor. If he was unable to pay, they increased the term and payable amount.

3. They used to sell a commodity on deferred payment basis, when the time of payment approached, the seller used to increase the amount due and give him more time. Suyūtī explains this practice in the following words: "They used to purchase a commodity on the basis of deferred payment, then on the date of maturity the seller used to increase the amount due in lieu of further delay"[10]. Thus, the increase of amount was not stipulated at the time of concluding contract of debt, but at the time of maturity of contract.

Ribā in Sunnah

The *aḥādīth* dealing with *ribā* are of two categories: First, those, which reaffirm the type of *ribā*, mentioned in the Qur'ān. The second categories are those that introduce a new form of *ribā*, not mentioned in the Qur'ān. This latter form of *ribā* is known as *ribā al-faḍl*.

A few of the *aḥādīth* relating to either category are reproduced below:

The First Category of Aḥādīth on Ribā

1. The Prophet (s.a.w.s.) is reported to have said in his last *ḥajj* Sermon (the farewell address):

   "Beware, all *ribā* outstanding from the *ribā* prevalent during the pre-Islamic era is void. You are entitled to your principal money. Neither shall you oppress nor shall you be oppressed.[11]

2. "Beware! All *ribā* of pre-Islamic era is annulled and the first claim o f *ribā* which I cancel is that of my uncle".[12]

3. From Jābir, who said: "The Messenger of Allah (s.a.w.s.) cursed the one who charges *ribā*; he who gives it; the one who

---

[10] Suyūtī, *al-Durr al-Manthūr*, Beriut: vol. 2, p.72.
[11] Muslim, *Ṣaḥīḥ*. Chapter of Hajj.
[12] Muslim, *Ṣaḥīḥ*. Chapter of Hajj.

records it; and the two witnesses; saying that "they are all equal"[13]

The Second Category of Aḥādīth on Ribā

1. From Abū Saʿīd al-Khudrī, who said: "The Messenger of Allah (s.a.w.s) said: "Do not sell gold for gold except when it is like for like; nor misappropriate one through the other; nor sell silver for silver except like for like; nor misappropriate one through the other; nor sell things that are absent for those that are present" [14]

2. From ʿUbādah Ibn Ṣāmit who said': "The Messenger of Allah (s.a.w.s.) said: Gold for gold, silver for silver, wheat for wheat, barley for barley, dates for dates, salt for salt, like for like, in equal weights, from hand to hand. If those species differ, then sell as you like as long as it is from hand to hand".[15]

These two *aḥādīth* provide that the following three transactions are usurious transactions.

i) A transaction of money for money of the same denomination where the quantity on both sides is not equal, either in a spot transaction or in a transaction based on deferred payment.

ii) A barter transaction between two weighable or measurable commodities of the same kind, where the quantity on both sides is not equal or where delivery from any one side is deferred.

iii) A barter transaction between two different weighable or measurable commodities when delivery from one side is deferred. [16]

---

[13] Bukhāri, *Ṣaḥīḥ, kitāb al-Buyūʿ*. Muslim, *Ṣaḥīḥ,*, Chapter on *Ribā*

[14] Muḥammad ibn Ismāʿīl Sanʿānī. *Subul al-Salām*. Beriut: Dār al-Fikr, 1938, vol.3, p.37

[15] Ibid, vol.3, p.37.

[16] Order of the Supreme Court's Appellate Bench on *Ribā*. *The News*, December 24, 1999.

Kinds of Ribā

There are two main kinds of *ribā: ribā al-Duyūn* and *ribā al-buyū' (ribā* of debt transactions and *ribā* of sale transactions) *ribā al-buyū'* is further divided into two kinds, i.e., *ribā al-faḍl* and *ribā al-nasā.*

I)- Ribā al-faḍl (ribā by way of excess):

It is the excess revealed through a *Sharī'ah* criterion stipulated in one of the two counter-values, in transaction of exchange. [17]

The *Sharī'ah* criterion in this definition refers to weight or measure of capacity or count. Thus, if two persons were exchanging wheat with each other, the quantity must be equal on both sides; if there is excess on one side, which would amount to *ribā. al-faḍl (ribā* by way of excess). *Ribā al-faḍl* takes place in a homogeneous exchange with increase from one side in terms of weight or measurement. In the above example if 5 kg wheat is exchanged for 6 kg wheat, that would amount to *ribā al-faḍl.*

II)- Ribā al-Nasā' (ribā of delay):

It is *ribā* by way of **defe**rment of completion of an exchange. *ribā al-nasā (ribā* by way of deferment) takes place when articles of the same genera or different genera, whether measured or weighed. are exchanged with deferment on one side, whether or not there is real excess in favour of either side. Thus, if 5 kg gold is exchanged for 5 kg gold with a delay of one year, it will amount to *ribā al-nasā'* because it has arisen from a period of delay.

Rationale Underlying the Prohibition of ribā al-faḍl

The rationale underlying the prohibition of *ribā al-faḍl* can be summarized in the following points:

1. In barter transaction, if the same commodity is exchanged it is likely that a party with ability to judge difference in quality will exploit the ignorance of less knowledgeable party in giving him less than the real value of the commodity. Therefore, the lawgiver has safeguarded him

---

[17] Kāsānī, *Badā'i' al-Sanā'i'*, vol.5, p.183.

against injustice and exploitation by stipulating that the exchange should be equal on both sides.

2. An unequal exchange of the same commodity gives way to hoarding, monopoly and profiteering. The rich man, for example, gives 1kg of superior dates for 5 kg inferior dates. What actually happens that all the inferior dates are transferred to the rich man at the cost of 1/5 amount of the superior dates with him, with the following results:

   i) A huge amount of dates has been stored with the rich man. He starts hoarding them.

   ii) The small quantity of the superior dates in the hands of a large number of poor persons will soon be finished. Only the inferior quality of dates will be left over in the market.

   iii) The rich man will monopolize the inferior dates and sell them in the market at very high rates, even higher than the normal market rates of the superior dates. [18]

3. By prohibiting *ribā al-faḍl*, i.e., unequal exchange of the same commodity, Islam has in fact encouraged the use of cash money. The Prophet (s.a.w.s) had instructed Bilāl (r.a.t.a.) to sell two measures of dates for money and then purchase superior ones with that money. Thus, the *aḥādith* relating to *ribā* seek to promote money as medium of exchange in the economy.

4. Deferred delivery brings undue benefit for one party. For example Mr. A sells $100 to Mr. B for Rs. 5500 to be delivered next year. By next year the exchange rate in the market has changed from 1 $ 55 Rs. To 1$ 65 Rs. But Mr. B will deliver Rs. 5500 only not Rs. 6500. This shows that benefit of change in exchange rate over the year went to one party i.e. in this case Mr. B. If exchange rate moved in

---

[18]Ghulām Murtazā, *Socio-Economic system of Islam*, Lahore: Malik Sons Publishers, 1990, pp. 34,35.

other direction, Mr. A would have been the gainer. In short one party will gain while the other will lose.

5. The restriction levied in the *aḥādīth* of *ribā al-faḍl* and *ribā al-nasā'*, seeks to forestall the entry of real *ribā* through the back door.

Underlying cause ('illah) of the prohibition of ribā al-faḍl and ribā al-nasā'.

The Muslim Jurists are unanimous on the point that prohibition of *ribā al-faḍl* and *ribā al-nasā* is not restricted to six commodities mentioned in the *ḥadīth*. The prohibition is extendable to other commodities, which resemble the six commodities with regard to the *'illah* (underlying cause).

The Jurists employ the method of analogical reasoning in extending the prohibition to other commodities besides the six commodities contained in the *ḥadīth* of 'Ubādah ibn Ṣāmit.

It is generally agreed that analogical reasoning is valid when the following conditions are met:

1. The *'illah* should represent the compelling factor which has motivated or is intended by the legal rule; it should be plain and consistent.

2. The same *'illah* should appear in both elements of analogy, object as well as subject. A mere resemblance between attributes is not sufficient.

3. The general rule governing the object of the analogy should be of general application and not restricted to a specific case.

The Jurists while agreeing on the application of the rule of prohibition to other commodities disagree on the underlying cause.

We now take up the viewpoints of the Jurists regarding the underlying cause which is at work behind the prohibition of *ribā al-faḍl* and *ribā al-nasā'*.

Hanafi View Point

The Hanafi Jurists consider the underlying cause to be similarity of species, i.e., the exchanged articles belong to the same genus and the similarity of the method of estimation, i.e., both articles. besides being of the same genus, are weighed or measured when they change hands.[19] According to this interpretation, all weighable articles such as iron and cotton if exchanged with each other, must fulfill the requirement of equality or sameness in quantity and simultaneous exchange. If the transaction fails to meet the first condition, it will amount to *riba al-fadl* and should the transaction fall of meeting second requirement that would rise to *riba al-nasā*. *Ribā* according to this viewpoint does not run in eggs because they are neither weighed nor measured rather, they are sold by count.

Shāfi'ī View Point

Shāfi'ī Jurists hold that the *'illah* for gold and silver is their being prices of the things or the currency-value (*thamaniyyah*) and for wheat, barley, dates and salt is food-value (*ṭu'm*). Thus, *ribā* runs in vegetables if two vegetables of the same kind are exchanged with each other either with excess or delay. since they belong to the class of foodstuff.[20]

Mālikī viewpoint

The Mālikī Jurists determine the *'illah* for gold and silver by their currency-value (*thamaniyah*), and for the remaining four articles by their food-value provided they can be stored for a reasonable time without perishing. Thus, *ribā* does not run in vegetables and fruits because these are perishable.

As regards Mālikīs, *'illah* for gold and silver can be extended to any modern currency. Imām Mālik is reported to have said:

> If the people of an age make currency out of the skins of camels, and that becomes prevalent among the people. I view its exchange with gold or silver with delay unlawful.[21]

---

[19] Kāsānī. *Badā'i' al-Ṣanā'i'*, vol.5, p.183.

[20] Khatīb Baghdādī, *Mughnī al-Muḥtāj*, vol 2, p.23.

[21] Saḥnūn, *al-Mudawwanah al-Kubār*, Beriut: Dār Ṣadir, n.d. vol. 8, pp.395,396.

This means that Imām Mālik applies the rules relating to *sarf* (money exchange) and *ribā* to all such articles, which assumes the status of currency.

The difference between the viewpoints of Imām Shāfi'ī and Mālik on the 'illah of gold and silver is that Imām Shāfi'ī while considering both metals as currencies, restricts this attribute of price-worthiness to these two metals. He regards these metals money by creation. To him, no other thing can assume this role. Thus the attribute operating in gold and silver, to Imām Shāfi'ī is not of general application. Imām Mālik, on the other hand, considers this rule, of general application and not restricted to a specific case. So a homogeneous exchange of currency should fulfill the requirements of equality in quantity and prompt delivery from both sides. In case of heterogeneous exchange (dollars with Rupees) the equality is not a requirement; however, it is necessary that both currencies be exchanged in the same session of Contract. Delay or deferment in delivery by either party would make it a contract of *ribā al-nasā*

Hanbalī View Point

Different versions relating to *'illah* are attributed to Imām Ahmad ibn Hanbal.

i) The *'illah* for gold and silver is twofold: the exchanged articles belong to the same genus and they change hands by way of weight. As for the other four articles quoted in the Hadīth, the *'illah* is again two fold; the exchanged articles belong to the same genus and they change hands by way of measure. This viewpoint is similar to that of the Hanafī School.

ii) The *'illah* for gold and silver is their currency-value (thamaniyyah), and for the remaining four articles, their food-value (ṭu'm). This version is close to that expressed by the Shāfi'ī and Mālkī jurists.

iii) The *'illah* for the four commodities is their being foodstuffs which are weighable and measurable; thus there is no *ribā* when the exchanged foodstuffs are neither measurable nor weighable, or when the exchanged counter-values are not foodstuffs.[22]

Some other Forms of Ribā

Under this title we will deal with some other forms of *ribā*, which are doubtful contracts from the *Sharī'ah* point of view. The contracts falling under this category conform to the requirement of the *Sharī'ah* with regard to *ṣīghah* (form of contract) but their objectives oppose the intention of the lawgiver, as they provide a legal device and subterfuge to circumvent the obstacles posed by *ribā* prohibitions. A majority of Muslims Jurists, therefore, regards such forms of contract invalid.

The Following are some of these contracts.

1. Bay' al-'Īnah:

Under this contract a person sells some object on credit for a certain price and then buys it back at a price less than the sale price on prompt payment, both transactions taking place simultaneously in the same session of contract. We can understand this from the following illustration.

A, sells a commodity to B for Rs. 100/- on a one-year's credit. A, than buys the commodity back for Rs. 80/- from B on immediate payment. In the above case, A is a creditor and B is a debtor. A has advanced loan of Rs. 80/- under the cover of sale transaction in which he earns a surplus of 20 rupees. Another form of *bay' al-'īnah* is to sell commodity on cash and then buy it back at a higher price to be paid at some specified time in future. In this case, the prospective debtor sells an object for cash to the prospective creditors. The debtor immediately repurchases the object for a higher amount payable at a future date. Thus the transaction amounts to a loan with object as security. The difference between the two prices represents the interest. It is called *'īnah* because the *'ayn* (substance) in this case returns to its owner. Financing under buy-back arrangement in Pakistan resembles this contract.

---

[22] Ibn Qudāmah, *al-Mughnī*. vol.6, pp.54-57.

The majority of Muslim Jurists consider this transaction invalid because the intended objective of the transaction opposes the objectives laid down by the Lawgiver. This form of transaction, in their view, is nothing more than a legal device aimed at circumventing the obstacle posed by the prohibition of *riba*. [23] These jurists establish the prohibition of this transaction by a tradition of 'A'ishah (God be pleased with her) when Umm Mahabbah informed her that she had a slave girl whom she sold on credit to Zayd ibn Arqam for eight hundred dirhams. Zayd soon decided to sell the slave, so Umm Mahabbah bought her back for six hundred on immediate payment. 'A'ishah (God be pleased with her) said, what you sold was bad, and bad was what you bought. Make it known to Zayd that his *jihad* alongside Messenger of Allah has been nullified, unless he repent". Umm Muhabbah asked her, " What if I should just take my capital from him". She replied, "Those who after receiving direction from their Lord desist, shall be pardoned for the past." Imam Shafi'i maintains that *bay' al-'inah* is permissible. The *hadith* of 'A'ishah is not established in his view.[24]

2. Bay' al-Wafa':

This is a transaction in which a person in need of money sells a commodity to a lender on the condition that whenever the seller wishes, the lender (the buyer) would return the purchased commodity to him upon surrender of the price. The reason for its designation as *wafa* is the promise to abide by the condition of returning the subject matter to the seller if he too surrenders the price to the buyer.[25] Like *bay' al-'inah*, this too is legal device for *riba*. The purchaser in this case is a creditor who benefits from the object held in his custody as pledge till the debtor pays him back his amount and retrieves his object. Islamic injunctions on pledge clearly provide that the creditor is not entitled to make profit out of the pledged property. Any profit drawn from it is interest.

---

[23] Zaki Badawi , *Nazariyyat al-Riba al-Muharram*, Cairo : al-Majlis al-A'la le re'ayah al-Funun,1940. p.203.

[24] Qurtubi, *al-Jam'i li Ahkam al- Qur'an*, Cairo:1353/1935, vol .3, pp.359,360..

[25] Ibn Rushd, *Bidayat al-Mujtahid*, vol.2, p.118.

3. Ḥaṭṭ wa ta'jjal:

Under this transaction the lender hastens the repayment of his delayed debt by taking an amount that is less than the value of the debt.[26] He accepts his money ahead of the time of maturity in lieu of discount on his principal amount. This is similar to present day practice of discounting of trade bills in the banks.

Viewpoints of Muslim Jurists regarding Ḥaṭṭ wa Ta'ajjal

The opinions of Muslim Jurists are divided on the legitimacy of *ḥaṭṭ wa ta'jjall*.

First Opinion:

Discounting for hastening the payment is permissible. This opinion is attributed to Ibn 'Abbās, Nakh'ī, Abū thawr and Zufar. They assert that the Holy Prophet (s.a.w.s.) had instructed Banī Naḍīr to reduce the amount owed to them and receive immediate payment. It is reported that when Banī Naḍīr were evicted from Madinah, a group of them came to the Holy Prophet (s.a.w.s.) with a complaint that they had been evicted at a time people owed to them money, whose payments were not yet matured. The Holy Prophet (s.a.w.s.) advised them to reduce the amount owed to them and demand prompt payment.

Second Opinion:

This opinion suggests that the practice of discounting for hastening the payment is not lawful. The majority of Muslim Jurists subscribe to this opinion. They put forward following arguments in favour of their standpoint:

1- A discount on the original amount for hastening the payment is similar to taking excess on the original amount. This is because in both the cases time is assigned a monetary value. Imām Sarakhsī said:

> "If a person is in debt of one thousand dirham for a specified period and he agrees with the creditor that he will pay him five hundred dirhams and will make payment to him ahead of time of maturity, it is not permissible, because the debtor has forfeited his right in time for five hundred

---

[26] Badawī. *Naẓaryyat al-Ribā al-Muḥarram*, p.205.

> and the creditor has also forfeited his right in five hundred
> in lieu of time, Hence it is an exchange of time for money,
> which is not lawful in our view"[27].

The real significance *ḥaṭṭ wa taʾjjal* (reduce and hasten payment) referred to in the *ḥadīth* is that the Holy Prophet (s.a.w.s.) had instructed the Jews to give up their claims of interest or excess over and above the principal amount and take back original amounts only before the time of maturity. In other words the Holy Prophet (s.a.w.s.) allowed them to receive their delayed debts before the time of maturity on the condition that they will reduce the amount of debt. The *ḥadīth* according to this interpretation does not suggest reduction in the original amount in return for immediate payment.

2-   The *ḥadīth* of *ḥaṭṭ wa taʾjjal* (discounting) came before the prohibition of *ribā*. The event of Banī Naḍīr took place in fourth year after Hijrah, then in the sixth year after *Ghazwah Khayber* came the prohibition of *ribā al-faḍl*. Thereafter, in the year ten after *Hijrah* the verses relating to *ribā* were revealed which contain final and conclusive prohibition of *ribā*. Thus, the *ḥadīth* of discounting is abrogated by the subsequent revelations on *ribā*.[28]

Third opinion:

This opinion suggests that discounting is permissible if it is affected without the condition of immediate payment. This means that if the debtor repaid his deferred debt before time of maturity and the creditor reduced some amount without its being a contractual obligation, then it is permissible, because former is not condition for latter.

Indexation of Loans and Ribā

Inflation and the consequent erosion. in the purchasing power of money is an important contemporary issue confronting Muslim Jurists, which has led to considerable debate and discussion. Inflation essentially harms the interests of the lender since he receives at the time of its return less money in terms of its purchasing power that he

---

[27] Sarakhsī. *al-Mabsūṭ*, vol.21, p. 31.

[28] Ibid .

had originally lent. Suppose one borrows one thousand rupees from another for a period of one year. After the year the rupees is devalued by 10 per cent. If the borrower pays the lender one thousand rupees as per agreement, then he is actually paying him 900 rupees only. This means that in terms of purchasing power of money, he is paying him less than what he has borrowed.

As a solution to this problem some Muslim Scholars suggest that the borrower should try to compensate lender for the loss of the value of money by giving such an extra amount, which at least offsets the drop that results from inflation. For this purpose, they have suggested that loans should be indexed to the rate of inflation in the economy.

In view of the above, indexation is characterized as "a scheme to link the nominal value of deferred payment to a suitable index of the purchasing power of money". [29]

A number of schemes of indexation have been proposed by economists, of which three are especially noteworthy. The first consists of linking indexation with general price level in the economy, represented through a basket of commodities known as the consumer goods basket. The second scheme consists of linking indexation with the price of some specific commodity, which has a stable value. In other words, it suggests that the loan should be presumed to have been offered in that commodity itself. The third scheme suggests that the loan should be offered and repaid in terms of specially introduced financial instruments, which have fixed value.

Muslim scholars are sharply divided regarding the validity and legitimacy of indexation of loans. A group of scholars favour indexation and does not see in it anything contrary to the injunctions of the Sharī'ah, rather these scholars find it in conformity with the principles of justice and fairness laid down in the Qur'ān and the Sunnah. Those who hold indexation of loans to be valid and legitimate in sharī'ah include scholars like Rafīq al-Miṣrī, Sulṭān Abū 'Alī, M.A. Mannān, Ziauddīn Aḥmad, Salīm Qureshī, 'Umar Zubayr,

---

[29] Munawar Iqbal," *Inflation. Indexation and role of Money"*,
    Paper presented in the workshop on Sharī'ah Position on Indexation,Jeddah. 1987 .

Gul Muḥammad, Mawlānā Muḥammad Ṭāsīn and several other scholars.

As against this, there is yet another group that maintains that the idea of indexation does not conform to the teachings of Islam. It involves an assumed positive return on loans. Those who maintain this viewpoint are:

Muḥammad 'Umer Chappra, Monzer Kahf, M. Nejatullah Siddīqī, Muḥammad Ḥasanuz Zaman, Mawlānā Taqī Usmānī, 'Alī Aḥmad Salūs, and some other prominent scholars. The council of Islamic Ideology of Pakistan has also expressed its opposition to indexation. The same view has been upheld by the Federal Sharī'at Court of Pakistan.

In the following lines an attempt will be made to explain the position of the Sharī'ah on the question and to analyse the arguments of the proponents as well as the opponents of indexation in the light of the general objectives of the Sharī'ah and the relevant texts of *Fiqh* relating to the repayments of debts and the exchange of currency.

Arguments of proponents

The arguments of proponents of indexation are summarised as follows:

1) Justice and Fairness: The Justice and fairness in mutual dealings are corner stones of the Islamic economic system. Qur'ān repeatedly enjoins upon believers to be just and fair in their dealings. It says, "God commands justice, the doing of good and liberality to kith."[30] It also says, "Be just, that is nearest to piety."[31] It further says, "You shall inflict no injustice and shall suffer none."[32] It is undoubtedly true that inflation causes both injustice and unfairness to the lender.

2) Principle of Redress of Harm: It is an accepted principal of the Islamic Sharī'ah that no damage should be borne nor should any be caused. Inflation causes a loss in the real value of monetary receipts while Indexation provides redress against such damage.

---

[30] Qur'ān, 16:90.
[31] Qur'ān, 5:8.
[32] Qur'ān, 2:279.

3) Giving Full Measures: Islam has strictly forbidden the practice of diminution in weights and measures, thereby depriving others of their due rights. In this regards the Qur'ān says, "And give full measure and weight with justice".[33]

This Quranic instruction of giving full measures is not limited to conventional weights and measures. It encompasses all measures of value. In modern economies, money is the biggest measure of value. Now in the period of inflation, the recipient does not receive what is really due to him. Indexation corrects this situation.[34]

Arguments of the opponents of Indexation

The most serious objection raised by the opponents of Indexation is that indexation involves an assumed positive return on loans. Hence it is a form of *ribā*. They do not favour the idea of compensating lender for the loss he suffers as a result of inflation. They find following demerits and flaws in the scheme of indexation, from the Islamic point of view.

1) Gharar and Jahl (uncertainly and lack of knowledge): It is a requirement of the *Sharī'ah* that both the values in an exchange contract (*'uqūd al-mu'awaḍāt*) should be clearly determined. Muslim Jurists are unanimous on the point that in a sale on deferred payment, if the price to be paid by the buyer is not fixed, it will render the contract void. Ibn 'Ābidīn says: "Fixation of price is a requisite for the validity of a contract of sale. If the price is left unspecified or market value is made the price of commodity then the contract will be invalid."[35] This shows that the obligation of the buyer in the contract of deferred payment should be fixed at the time of making the contract. In the case of indexation, however, the liability of the debtor is known only on the date it is due.

2) Injustice and Unfair: That the element of injustice and unfairness is inherent in the indexation will be evident from the following:

---

[33] Qur'ān, 6:152.

[34] Munawar Iqbal, *Inflation, Indexation and role of Money.*

[35] Ibn 'Ābidīn, Radd al-Muḥtār, vol.5, p.60.

(i) In the Islamic Law of indemnity the one who has caused wrong to someone is responsible for redressing or compensating that wrong. Inflation and the consequent damage to the money of lender is never an act of the borrower. This loss would have happened even if the lender had not lent his money. Hence, why should the borrower be held responsible for the loss and be asked to pay any compensation? Such a scheme obviously causes harm to the borrower.

(ii) The basket of consumers' goods which is the most popular method of indexation does not provide a just and fair standard for determining the purchasing power of money To quote the words of Ḥasanuz Zamān:

> "This basket represents the consumption habits of an average person, which does not necessarily represent the habits of actual men and women living in a society. This average will be fair for some but an unjustifiable favour for some others." [36]

To explain this point further, it needs to be pointed out that a large majority of our population does not consume most of the goods contained in the basket. Their basket is generally restricted to a few things only such as cooking oil, soap, pulses, and flour. The consumer's basket, on the other hand, consists of about forty items, which are hardly consumed by the majority. If such a basket were adopted as a standard to determine the purchasing power of money, it would be unjust and unfair to many people.

The Element of Ribā al-Faḍl

Indexation also contains the element of *ribā al-faḍl*. It involves an excess in one counter value in the exchange of two commodities of the same genus and conflicts with the *ḥadīth* which requires that a fungible good is to be returned by its like, and good quality and bad quality have no relevance for such a contract. Thus, darkened silver

---

[36] S.M. Ḥasanuz Zamān, *Indexation of Financial Assets*, an Islamic Evaluation, Islamabad, International Institute of Islamic Thought, 1993, p. 40.

has the same value in weight as polished silver. There is a consensus among the *fuqahā'* that the sameness in the tradition mentioned above, means sameness in kind and quantity, not in value.

Rules for exchange of fungible goods

The *fuqahā'* are so emphatic about "sameness" that they have ruled out all considerations of value or quality. In order to realize this objective they have laid down very clear rules so as to ensure the sameness of quantity. Ibn Qudāmah has mentioned some of these rules:

(1) The loan of the *dirham* of unknown weight is not permissible.

(2) If *dirhams* are lent by weight, they should be returned by weight.

(3) If *dirhams* are lent by counting their repayment must be by counting.

(4) The borrower will be required to return the same quantity, which he borrowed regardless of any change in price.[37]

It is due to this requirement of sameness that the Shāfi'ī Jurists invalidate the loan of non-fungible goods because sameness cannot be realized in it. The workshop on indexation organized by the Islamic Development Bank in Jeddah in 1987 emphasized this point in the following words:

> "In the context of indexation, the scholars attending the workshop emphasized that the word "*mithl*" referred to in the tradition of the Prophet Muhammad (s.a.w.s.) on *ribā* means sameness in kind and quantity according to the Sharī'ah. Sameness in quantity means sameness in weight, measure or number, not sameness in value. This is in adherence to what the *Sunnah* has indicated and it is in compliance with what the *Ummah* has agreed upon unanimously and what it has been practicing."[38]

---

[37] Ibn Qudāmah, *al-Mughnī*, vol .4 p. 210.
[38] Recommendations of workshop on Sharī'ah Position on Indexation (April 25 -28, 1987) Organized by Islamic Development Bank, Jeddah,1987.

It is evident from the above that the Sharī'ah disallows any excess over and above the principal sum in all circumstances. The additional amount received by the lender through indexation falls under the purview of the *ḥadīth* which declares that each loan that entails some monetary benefit is a kind of *ribā*.[37] In fact indexation is an attempt to provide justification for banking interest. A bank may claim that the excess paid to the depositor is compensation for the loss suffered by the latter during the period money remained in custody of bank, and it is not *ribā*. As such, this device opens the back door for interest.

No doubt constant rise in prices inflicts great harm on the majority of people. It especially harms people with limited and fixed incomes and prevents the equitable distribution of wealth in the society. Inflation is a social evil that adversely affects almost all the members of the society. Thus, it is not merely an individual's problem. It would be unjust as well as irrational to hold only one party of the contract, namely the borrower, responsible for this phenomenon and ask him for compensation. Such an attitude will only further widen the area of injustice instead of narrowing it down. It is the obligation of the state to control prices and adopt measures that would reduce the level of inflation.

Conclusions

1. *Ribā* is defined as an increase in the principal, stipulated in loan transaction.

2. The Qur'ān has dealt with the issue of *ribā* in *Sūrat al-Rūm* (Verse 39), *Sūrat al-Nisā* (Verse 161), *Sūrat Āl - 'Imrān* (Verse 130) and *Sūrat al-Baqarah* (Verses 275-281).

3. The Aḥadīth dealing with *ribā* are of two categories:

    (i) Those, which reaffirm the type of *ribā* mentioned in the Qur'ān.

    (ii) Those that introduce new forms of *ribā*. i.e., *ribā al-faḍl* and *ribā al-nasā'*

2. *Ribā al-faḍl* takes place in a homogeneous exchange with increase from one side in terms of weight or measurement.

3. *Ribā al-nasā'* takes place when articles of the same genera or different genera are exchanged with deferment from one party.

4. The prohibition of *ribā al-faḍl* and *ribā al-nasā'* seeks to forestall the entry of real *ribā* through the back door.

5. The prohibition of *ribā al-faḍl* is not restricted to six commodities. It is extendable to commodities. which resemble the six *rabwī* commodities with regard to underlying cause.

6. The Muslim Jurists have provided different underlying causes of the prohibition of *Riba al-fadl and Riba al-Nasā'*.

7. Other forms of *ribā* are: *bay'al-'īnah* (buy-back agreements), *bay'al-wafā* and *ḥaṭṭ wa Ta'jjal* (discounting for hastening the payment).

is for a particular author and it turns out to be of another author, he suffers from mistake of substantial quality.

EFFECT OF CONTRACT WITH MISTAKE

The Muslim jurists are unanimous on the point that a mistake bearing on genus renders a contract invalid as in the case of corundum.[4] As for mistake that relates to substantial quality, they hold that it makes contract voidable at the option of the party that suffered from mistake.[5]

The distinction between the categories of substantial and non-substantial has been made mainly with regard to usufruct of the object – the use to which it is intended to be put; and principally to the object the contracting party has in mind when he forms the contract. The quality must, therefore, be material in the mind of contracting party who is claiming the mistake: this is so whether it is clearly stated or merely implied. An instance is the buying of an animal for its meat, which the purchaser later discovers to be blind. Here, the purchaser cannot avoid the contract, because the defect of blindness is hardly pertinent to the intended use of the subject matter of the transaction, that is, to obtain meat.[6]

If the species of the object is the same, but an appreciable difference exists between the thing contracted for and the usufruct of the intended object, then the contract is again voidable by virtue of mistake as to meaning (substance). For instance a cloth is sold in a different colour or pattern to the one intended and it is not in accordance with the purpose of the contract.[7]

The mistake with regard to substantial quality affects those contracts only which admit of revocation such as commutative contracts. It, however, does not affect the contracts, which do not accept revocation such as contract of marriage. Thus, a marriage

---

[4] Zaylaʿī, *Tabyin al-Ḥaqāʾiq*, vol.4, p 52.
[5] Zuhaylī, *al-Fiqh al-Islāmi wa Adillahtuhū*, vol. 4, p.217; Madkūr, *al-Madkhal*, p.646.
[6] Rayner, *Islamic Law of Contract*, p.180.
[7] Ibid. p.181.

CHAPTER-10

DEFECT OF CONSENT AND ITS EFFECT ON CONTRACT

As mentioned earlier, consent of the parties forms the basis of a contract. A contract is considered valid only when it is concluded by a free consent. A defect of consent leading to nullity of contract arises when a party gives his consent as a result of mistake, fraud and duress or coercion. In these circumstances the contract becomes viodable at the option of the party whose consent was so obtained.

In the following lines we will discuss mistake, fraud and coercion and their effect on the validity of contract.

I. Mistake (Khaṭā'):

Mistake is generally defined as a "belief that is not in accord with the facts".[1] Mistake conceived by Muslim Jurists relates either to genus (substance) of the object or its substantial quality. An example of the former is sale of corundum (*yaqūt*). If a stone is sold as being corundum but turns out to be only glass the sale is void, the reason being the difference between glass and corundum.[2] An example of a mistake in the substantial quality is where a person purchases a piece of cotton as Egyptian cotton, which turns out to be Japanese Cotton.[3] Similarly, when a person purchases a book believing that it is for a particular author and it turns out to be of another author, he suffers from mistake of substantial quality.

---

[1] Sanhūrī, *Maṣṣadir al-Ḥaq*, vol.2, p.104.

[2] Sarakhasī, *al-Mabsūṭ*, vol. 13, pp. 12-13.

[3] Zaydān, *al-Madkhal li dirasat al-Sharī'ah al-Islamiyyah*, p.353.

contract cannot be revoked on the grounds of absence of required quality in the wife in the opinion of Ḥanafī jurists. Imām Aḥmad, on the other hand, holds that the husband has right to revoke the contract if he entered the contract relying on the words of guardian that she is beautiful but she appeared ugly, or she is virgin but it appeared that it is her second marriage.[8]

The mistake concerns non-substantial quality where the object is of the same substance as that contracted for, and the representation made by the seller as to its quality is false. For instance, a seller presents an object as a ruby, which is later found to be yellow. Here, the sale is valid but not binding on the purchaser because the mistake is not about the substance of the object nor is it deemed to have affected the usufruct intended by the purchaser and the true sale.[9]

A reference to the Egyptian civil code would be quite relevant to know as to which mistake affects a contract. This law determines that a mistake is essential when:

i) It has bearing on the quality of goods, which the parties have considered essential or which must be deemed essential, taking into consideration the circumstances surrounding the contract and the good faith that should prevail in business relationship.

ii) It has a bearing on the identity, or on one of the qualities of the person with whom the contract is entered into, if this identity or this quality was the principle factor in the conclusion of the contract".[10]

II. FRAUD (Tadlīs, Taghrīr, Khilābah):

Fraud is another cause of nullity of an agreement. It occurs when the conduct of one of the parties is such that without it the other party would not have contracted.

---

[8] Ibn Qudāmā, *al-Mughnī*, vol. 6, p.526.

[9] Rayner, *Islamic Law of contract*, p.182

[10] *Egyptian Civil Code*, Article 121 (a) & (b).

"Fraud is to induce a person by some deceptive means with a view to obtain his consent to a contract without which he would not have consented to the contract".[11] If what is so represented by words or conduct, be false, that is, not in agreement with the facts and the person making such representation is aware of it, the representer is said to be guilty of fraud.

Fraud in Islamic Law includes the misrepresentation of Western Law, which is defined as "a false statement of fact, made by one party before or at the time of the contract which induces the other party to enter into the contract".[12] The act of fraud which gives innocent party right to revoke the contract, must fulfill following conditions:

i)   Misrepresentation of a material fact must occur,

ii) There must be an intent to deceive,

iii) The innocent party must rely on misrepresentation,

iv) The innocent party must suffer an injury. Thus, fraud alone does not cause the annulment of contract.

Traditional Forms of Fraud In Islamic Juristic Literature

The Muslim Jurists have discussed various forms of fraud, some of them are as follows:

1. Taṣriyah:

It is to tie the udder of a she-camel or sheep to allow the animal's milk to accumulate in her udder so as to give a false impression to the intending buyer of a very productive milk-yield. In this respect the Holy Prophet (s.a.w.s) says:

> "Do not tie up the udder of she-camels and sheep. If any one among you buys a she-camel or sheep whose udder have been tied up, has option (of annulment) after milking

---

[11] *The Law of Business contracts*, p.102.

[12] Zarqā, *al-Madkhal al-Fiqhi al-'Amm*, vol. 1, p.374.

it; either to retain it or to return along with a measure of
dates (in lieu of the milk consumed by the purchaser).[13]

The act of *Tasriyah* renders the contract voidable at the
option of the buyer, who has suffered lesion from this fraud. This is
the viewpoint of the majority. Hanafī jurists do not approve
annulment of contract. They allow the defrauded party to claim
undue increase from the seller.[14]

2. Najāsh or Tanajush (False bidding to raise price):

It is to offer a high price for a commodity without any intention to
buy it, the sole aim being to cheat somebody else who really wanted
to buy the commodity. The Holy Prophet (s.a.w.s) has prohibited
this practice. It is related on the authority of Abū Hurayrah (r.a.t.a)
that the Prophet (s.a.w.s) said: 'O people! With a view to bargaining
with the people who come with their animals laden with
commodities for sale, do not go to meet them (outside the town) and
if a person is bargaining with another, do not interfere by bidding
higher.[15]

Najāsh or *Tanajush* is a vitiating factor of contract and renders
the contract voidable. *Tanajush* gives a buyer right to revoke the
contract. This is the viewpoint of majority of Muslim jurists. Shāfi'ī
jurists do not acknowledge this right for the buyer.[16]

3. Ghabn Fāhish:

Ghabn fāhish means excessive loss suffered by a party to the
contract as a result of concealment or misrepresentation, or
deception or fraud practiced by the other.

---

[13] San'ānī, *Subul al-Salam*, vol.3, p.26.

[14] Ibn 'Ābidīn, *al-Durr al-Mukhtar*, vol.4, p.101.

[15] San'ānī, *Subul al-Salam*, vol. 3, p.18.

[16] Zuhaylī, *al-Fiqh al-Islām i*, vol.4, p.223.

Explanation: Whether the loss is excessive/exorbitant or not is to be ascertained in view of the market value of the subject matter. Article 146 of Jordanian Civil code States: "Evaluation concerning *Ghabn Fāḥish* in real estate or other property is a matter for the estimators alone".

Ghabn is regarded light (*yasir*) if the difference between the price at which goods were sold and their real market value is so small that the merchants do not generally take it into account in their dealings. For instance a book worth Rs. 100/- is sold for Rs. 110, it will not be a Ghabn fāḥish but if it if sold for Rs. 150/- it will amount to *Ghabn Fāḥish*.

Effects of Ghabn Fāḥish : Ḥanafī viewpoint

The Ḥanafī jurists are of the view that excessive loss suffered by a party alone is not a cause of nullity of contract. It annuls the contract only when it is caused by a fraud, or misrepresentation. For example, A sells a watch worth Rs. 300/- for Rs. 600/- to B claiming that market value of such watch is 700/- rupees. B relying upon the words of A purchases it for Rs. 600/-. B has suffered from *ghabn fāḥish*, which is a result of fraud. Such *ghabn fāḥish* gives him right to revoke the contract.[17] In this respect the *Majallah* states:

> "If there is an excessive lesion without fraud in the
> sale, the person who has suffered loss cannot annul
> the sale.[18]

There are, however, certain cases in which excessive loss of a party alone without fraud affects the contracts such as the sale of *waqf* property or the property of *bayt al-māl* or the property of minor or insane. If the property of these people and institutions is

---

[17] Ibn 'Ābidīn , *al-Durr al-Mukhtar*, vol.4, p.166.
[18] *Majallah*, Article 356.

sold with *ghabn fāḥish*, i.e., at a much lower price as compared to its market value, the sale will be revoked.[19]

Ḥanbalī viewpoint

Ghabn fāḥish affects the contracts and makes it voidable at the option of the party which suffered lesion irrespective of the fact that it is a result of fraud or otherwise.[20]

Shāfiʿī viewpoint

The Shāfiʿī jurists do not admit the right of revocation for the buyer. They say that the lesion has occurred because of the negligence of buyer. Thus, he alone is responsible for the loss.[21]

4. Talaqqī al-Rukbān

It is another form of fraud and misrepresentation. It is a transaction where a city-dweller takes advantage of the ignorance of a bedouin carrying objects of prime and general necessity for sale and cheats him in the course of the sale. The shrewd city-dweller goes out of town to meet the bedouin merchant and buys his goods at a cheap rate, depriving the latter of the opportunity of first surveying the market to acquaint himself of the current market rate. The Holy Prophet (s.a.w.s.) said:

> "It is forbidden to meet the riders (i.e. the traders) on the road (for the purpose of taking undue advantage). Whosoever meets a trader on road and buys goods from this trader, the vendor has the right of option and cancellation of such deal when he arrives at the market".[22]

5. Inflated Price in Trust Sale:

Another form of fraud is where the seller in a trust sale, sells goods at an inflated price to buyer. The buyer bases himself on the price the

---

[19] Ibid, Article 356.
[20] Ibn Qudāmā, *al-Mughnī*, vol. 4, pp.212-218.
[21] Shirbīnī, *Mughnī al-Muḥtāj*, vol. 2, p.36.
[22] Ṣanʿānī, *Subul al-Salām*, vol. 3, p.21.

seller claims to have himself paid in order to suggest to him a purchase price.[23]

In trust sale the buyer takes the declaration of the person selling on trust. The latter's declaration may, of course be a lie, for he may in fact have acquired the article at a much lower price than the one he claims in order to make a large profit.[24]

Following are kinds of trust sale:

a) *Tawliyyah*: Resale at cost price.

b) *Murābaḥah*: Resale with profit Increase.

c) *Wadīah*: Resale with loss.

The fraud in trust sale renders the contract voidable at the option of buyer. He may either revoke the contract or claim reimbursement of undue increase from the seller.   Ibn 'Ābidīn states that if the amount of deception is one-fourth of the original, the buyer has the right to devalue one-fourth of profit from the stated price.[25]

Some Jurists suggest that the swindled purchaser should either cancel the sale completely or retain the goods at stated price. He does not have the option of devaluation of undue increase.

6. Tadlīs bi al- 'Ayb (Fraud with defect):

Soundness of the object is an implied condition of the contract. It is not permitted for a person to sell a defective object knowingly. Whatever may be the cause of diminishing the price amongst merchants is considered as a defect. A buyer discovering a defect in the article purchased is at liberty to return it to the seller, unless he was aware of the defect before hand.

---

[23] Zuhaylī, *al-Fiqh al-Islamī wa Addillatuhū*, vol. 4, pp.710-711.

[24] Sanhūrī, *Maṣadir al-Ḥaq* vol. 2, p.158.

[25] Ibn 'Ābidīn , *al-Durr al-Mukhtār*, vol. 4, p.155.

A purchaser is entitled to compensation for a defect in an article where it has sustained a further blemish in his hands, but he cannot in this case return it to the seller. He is also entitled to compensation if the return be rendered impracticable by any change in the subject.

Coercion (Ikrāh)

Sarakhsī defines coercion in the following words: "By coercion one designates the action of one person against another suppressing the consent of this latter person or vitiating his consent".[26] Zayla'ī defines *ikrāh* as: "An action directed against a person, which suppresses his true consent".[27] According to the *Majallah, ikrāh* is to compel, without right, a person to do a thing without his consent or by fear".[28]

In modern Law coercion is some element of force, either physical or economic used to suppress one party's consent to choose whether or not to enter into a particular contract. Under such circumstances the contract is voidable at the instance of the innocent party.[29]

Conditions of effective coercion

Following are conditions, which give rise to annulment of contract under coercion:

i) Coercion should be legally unjustified.

ii) It should emanate from a party who has the power to execute his threat, that is, it must be realistically practicable.

---

[26] Sarakhsī, *al-Mabsut*, vol. 14, p.39.

[27] Fakhr al-Dīn 'Uthmān ibn 'Alī Zayla'ī, ,*Tabyīn al-Haquiq*,Būlāq: al-Maktabah al-Kubrā al-Amīriyyah, 1313-1315, vol. 5, p.181.

[28] *Majallah*, Art. 948.

[29] *Business Law*, p.116.

iii) It must be of such a nature as to intimidate the victim: that is, it must be of significant and imminent danger.

iv) The compelled person must believe that if he does not comply with the compeller's demands, the harm promised by the compeller will be inflicted upon him.

Kinds of Coercion

Coercion is divided into two kinds:

1. Perfect Coercion (Ikrāh Tāmm): It leads to destruction of life, or loss of limb or one of them. It annuls the juridical act done under constraint.

2. Imperfect Coercion (Ikrāh Nāqis): This causes only grief and pain. It is compulsion, which is by things like a blow or imprisonment. Imperfect or minor coercion also annuals consent, but supposes that the contracting party who suffered this coercion could still exercise his free will. Such would be the case if he was threatened with blows not liable to cause his death or to cripple him.[30]

Effects

The opinion of Jurists is divided on the validity of contract with coercion. Ḥanafī Jurists maintain that contract concluded under coercion is valid because it has been agreed to by intention of the party, even though the consent was not freely given. In the opinion of these jurists coercion does not render the contract void but merely voidable. It gives rise to effects, which are assigned to voidable contracts. The party whose consent was obtained through coercion has the right either to ratify it in which case it will become binding

---

[30] Zaydān, *al-Madkhal*, p.361.

or to annual it.[31] Imām Zufar considers such contract suspended (*mawquf*) subject to ratification.

The viewpoint of the Mālikī jurists on the effect of a contract concluded under coercion is similar to that of the Hanafī School of Law. They regard it a valid contract but non-binding. The party, who has been coerced, has the right to revoke it. The Shāfi'ī and Hanbalī jurists regard the act under coercion non-existent since the essential condition of the juridical act, i.e., the will, is vitiated.[32] The Shāfi'īs argue that *khiyar* and consent are interdependent concepts and cannot operate independently in the intention to create legal relations.[33]

Conclusion

1. A defect of consent leading to nullity of contract arises when a party gives his consent as a result of mistake, fraud and coercion.

2. Mistake is a belief, which is not in accord with the facts. It relates either to genus of the object or its substantial quality.

3. The mistake bearing on genus renders the contract invalid while the mistake relating to substantial quality makes contracts voidable.

4. Fraud is to induce a person by some defective means with a view to obtain his consent to a contract without which he would have not consented to the contract.

5. Traditional forms of fraud include;

   i) *Tasriyah*

   ii) *Najash* (false bidding to raise price)

---

[31] Zarqā, *al-Madkhal*, vol. 1, p.371.

[32] Zahaylī,, *al-Fiqh al-Islam i*, vol.4, p.216.

[33] Ibid.

iii) Ghabn Fahish

iv) Talaqqi al-Rukban

v) Inflated price in trust sale

vi) Tadlis bi al -'Ayb

6. Coercion refers to an action of one person against another suppressing the consent of this latter. It is a cause of nullity of contract.

CHAPTER-11

EXTRINSIC CONDITIONS, AND THEIR EFFECT ON THE CONTRACT

The opinion of Muslim Jurists is divided on the extent of freedom enjoyed by the contracting parties to insert extrinsic or ancillary conditions in the contract. The reason for emphasising this issue is that the Lawgiver has assigned certain legal effects to contracts while the extrinsic conditions remove or modify these effects. For example the effect of sale is to transfer ownership of the goods sold and their usufruct to the buyer immediately. Now if a person sells a car to another on the condition that he (seller) reserves right to use it for a month. This condition has direct bearing on the effects of the contract because it delays the effects of the contract. Is such condition valid? In other words can contracting parties by their mutual consent agree to a condition, which may change and modify the effects, which the *Sharī'ah* accords to contract?

The Jurists have differed among themselves on this point. One school, which emphasises the supremacy of the autonomy of the will of contracting parties, holds that the parties are free to insert any condition. They deem every clause or condition in the contract valid provided it does not contradict any text of the Qur'an and the Sunnah. Another school has adopted a very rigid and extreme position. This school holds that conditions are generally not valid except where the text provides for them.

A third school while favouring the position held by the second school that the contracting parties do not have the right to modify the effects of contracts, allow for some conditions, which either confirm the effects or are normally recognised, in the commercial usage. Unlike the first school, this school is rather restrictive which does not accept conditions except those, which conform to the principles laid down by this school for admissibility of conditions. Now we discuss these viewpoints and their arguments in detail.

Viewpoint of Ẓāhirī Jurists

Ẓāhiī jurists impose total ban on ancillary conditions except the conditions, which are approved by the text. To these jurists basic presumption of law is that all contracts and conditions are prohibited except that which is established by the text or *ijmā'* (consensus of opinion).[1]

Their Arguments

1. Holy Prophet (s.a.w.a) said, "He who performs an act we have not ordered him, his act is null and void".[2]

2. Holy Prophet (s.a.w.a) said: "A loan made at the same time as a sale is illicit. Two conditions in a sale are not allowed nor is profit without corresponding liability and sale of what is not possible"[3]

Thus, the Ẓāhiī Jurists invalidate all such conditions, which do not figure in the Qur'ān and the Sunnah, or they introduce modification to the effects of a juridical act.

Ḥanbalī Viewpoint

The Ḥanbalī viewpoint represents a very liberal approach as it acknowledges complete autonomy of will in contracts and transactions.[4] To Ḥanbalī jurists general rule with regard to contracts and conditions is permissibly unless a text from the Qur'ān or the Sunnah or a valid consensus makes them invalid. They do not demand a text providing for permissibility, as it is demanded by the Ẓāhiī Scholars. Thus, to combine two contracts in one or to sell with the condition of loan from buyer are not valid conditions because the text has explicitly prohibited it. Apart from it all other conditions are permissible. It is, therefore, permissible for a woman to stipulate in marriage contract that her husband will not compel her to leave her hometown. It is also permissible to stipulate that he will not marry

---

[1] Ibn Ḥazm, *al-Muḥallā, vol.* 2, p. 412.

[2] *Iḥkām fī Uṣūl al-Aḥkām,* vol. 5, p.32; *Taysīr al-Wuṣūl 'ilā Jāmi' al-Uṣūl.* vol. 1, p.63.

[3] *Nayl al-Awṭār*, vol. 5, p.190.

[4] For Ḥanbalī Viewpoint see Ibn Taymiyyah, *Naẓriyyat al-'Aqd*, p.15,16; and *Fatāwā 'ibn Taymiyyah* vol. 3, p.323.

another woman. Such condition would be binding upon husband and give her right to revoke contract if he does not honour it. They also allow the seller of a house to stay in the house sold for some specified time as a part of contractual condition.

Their Arguments

1. The Qur'ān says: "O you who believe: fulfill your contracts".[5] It also says: "And fulfil every promise, because every promise will be inquired into".[6] In these verses Allah has ordered believers to fulfill their obligations and undertakings towards each other and prohibited from violating them. This includes conditions the parties insert in the contract by their free will.

2. The Holy Prophet (s.a.w.s) said: "Muslims are bound by their stipulations unless it be a condition which turns *ḥarām* into *ḥalāl* or *ḥalāl* into *ḥarām*."[7]

   This *ḥadīth* allows inserting conditions in contract, and the parties are bound to abide by it. The only limitation imposed on the parties is that they should not insert a condition, which is inconsistent with the injunctions of Islam.

3. As regards the *ḥadīth* which declares all such conditions void, which do not exist in the Book of God, these jurists, argue that prohibition contained in it is applicable to those conditions only which are against the Book of Allah, i.e.,against its injunctions. The meaning of *ḥadīth* in the light of this interpretation would be that if someone stipulated for a thing which is not recommend in His book, this act on his part will be regarded null and void.

4. The Ḥanbalīs differentiate between *'ibādāt* and *mu'āmlāt*. *'ibādāt* are established by the explicit injunctions of the *Sharī'ah*. As for *Mu'āmlāt* (transactions) the governing principle is permissibility and absence of prohibition.[8]

---

[5] Qur'ān, 5:1.
[6] Qur'ān, 17:34.
[7] Shawkānī, *Nayl al-Awtār* vol. 5, p.255.
[8] Ibn Taymiyyah, *Fatāwa*, vol. 29, pp. 16-18; *Naẓriyyat al-'Aqd*, p. 314.

Viewpoint of Ḥanafī, Shāfi'ī and Mālikī Jurists

The jurists of these schools divide the condition into three kinds.[9]

a) Valid Conditions: Valid conditions are further divided into four categories:[10]

> i) Conditions, which confirm the effects, attributed to juridical act by the *Sharī'ah*. Such conditions strengthen the purpose of contract. The condition, for example, to sell on the condition that the seller will not hand over good to buyer unless he pays the price is a valid condition because it stresses and confirms the effects of contract and realizes its objective.

> ii) Condition, which is admitted explicitly by the *Sharī'ah*, such as the option of stipulation, reserved for a party to revoke or ratify a contract within three days. Such condition is valid because the *Sharī'ah* has sanctioned the option of stipulation (*khiyār al-sharṭ*) and option of inspection (*khiyar al-ru'yah*).

> iii) A condition, which is intimately, connected with the contract such a pledge of security in a contract of surety.

> iv) The Ḥanafī jurists also allow a condition, which has been established by custom. A modern example of such condition is to purchase air-conditioner with the condition that the company will be responsible for its repair for two years.

b) Irregular Condition:

A condition is regarded irregular if:

> i)   it is repugnant to requisites of the contract;

---

[9] Madkūr, *al-Madkhal Li al- Fiqh al-Islāmī*, p. 664. See for details: Sarakhsī, *al-Mabsūṭ* vol. 13, pp. 14-28; Ibn al-Humām, *Fath al-Qadīr*, vol. 5, p.314; Ibn 'Ābidīn, *Radd al-Mukhtar*, vol. 4, p.126

[10] See 'Ādil Muṣṭafā Basyūni, *Al-Tashrī al-Islāmī wa al-Nuẓum al-Qanūniyyah al-Waḍ'iyyah* , p.152,153

ii) it is irreconcilable with the purpose and effects of contract;

iii) it is not allowed by the *Sharī'ah;*

iv) it is not allowed by custom and usage;and

V) it gives undue advantage to one of the contracting parties

The *ḥukm* of such condition is that it renders the entire juridical act invalid. It especially affects commutative contracts. The condition by an owner of a house to stay in the house sold for one year is an irregular condition, which effects whole contract and renders it invalid. But it does not affect gratuitous contracts. The contract containing such condition remains valid, the condition alone is regarded null and void. The reason for the difference between commutative contracts and gratuitous contracts is that in the former case the condition disturbs balance of benefits involved in the contract. It gives one of the parties an advantage that is not balanced by a corresponding gain or benefit of the other. On the other hand, gratuitous contracts do not involve bilateral benefits, so no question of the disruption of equilibrium arises. An irregular condition in gratuitous contract, therefore, does not nullify whole juridical act.

c) Void Conditions:

It is a condition, which directly infringes any rule of the *Sharī'ah,* or inflicts harm on one of the two contracting parties or derogates from completion of contract, such as the condition imposed by the seller that the purchaser will not sell it further to any party. The condition, which brings benefit for one of the two contracting parties and disturbs the equivalence of benefits, is, in fact, a kind of *ribā* and is, thus, considered null and void.[11]

The *ḥukm* of a contract with a void condition is that the condition is severable from the contract, it does not nullify the whole contract.The condition alone will be regarded null and void.

---

[11] Zaydān, *al-Madkhal,* p.398.

Meaning of two conditions in sale and two transactions in one:

The tradition prohibiting the two conditions and two transactions referred to above has been interpreted by the jurists in a number of ways. Sarakhsī, a Ḥanafī jurist, commenting on the tradition says:

> "The description of the two conditions in sale is to say (So much for cash and so much for delay)The contract here is *fāsid* because the buyer did not specify the price at which he has agreed to purchase goods. Thus, the cause of irregularity of this contract is indeterminacy with regard to price of goods. "[12]

In regard to the legal status of two transactions in one Imam Shāfi'ī is reported to have stated his opinion in the following words:

> It carries two interpretations: first, I sold you this commodity for two thousand on credit and one thousand in cash and sale is binding and irrevocable at one of the two prices. The sale is void because contract is contingent upon an unspecified thing. Second: I sell you my house on the condition that you sell your horse to me. This is invalid because it involves exploitation of buyer who is compelled to purchase a thing, which he does not want. It also contains *gharar* because the seller does not know whether the second sale will take place or not.[13]

This sale is invalid in the Ḥanbalī School as well because of the element of *gharar*.[14]

Conclusion

1-The opinion of Muslim jurists is divided on the legality of extrinsic conditions in a contract.

2- The Ḥanbalī Jurists emphasise the supremacy of the will of contracting parties and allow every condition and stipulation in a contract as long as it does not contradict any text from the Qur'ān or the Sunnah.

---

[12] Sarakhsī, *al-Mabsūṭ*. vol. 14, p. 0
[13] Shīrāzī , *al-Muhadhdhab*. vol. 1, p.267
[14] Ibn Qudāma , *al-Mughnī*. vol. 4, p.234.

3- The Ẓāhirī Jurists impose total ban on extrinsic conditions. They accept only those conditions, which are approved by the explicit texts of the Qur'ān and the Sunnah.

4- The Ḥanafī, Shāfi'ī and Mālikī Jurists divide conditions into valid, irregular and void.

5- Valid conditions are those, which confirm the effects, attributed to juridical act by the *Sharī'ah* and which are admitted explicitly by it, such as the option of stipulation.

6- A condition is regarded irregular if:

i) It is repugnant to requisites of the contract

ii) It is irreconcilable with the purpose and effects of contract

iii) It is not allowed by the *Sharī'ah*

iv) It is not allowed by custom and usage

v) And it gives undue advantage to one of the contracting parties

7- Void Condition is a condition, which directly infringes any rule of the *Sharī'ah*, or inflicts harm on one of the two contracting parties or derogates from completion of contract.

CHAPTER -12

ISLAMIC LAW OF OPTIONS (KHAYĀRĀT)

Muslim jurists have suggested number of devices to safeguard contracting parties against hasty undertaking. These devices give a party who signed contract unwisely and then regretted his haste on seeing some lesion or fraud, an opportunity to ponder over his transaction and revoke the contract. These devices are called *Khayārāt* (plural of word *Khiyār)*, i.e., options in Islamic Law. They have been designed to maintain balance in transactions and to protect a weaker party from being harmed. They constitute preventive measure against error, defect in goods, want of knowledge concerning quality of things. lack of desired quality. The meaning of *Khiyār* is that a contractor has right to ratify the contract or to annual within the period of option.

Kinds of Options

The options allowed in Islamic Law are as under:

1) *Khiyār al-Shart* (Option of condition)

2) *Khiyār al-Ta'yīn* (Option of determination)

3) *Khiyār al-'Āyb* (Option of defect)

4) *Khiyār al-Ru'yah* (Option of inspection)

5) *Khiyār al-Waṣf* (Option of Description) [1]

These options are established either through the rule of the *Sharī'ah* or the agreement between the parties. Options of defect and option of inspection have been granted by the *Sharī'ah* while the

---

[1] Zuḥaylī. *al-Fiqh al-Islāmī wa Adillatuhū,* vol. 4; p.250.

option of stipulation, option of determination, and option of description are established by agreement.[2] Some modern authors class option of condition under first category.

1) *Khiyār al-Sharṭ* (Option of condition):

Khiyār al-Sharṭ is that option through which one party or both of them stipulate for themselves or for someone else the right to revoke the contract within a determined period.[3] For instance, the purchaser says to the seller "I purchased this thing from you but I have the right to return it within three days". As soon as the period is over the right to revoke, derived through this option, lapses The result of this option is that contract which is binding initially becomes non-binding with the stipulation of this option.

Legality of khiyār al-sharṭ

It is reported that the Holy Prophet (s.a.w.s) granted this option to Ḥibbān ibn Munzir who complained that he was defrauded each time he made a purchase. He was directed by the Holy Prophet (s a w s) to say whenever he made a purchase "No Cheating, and I reserve option for three days".[4] The purpose of option is to give chance to a person who suffered some loss in transaction to revoke contract within stipulated time. The option is stipulated normally at the time of the contract. According to Imām Shāfiʿī and Imām Aḥmad it should be stipulated at the time of contract. Other jurists allow it even after the contract has been concluded, as long as the parties are in the same session of contract.

Contract in which *khiyār al -sharṭ* is permitted

Khiyār al sharṭ is permitted in - those contracts, which accept revocation like sale, hire, *muzāra'ah* (crop sharing). It cannot be stipulated in those contracts, which do not accept revocation such as divorce, manumission etc.

As regard those contracts, which are revocable by nature like agency, and partnership, the stipulation of *khiyār al-sharṭ* would be

---

2 Hassan.*al-Madkhal*, p.455.

[3] Zuhaylī, *al-Fiqh al Islāmī wa Adillatuhū*, vol. 4, p.254; See also
Zaydān, *al-Madkhal*, p.377.

[4] Shawkānī, *Nayl al-Awṭār* vol. 5, p.182.

futile as they can be revoked at the will of either party. It is also not permitted in contracts of *salam* (sale of future goods)[5] and *ṣarf* (money exchange) .

For whom the option is stipulated

The option can be stipulated by one of the parties for himself or for a third party. The third party then becomes the *wakīl* of the party for purpose of exercising the option but it does not prevent the party from exercising the option himself.

Maximum period of khiyār al -sharṭ

There is agreement amongst the jurists that *khiyār al- sharṭ* can be stipulated for a period of three days or less. This agreement is based on the tradition quoted above.

The jurists disagree as regards any period over three days. Imām Abū Yūsuf and Mohammad and the Ḥanbalīs are of the opinion that it is permitted to lay down a period of more than three days without any restriction of the maximum period.[6] Imām Abū Ḥanīfah and Shāfi'ī do not allow it for more than three days. The reason is that *qiyās*, i.e general rule prohibits the stipulation of *khiyār* altogether, which is then permitted as an exception from the tradition. The necessity has been acknowledged as three days by the tradition and cannot, therefore, be extended beyond such period.[7] According to the Mālikīs the period of *khiyār* varies from case to case. Thus, it may be one day when a piece of cloth has been purchased and may be one or two months when a house has been purchased.[8]

---

[5] Abū Zahrah. *al-Milkiyyah wa Nazariyyat al-'Aqd* p. 393.

[6] Ibn Qudāma. *al-Mughnī* vol. 3, p.585.Kāsānī. *Badā'i' al-Sanā'i'* vol. 5, p.174

Shirbīnī. *Mughnī al-Muhtāj*, vol. 2, p. 47; Kāsānī. *Badā'i' al-Sanā'i'* vol. 5, p.174.

[8] Ibn Rushd. *Bidāyah al-Mujtahid*, vol. 2, p.208.

Effect of the contract with khiyār al-shart

The difference between the jurists as regards the *ḥukm* of the contract can be reduced to two opinions.

First Opinion: The effects do not come into operation during the period of the option. The contract remains suspended *(mawqūf)* during the period of the option or till such option is exercised. Thus right in the property is not transferred to one in whose favour the option has been stipulated.

Second Option. The effects come into operation but the contract is now not binding or *ghayr lāzim* and can be revoked during the period of the option by the one in whose favour the option has been stipulated.

The option may be exercised expressly or impliedly. Revocation does not require the *ḥukm* of the court to become effective. Ratification may also be expressed or implied [9]

Termination of the Option

The option ceases to be applicable in the following cases

> **i) Death of one in whose favour the option was operating:** In such case the option becomes extinct and the contract is now binding as regards the representative of the deceased. The exercise of the option is a personal right and cannot pass to the heirs According to the Mālikīs and Shāfi'īs on the other hand, it is right which can be inherited and the heirs can exercise the option within the stipulated period.

> **ii) Termination of the Period:** On termination of the period the contract becomes binding and irrevocable.

> **iii) Destruction of the subject matter:** In this case also the contract becomes binding.

Hassān *al-Madkhal.* pp 456,457

2) Khiyār al-Ṭa'yīn (Option of designation):

Option of designation is the right of buyer to choose, designate or determine within a pre-stated time one object out of two or more which are proposed to him. The basic rule is that the subject matter must be known. i.e., ascertained at the time of contract. There is, however, a genuine need of the people to buy an unascertained thing out of a number of ascertained things with a right to ascertain the exact thing later. For example one buying a car out of three vehicles offered for fixed price, gets opportunity through this option to have cars examined by a specialist and choose one of them. The reserving of the right to ascertain the bought item later is known as the *Khiyār al-ta'yīn* or the option of ascertainment

This option is imposed by the buyer only and it results in making a binding contract non-binding in favour of the buyer.

Effects of the Option

The general rule is that the goods being purchased must be ascertained at the time of the contract. On the basis of this rule the Shāfi'īs and the Ḥanbalīs do not permit the stipulation of the option of ascertainment. The option if stipulated would make the contract *bāṭil*. The Ḥanafīs and Mālikīs allow this option because one may be in need of consulting other or for pondering over the purchase and at the same time he does not wish to lose the bargain also. It may also happen that he is the agent of someone and wants to refer the matter to his principal.[10]

The option is allowed as an exception through *istiḥsān* (juristic preference) against *qiyās* (general rule) and its operation is very narrow being permitted mainly in the contract of sale. Again it is permitted to the buyer only as the necessity on which it is based cannot be established for the seller according to the majority of the Ḥanafīs

Duration of Khiyār al-ṭa'yīn

Those who maintain that *khiyār al-ta'yīn* is a condition, which operates within *khiyār al-shart*, or is a kind of *khiyār al-shart* grant the same period as stipulated for the *khiyār al-shart*. Thus the maximum

---

[10] See Kāsānī. *Badā'i' al-Sanā'i'*, vol. 5. P 158; *Dasūqī 'Ilā al-Sharḥ al-Kabīr*, vol. 3, p. 91.

period is three days according to Imām Abū Ḥanīfah and unlimited according to Imām Abū Yusuf and Muḥammad. Another opinion within the Ḥanafī School is that *khiyār al-ta'yīn* is independent of *khiyār al-sharṭ* and thus has no fixed period.[11]

Conditions of Khiyār al-ta'yīn

i) The number of unascertained items should not exceed three i.e., those out of which one has to be ascertained. The reason is that necessity does not go beyond three.

ii) There should be a difference in value between the three items and the price of each must be known.

iii) The period of the option should be determined within the confines of the *khiyār al-sharṭ* (majority opinion).[12]

Effects of the Khiyār al-ta'yīn

A contract witn this option is binding for the seller and non-binding for the buyer. As the *khiyār al-ta'yīn* operates within the *khiyār al- sharṭ* it is possible for the buyer to revoke the purchase in all three items.

On the termination of the period the contract becomes binding and it is now necessary for the buyer to ascertain one of them. This is the opinion of the Ḥanafīs. The Mālikīs maintain that on termination of the period, the sale is void in all items. In other words the option must be exercised within the period otherwise the contract is void. Some of the Ḥanafīs who maintain that *khiyār al -ta'yīn* in not a part of *khiyār al-sharṭ* are of the opinion that the contract cannot be revoked in all items and one item must be ascertained.

Factors terminating the option

i) Exercise of the option whether express or implied.

ii) Destruction of one of the items

---

[11] Kāsānī. *Badā'i' al-Ṣanā'i'*. op. cit. vol. 5. p. 158.
[12] Madkūr. *al-Madkhal li al-Fiqh al-Islāmī*. p.680: See also Zaydān. *al-Madkhal li Dirāsāt al-Sharī'ah*, p.381.

a) In possession of the buyer: The goods destroyed become ascertained and the buyer is liable for the price.

b) In possession of the seller: Buyer has a choice to accept what remains or to call off the contract.

iii) Death of one who possessed the option. The contract becomes non-binding for the heirs and right of revocation lapses. The heirs must ascertain one item.

3) *Khiyār al -Ru'yah* (Option of Examination):

Option of examination is the right accorded to a person buying or brings anything not yet present at the moment of the signature of the contract to confirm or cancel the said contract after inspecting the object.

Knowledge of the subject matter at the time of contract is an essential condition. Such knowledge is possible through an examination of the subject at the time of the contract or by description in a manner, which removes all kinds of *jahālah* (want of knowledge).

Some of the jurists consider examination at the time of contract essential and any condition permitting examination later would make the contract *bāṭil*. The Ḥanafīs allow the sale of things, which have not been seen or examined at the time of the contract and grant an option to the buyer to examine the goods later. If he finds the goods or property to his liking, he may accept them and in the alternate he may revoke the contract. This is known as the option of examination or *khiyār al- ru'yah*.

Opinions of Fuqahā regarding option of examination:

There are two opinions relating to the *khiyār al- ru'yah* which are summarised below.

Option 1. The Shāfi'īs are of the view that the contract in which the subject matter has not been examined is not valid.[13] Thus they reject the validity of *khiyār* al-ru'yah. They argue on the basis of the tradition, " do not sell what you do not have".[14]

---

[13] Shīrāzī. *al-Muhadhdhab* vol. 1. p. 263.
[14] Shawkānī. *Nayl al- Awṭār*.vol.5.p.164.

The Mālikīs agree with the Shāfi'īs in general but when examination at the time of the contract becomes impossible or is likely to result in grave loss (e g exposure of a very expensive piece of cloth time and again for buyers) they allow sale by minute description. In such case the buyer may exercise option of inspection and reject the object if it does not conform to description [15]

The Ḥanbalīs maintain that sale must be through examination at the time of the contract and if this is difficult. sale may be by description. Thus they reject *khiyār al -ru'yah* also.

Option 2

The Ḥanafīs differing with the other schools maintain that the contract in which the buyer has not seen the goods is a contract which is valid and enforceable but is non-binding and the buyer has the option to revoke it upon examination. This is known as the *khiyār al -ru'yah*. It is very important to note here that through this option the buyer can reject the goods upon examination even if the goods were described minutely and are found to conform to the description upon examination This option can be stipulated for the buyer only.

The Ḥanafīs argue that the tradition. "Do not sell what you do not possess" applies to one who does not own the goods and has not capacity to deliver. It does not apply to the goods. which cannot be seen at the time of the contract. They also quote in support a tradition to the effect that: "He who buys a thing which he has not seen has an option upon seeing it" [16]

They also base its legality on a judgement against Ḥaḍrat 'Uthmān (r.a t.a) who had sold land to Ḥaḍrat Ṭalḥah Either had not seen the land Some one said to Ṭalḥah "you have made a bad bargain" He replied". I have not seen the land and thus have an option". Jubayr ibn Mut'am arbitrated the dispute and allowed Ṭalḥah right of option The course taken by this litigation without any objection on the part of the companions is said to have established right of option of examination for buyer. [17]

---

[15] Ibn Rushd. *Bidāyat al-Mujtahid* vol. 2. p. 155.
[16] Madkūr. *al-Madkhal li al- Fiqh al-Islāmī*. p.686.

[17] Abū Zahrā . *al-Milkiyyah wa Nazariyyat al-'Aqd* p.398.

Conditions related to the option

i) The buyer must not have seen the goods. which are the subject matter of contract.

ii) The contract must be in property. which is specified. and not in that which is sold by description. Things specified are like houses. land horses. etc. which possess their own individuality.

Effects of the option of examination

The option makes the contract non-binding. The seller cannot revoke such a contract. which is binding for him even if he has not seen his own property. The property passes to the buyer and the contract is non-binding

Facts terminating the option

1. The option ends with the examination of the subject matter. There is no fixed period for the option. however. once the goods have been examined. the option is terminated.

2 The option lapses if the subject matter is destroyed. The contract becomes irrevocable upon destruction of the subject matter.

3. The death of the buyer makes the contract binding for the heirs of the buyer.

4. If the buyer examines the property and disposes it off. the contract becomes irrevocable.

4). Khiyār al-'ayb (option of defect)

It is a right given to a purchaser in a sale to cancel the contract if he discovers that the object acquired has in it some defect diminishing its value.[18] The option has been imposed by the law itself and the parties do not have to stipulate it. It is thus a necessary

---

[18] Kāsānī. *Badā'i' al-Ṣanā'i'* vol. 5.p. 247.

condition of the contract. The goods are liable to be rejected if undeclared defects are discovered. When the seller specifically states that he is not responsible for any defects then the buyer acts at his own risk and goods cannot be rejected

This option is based on the traditions:

i) "He who defrauds another is not from amongst us"[19]

ii) "It is not permitted for seller to sell things which are defective unless he points it out to him"[20]

The option operates in favour of one buying or hiring property. The option is valid in case of goods, which need to be specified like a house, land or any room, which has its own individuality.

Conditions for exercising option of defect:

1) The defect should be such which causes decrease in the sale of the property. The defect may be obvious or hidden.

2) The defect should have existed prior to the contract. A defect appearing later after delivery is not valid for purpose of the option.

3) The defect should continue after delivering till the time of the exercise of the option. If the defect disappears before this, there is no option.

4) The buyer should have no knowledge of the defect at the time of the contract or at the time of delivering.

5) **There should** not be any agreement of non-guarantee. If **the purchaser** who by an agreement of non-guarantee **expressly** exonerated the seller of any responsibility for **defect in the** article sold, then he cannot in future avail **himself of the** option of defect.

---

[19]Bukhārī. *Sahīh* quoted from *Jam' al-Fawā'id*. Hadīth No. 4668

[20] Shawkānī. *Nayl al-Awtār*. vol. 5. p. 224.

Effects of Option of Defect

The contract with the option of defect is revocable. The purchaser of an object with defect has the choice to confirm the sale or to cancel it. This is the majority opinion. The Mālikī jurists distinguish between the minor (*yasīr*) defect and major (*fāhish*) defect and propose that if the defect is minor, the buyer may confirm the sale while being returned part of the price paid in proportion to the extent of the defect. In case the defect is major, he has the choice either to cancel it or confirm it without compensatory restitution. The Ḥanbalī jurists hold that the buyer of an object with defect whether minor or major, may confirm the sale while being paid the difference between the price of the article in perfect condition and its price with defect.

Factors terminating the option

i) Acceptance of object with defect by the buyer

ii) Destruction of the object in the hands of buyer.

The death of buyer does not terminate the option. The right in such case inherited by the heirs.

Conclusion

1- Islamic law of option provides a device to safeguard contracting parties against hasty undertakings.

2- The options allowed in Islamic law are

(i)   Option of condition

(ii)   Option of determination

(iii)   Option of defect

(iv)   Option of inspection

(v)   Option of description

3- The option of inspection and option of defect are granted by the *Sharī'ah* whereas the options of condition, determination and description are established by the mutual agreement.

CHAPTER -13

CLASSIFICATION OF CONTRACTS

The modern Muslim jurists have classified contracts from various perspectives to facilitate understanding. One classification is according to their function and purpose and the other is according to their time of completion.

A- Classification according to function of contract:

Contracts from this perspective are divided into the following seven categories:

1. *Tamlīkāt* (contract for alienation of property): The contract falling under this category aims to make a person owner of a thing or its usufructs. They may be for consideration and without consideration. In the former case, they are designated as *'uqūd al-mu'āwaḍāt* (commutative contracts) such as sale, hiring, *ṣarf* (money changing), *ṣulḥ* (composition), *'istiṣnā* (manufacturing contract), *muzara'ah* (cultivation) and *musāqāh* , in the latter case, they are called *'udūd al-tabarru'āt* (gratuitous contracts) such as gift, bequest, *waqf* (religious endowment) *'āriyah* (commodate loans) and *ḥawālah* (assignment of debt). Sometimes a contract begins with donation and ends up with exchange. Thus at the final stages it becomes a commutative contract such as contract of loan and surety by the orders of debtor.

2. *Isqāṭāt* (contracts extinguishing rights):

> The object of such acts and contracts is to extinguish established rights. They may be with consideration and without consideration. The examples of first kind are divorce without consideration, manumission, remission of debt, withdrawal of the right of *shufa'ah* (pre-emption), whereas the divorce for consideration and accepting blood money instead of *qiṣāṣ* are the examples of second kind.

3. *'Iṭlāqāt* and *Tafwīḍh* (contracts of authorisation): The purpose of these contracts is to delegate power and authority to a party to carry

out a transaction which was not permissible for him before this delegation, like agency, permission to a person placed under interdiction person for dispositions.

4. *Taqyīdāt* (contracts restrictive of the rights of others): The principle feature of these contracts is to restrict the liberty of a person and prevent him from the right of disposal and use of property such as preventing insane, lunatic, minor and insolvent person from dispositions.

5. *Tawthīqāt*(contracts of guarantee) The purpose of such contract is to secure the debt of creditors. The contracts which serve this purpose are *kafālah* (suretyship), *ḥawālah* (assignment of debt) and *rahn* (pledge).

6.*Ishtirāk (partnership):* The purpose of contracts falling in this category is to share the profit of a business such as *mushārakah, mudhārabah, muzāra'ah.*

7. *'Uqūd al-Ḥifz (deposits and bailments).* These contracts aim at safeguarding the property of a person like deposit and bailment.[1]

A contemporary scholar Muhammad Salām Madkūr has treated *'uqūd al-mu'awadāt* and *'uqūd al-tabarru'āt* separately instead of classing them under *tamlīkāt.*[2] The contracts according to his scheme are as follows:

I-*'Uqūd al-Mu'āwadāt* (commutative contracts):

These contracts contain exchange of counter values from both the contracting parties such as contract of sale, and *iājrah* (hiring). *'Uqūd al- mu'āwadāt* includes the following contracts:

❑   Contract of Sale: Contracts of sale are further classified as under:

a) Classification according to object:

◆ *Muqāyadah* (barter)

---

[1] Zuhaylī, *al-Fiqh al-Islāmī wa adillatuhū,* vol. 4.

pp. 244,245.Zaydān, *al-Madkhal,* pp. 375,376

[2] Madkūr, *al-Madkhal,* pp. 595,596.

* *Ṣarf* (money changing)

* *Salam* (sale with immediate payment and deferred delivery)

* *Bay' Mu'ajjal* (deferred payment sale)

* *Bay' Muṭlaq* (sale of object for money)

b) Classification according to price:

* *Tawliyah* (resale at cost price)

* *Murābḥah* (resale at cost price plus some profit)

* *Wadī'ah* (resale with loss)

* *Musāwamah* (resale with agreement that no reference be made to the original cost price).

❑ Contract of Hiring: This may be divided into

* *Ijārat al-Ashkhāṣ* (rendering services)

* *Ijārat al-Ashyā'* (letting things)

❑ Loan Contract

❑ *Istiṣnā'* (contract of manufacturing)

II- *'Uqūd al-Tabarrū'āt* (gratuitous contracts): The main feature of these contracts is donation of property. The donor transfers ownership of that property to a party without consideration. Following contracts fall under this category.

* *Hibah* (gift)

* *Waṣiyyah* (bequest)

* *Waqf* (endowment)

* *Kafālāh* (guarantee)

* *'Āriyah* (commodate loan)

III. *'Uqūd al-Isqaṭāt* (relinquishment of rights) such as

* Remission of debt

* Relinquishment of right of pre-emption.

IV. *'Uqūd al-Iṭlāqāt* (authorization) such as:

   ♦ *Wakālah* (agency)

   ♦ *Īṣā'* (making a person guardian)

   ♦ Removal of interdiction from discerning minor.

   ♦ Manumission

V. *'Uqūd al-Taqyīdāt* (contracts restrictive of the rights of others) such as:

   ♦ Dismissal of agent.

   ♦ Dismissal of guardian and superintendent of *waqf* from their offices.

   ♦ Interdiction of minor from disposition

   ♦ Interdiction of insane. lunatic. insolvent etc.

VI. *'Uqūd al-Sharikāt* (contracts of partnership.

   They include:

   ♦ *Sharikat al-mufāwaḍah*

   ♦ *Sharikat al-'inān*

   ♦ *Sharikat al-wujūh*

   ♦ *Sharikat al-a'māl*

   ♦ *Sharikat al-muḍarabah*

VII. *'Uqūd al-ḍamanāt* (contracts of suretyship)

   They include:

   ♦ *Kafālah*

   ♦ *Ḥawālah*

   ♦ *Rahn*

VII. *'Uqūd al-Istiḥfazāt* (contract of depositing)

Sir Abdur Rahim has rather followed legalistic approach and classified Islamic contracts as follows.[3]

1. Alienation of property for exchange, namely

♦ sale

♦ without exchange, namely *ribā* or simple gift

♦ by way of dedication, namely *waqf.*

♦ to create succession, namely bequest.

2. Alienation of Usufruct

♦ In exchange for property namely *ijārah* which includes letting things movable and immovable for hire, contracts for rendering services such as for carriage of goods, safe custody of property, domestic and professional services.

♦ Not being in exchange of property, for example; commodate loans and deposits.

3. Contracts for securing the discharge of an obligation, namely; pledge and suretyship.

4. Contracts for representation namely; agency and partnership.

B- Classification of contracts with regard to time of completion:

Having regard to time of completion, the Muslim jurists have divided contracts in to the following three kinds.[4]

1.Al-'Aqd al-Munjaz (Contract Immediately Enforceable):

It is a contract, which unconditionally becomes complete after the offer is accepted and its consequences in the form of obligation ensue immediately. Thus a contract will be regarded *'aqd munjaz* if:

---

[3] Sir Abdur Rahim *'Muhammadan Jurisprudence*, Lahore: All Pakistan Legal Decisions, 1977,pp.227, 228.

[4] Madkūr, *al-Madkhal* , p. 611.

i. It is free from any option reserved for a party like option of the buyer to revoke contract within three days.

ii. It does not depend upon ratification by the party concerned. For example, the contract concluded by a discerning minor or the one placed under interdiction due to idiocy and lunacy, is suspended till it is ratified by their respective guardians. Similarly the contract made by a *fuḍūlī* (unauthorized agent) is also a suspended contract, which is enforceable only on ratification by the principal. The sale of mortgaged property also remains suspended till the mortgagee forgoes his claim upon the property and ratifies the contract.

iii. It is not contingent upon a condition or happening of an uncertain event in future i.e. I sell you my house if A sold his house to me. As general principle, Muslim jurists hold that a valid contract should give rise to the effects assigned to it by the Lawgiver immediately. It is for this reason that majority of jurists do not admit of suspended contracts because such contracts cause delay in the enforcement of contracts.[5] Ibn al-Qayyim and Ibn Taymiyyah, however, approve contingent contracts and regard them valid.[6]

2. Al'Aqd al-Muḍāf li al-Mustaqbal. (Contract Effective From Future Date):

Such contract is not valid according to majority of the jurists since they hold that the effects should ensue immediately without any delay.[7] They, however, allow the contracts made on usufructs to be effective from future date like the contract of leasing, manufacturing because a person does not own usufructs immediately as he does in the case of sale contract, but he owns them gradually, so the future time is considered in such contracts. *kafālah* (suretyship) and *ḥawālah* (assignment of debt) are also considered to be the contracts of above-

---

[5] See Ibn Humām, *Fath al-Qadīr* Vol. 5, P. 195; Nawawī,
    al-Majmū' vol. 9, p. 340; Ḥajawaī, *al 'Iqnā'*, vol. 3, P. 157;
    Ibn Qudāma, *al-Mughnī*, vol. 6, p. 599.
[6] Ibn al-Qayyim, *I'lām al-Muwaqqi'īn* vol. 3, p.237.
Darīr, *al-Gharar fi al-'Uqūd*, pp. 4-5.

mentioned category. A *kafīl* (surety) is not required to pay debt immediately when the contract is concluded. So it is valid if the surety were to say to the creditor "if your debtor did not pay off his debt to you by the beginning of next month, then I will make this payment". Similarly the agency, divorce and *waqf* are valid from future date. Contract of bequest also by its nature admits of delay, as it cannot be enforced in the life of legator. The contract of *ijārah* partakes the attributes of both the *'aqd munjaz* and *gayr munjaz*.

The contract of sale in the opinion of all the jurists is immediately enforceable contract, thus it is not permissible to say "I sell you this house of mine in the beginning of next year". The jurists see in this postponement and delay an element of *gharar* (uncertainty). It is like a contract which is contingent upon an uncertain event which the parties do not know whether it will occur or not or it is dependent upon condition about which the parties do not know whether it will be fulfilled or not.[8]

But the fact is that there is substantial difference between *'aqd muḍāf* (effective from future date) and *'aqd mu'allaq* (contingent upon event or condition) in that in the former case the parties clearly know the time of performance of obligation whereas in latter case they do not know as to when it will be performed and whether or not it will be performed. Commenting on the viewpoint of jurists, Dr. Muḥammad Ṣiddīq observes: " Indeed the only *gharar* in a future contract lies in the possible lapse of interest of either party which may affect his consent when the time set therein comes. If someone buys something by *'aqd muḍāf* and his circumstances change or the market changes bringing its price down at the time set for fulfillment of contract, he will undoubtedly be averse to its fulfillment and will regret entering into it. Indeed the object may itself change and the two parties may dispute over it".[9]

---

[8] Madkūr , *al-Madkhal*, p.614.

[9] Darīr, *al-Gharar fi al-'Uqūd*, p. 19.

It is pertinent to note that Ibn al-Qayyyim and Ibn Taymiyyah do not subscribe to majority's viewpoint. They maintain that *'aqd muḍāf* is permissible, without distinction between sale contract and leasing contract.

3.Al-'Aqd al-Mu'allaq (contingent contract):

It is a contract, which is contingent upon happening of an uncertain event. Such contract takes effect on the happening of contingency. According to the majority the contingent contract are void especially when they belong to the class of commutative contracts such as sale and leasing. The reason is that the contracting parties do not know whether the event will occur or not. and whether the contract will be subsequently enforced or not. It is also possible that one of the contracting parties may change his mind when the event occurs. According to Hanfi jurists even the gratuitous contracts are not permissible if made to take effect on the happening of contingency. Thus, it is not permissible to make a gift dependent on entrance of Zayd or the arrival of Khalid. Similarly in *waqf*, it is essential that the appropriation should not be made to depend on contingency. There are. however, some contracts, which are allowed to be made contingent upon uncertain event such as agency, bequest, and suretyship assignment of debt, manumission and divorce. Thus it is allowed to say to wife, "if you leave my house, then you are divorced" or to say to prospective agent, "if I traveled abroad, then you will be my agent". Ibn al-Qayyim diverging from the majority position held that the contingent contracts are valid. He does not see any *gharar* in them.[10]

Conclusion

1. The contracts with regard to the object, principal features of contract have been classified as follows:

   i) contracts for alienation of property:

   ii) contracts extinguishing the established right:

   iii)contracts of authorization:

---

[10] Ibn Taymiyyah. *Nazariyyat al-'Aqd*, p.227.

    iv) contracts of partnership;

    v) contracts of guarantee;and

    vi) contracts for safeguarding the property of a person.

2. According to some scholars they are classified as under:

    i) commutative contracts such as sale, hiring ;

    ii) gratuitous contracts such as waqf, gift ;

    iii) contracts of trust such as agency depositing ;

    iv) contracts of partnership such as *sharikah, mudārabah, muzāra'ah* ;and

    v) cont.acts of Suretyship such as guarantee, assignment of debt and pledge.

3. Contracts with regard to time of completion are divided into the following three kinds:

    i) *'Aqd Munjaz* (contract immediately enforceable);

    ii) *'Aqd Mudāf li al- mustaqbal* (contract effective from further date);and

    iii) *'Aqd Mu'allaq* (contingent contract).

COMMUTATIVE COTRACTS

I. CONTRACT OF SALE
II. CONTRACT OF LEASING

CONTRACTS OF PARTNERSHIP

I. SHARIKAH
II. MUDĀRABA

CONTRACTS OF SURETYSHIP

I. KAFĀLAH
II. HAWĀLAH
III. RAHN

CHAPTER-14

CONTRACT OF SALE

The contract of sale is one of the most important contracts for the exchange of goods. It is defined as "an exchange of a useful and desirable thing for similar thing by mutual consent in a specific manner.[1] The word "useful" excludes from the purview of definition unuseful transactions such as the sale of one rupee for one rupee. While the word "desirable" excludes things such as carrion and dust from being valid objects of sale, as these things are not desired by the people. The words "in a specific manner" signify the modes of conveying consent such as offer and acceptance, and conduct.

Some jurists have added the words "for the alienation of property"[2] to the above mentioned definition to denote that the purpose of such a contract is to transfer property in goods to the buyer, and in price to the seller. Thus, the complete definition of sale will be as follows: "Exchange of useful and desirable thing for a similar thing by mutual consent for the alienation of property". It can also be defined as "exchange of property for property with mutual consent".

Definition of Māl (Subject-matter)

According to the Ḥanafī School, *māl* is that which is desired by the people and stored for use at a time of need.[3] It does not treat benefits and incorporable rights as *māl*. The Shāfiʿī jurists on the other hand include benefits in the definition of *māl*. To them the sale contract

---

[1] Kāsānī, *Badā'i' al-Ṣanā'i'*, vol. 5, p. 133: Ibn al-Humām *Fatḥ al-Qadīr* vol, 5, p.73.

[2] Shirbīnī, *Mughni al-Muḥtāj* vol.2:2, Ibn Qudāmā, *al-Mughnī* vol. 3, 559.

[3] Ibn ʿAbidīn, *Radd al-Muḥtār* vol.4.p.3.

contains both transfer of ownership in goods and transfer of ownership in benefits.[4] The Mālikī jurists. like Ḥanafī jurists do not regard benefits and incorporeal rights as *māl* and consequently do not allow their sale.

Dissatisfied with the definitions of *māl* in early jurisprudence. Muṣṭafā Zarqā. a renowned scholar. has applied *māl* to every thing that has legal and material value among the peoples.[5] The property in this sense refers to any tangible or intangible thing that gives determinate capacity to a person to use it to the exclusion of whole world. It includes both abstract and unreal rights It applies equally to the objects. which have perceptible existence in the outside world as well as to intangible property such as trademarks and intellectual property.

Classification of Māl

Property has been classified in different ways:

I. Movable and Immovable:

There are two principal classes of property movable (*manqūl*) and immovable (*ghayr-manqūl*). By immovable is primarily meant land and along with it all permanent fixtures. such as buildings. The characteristic of movable property is that it may be removed from one place to another place. Movable property is classified as follows:

    a) *Makīlāt* or things. which are ordinarily sold by measurement of capacity.

    b) *Mawzūnāt* or things. which are sold by. weight.

    c) *Madhrū'at* or things which are estimated by linear measurement.

    d) *'Adadiyyāt* or things sold through counting.

All articles of the nature of *makīlāt. mawzūnat. madhrū'at.* and *'adadiyyāt* are comprehensively called *muqaddarāt.*

---

[1] Shirbīnī. *Mughnī al-Muhtāj* vol.2. p.3.

Muṣṭafā Ahmad Zarqā, *al-Madkhal al-Fiqhī al-'Ilm,* Demascus: Matba'ah Tarbīn. 1968. Vol.3. P 122.

II. Fungible or Similar (Mithlī) and non-Fungible or Dissimilar (Qīmī):

An article is said to belong to the class of similar *(mithlī)* if the like of it can be had in the market without there being such difference between the two as people are apt to take into account in their dealings. A thing belongs to the class of dissimilar if the like of it is not available in the market or if it be available, it is with such difference between them as people are wont to take into account in fixing the price.[6]

III. Determinate ('Āyn) and Indeterminate (Dayn) property.

Connected with the division of things into similar and dissimilar is the division of property into *'ayn* that is, specific or determinate and *dayn* or non-specific or indeterminate property. The chief distinguishing test is when a man is to get certain property from another who either borrowed it from him or took it by force, whether he is entitled to recover it in species or not. If he is, then it is called specific or determinate and if he is not, it is called non-specific or indeterminate.

Articles of the class of similar cannot, as a rule, be recovered specifically, and are thus regarded as *dayn* or indeterminate property. Hence, gold and silver in the shape of coins or otherwise, grain, oil and the like are *dayn* or indeterminate property. Therefore, if a man sells an article for one hundred dirhams out of a bag of money pointed out to him by the buyer, he does not become entitled to be paid out of the identical bag but his claim will be satisfied on being paid an equivalent amount. Generally speaking all indeterminate property rests on the mere responsibility or obligation of the person from whom it is recoverable.[7]

Conditions for Validity of Sale

1. Contracting parties should posses legal capacity necessary for concluding contract, i.e., they should be competent to conclude the contract.

---

[6] See 'Abd al-Rahīm *Muhammadan Jurisprudence.* p. 211.

[7] Ibid, p. 212.

2. The Commodity should be any thing in which transactions are permissible in the *Sharī'ah*. This means that it should be a pure substance ritually and legally clean. Therefore, any substance, which is religiously and legally unclean and upon whose disposal there are restrictions cannot serve as an object of sale: e.g. wine, pig, intoxicants, blood, and the carcasses of an animal are not valid objects of sale.

3. The merchandise must be either in actual existence or it should be capable of being acquired and delivered to a buyer in the future.

4. The transactions, which involve an element of uncertainty and risk with regard to the existence and acquisition of subject matter, are forbidden in Islamic Law. Examples are as follows:

    i) The sale of fish in water

    ii) Sale of a foetus in the womb

    iii)Sale of milk in the udder of an animal

    iv)Sale of fruit on a tree at the beginning of season when their quality cannot be established.

    From this it may be concluded that only that non-existent thing is excluded from the purview of a valid transaction, which involves an element of uncertainty. Things, which can be produced and manufactured in future, are the valid objects of sale as they are free from the attribute of uncertainty.

5. Goods should be owned by someone. If one sells something before acquiring ownership, such sale is invalid. Things in which no real ownership can be established, e.g., pious endowment (*waqf*) or public property are also excluded from being the subject matter of sale contract.

6. The item should be possessed by the owner. It is a necessary condition so that he is able to deliver it to the purchaser in the event of the sale contract. Things, that are not in actual possession, such as a thing lost or usurped, cannot be made the subject matter of a contract. Besides, the Holy Prophet (s.a.w.s) has prohibited the sale of foodstuffs before taking their possession. Other things can be validly sold before taking their possession if the vendor can subsequently deliver them to the purchaser.

7. The item of sale should be known to the contracting parties. This requires that their subject-matter should be ascertained. It can be realized through examination of the object if it is present in the session of contract or through a precise description if it is not available at the time of the contract. The description should be detailed enough to do away with all vagueness and uncertainty. The majority of the jurists allow it. The Shāfi'īs do not allow sale by description and stipulate actual examination at the time of the contract as a necessary condition. Sale by description confers the "option of description" upon the buyer, whereby he can reject the goods if they do not conform to the description.

8. The conditions of property have been discussed in detail in Chapter-III under the title Elements of Contract: Subject-matter.

9. Consideration may be deferred to a fixed future period but it cannot be suspended on an event the time of the occurrence of which is uncertain. Thus, it is not lawful to suspend payment until the wind shall blow, or until it shall rain; nor is it lawful even though the uncertainty be so inconsiderable as almost to amount to a fixed term. Thus, it is not lawful to suspend payment until the sowing or reaping time.

10. The sale contract should be absolute and not contingent upon a future event. For example, A says to B, "If X wins election, my car stands sold to you". Such a contract is invalid.

11. The sale must be instant. The majority of the jurists are of view that sale contract must come into effect immediately on the conclusion of the contract. Its effects cannot be postponed to a future date. Thus, it is not valid to make contract effective from some specified date in future.

Some expressly prohibited sale contracts of Islamic law

1. Bay' al-Mukhāḍarah :

It refers to sale of fruits on tree before their benefit is evident since they are not free from being spoiled. It is narrated by Anas ibn Mālik that God's Messenger (s.a.w.s) forbade the sale of fruit till they were almost ripe. Allah's Messenger further said: "If Allah spoiled the fruits what right would one have to take money of one's brother"?[8] *Mukhāḍarah* also refers to the sale of grain or vegetables before they are ripe.

2. Bay' al-Juzāf:

This applies to sale of foodstuffs at random or haphazardly. It is a sale of goods, which are not determined as to their quantity.

3. Bay' al-Munābadhah (throw sale):[9]

a) Such a sale is affected simply by two parties mutually exchanging their goods without any examination by either side.

b) Sale is completed when the seller throws down the goods with no opportunity for the purchaser to see it.

4. Bay'al-Mulāmasah:[10]

This is to buy an object by merely touching it, without examining it. It is a sale of a piece of cloth already folded, that is bought by merely touching it, and renouncing in advance the right to revoke on inspection.

5. Bay'al-Muhāqalah:[11]

Sale of wheat in exchange of wheat in ear to be estimated by conjecture.

6. Bay'al-Muzābanah:[12]

Sale of fresh fruits in exchange of dry fruits in a way that the quantity of dry fruit is measured while the quantity of fresh fruits is uncertain.

---

[8] Bukhārī, *Ṣaḥīḥ* as quoted in Shavkānī, *Nayl al-Awṭār*, vol.5, p.183.

[9] Ibid. vol.5, p. 159.

[10] Ibid.

[11] Ibid

[12] Ibid

7. Bay' al-Ḥaml:

Sale of what a female animal bears in the womb.

8. Bay' al-Ḥasāt: [13]

In this form a sale is affected by saying: "of these pieces of cloth, I sell you the one upon which falls pebble thrown in the air".

9. Mu'āwamah: [14]

The selling of fruits on tree in advance for two or three years.

10. Darbat al-Ghā'is : [15]

Such a transaction is affected by saying: "I dive into the sea, if I have anything (pearl), it will be yours at such and such price".

11. 'Asb al-Faḥl:

This refers to renting service of a male animal to cover female animal. The Holy Prophet (s.a.w.s) is reported to have prohibited such contract and disallowed receiving price or cost of this service. [16]

12. Sale of fish in water:

This type of sale was commonly practiced by Arabs in pre-Islamic period. Holy Prophet (s.a.w.s) forbade such contracts. [17]

13. Bay'Ḥabl al-Ḥabalah:

This refers to sale of younglings to be brought later from the foetus of an animal. [18]

---

[13] Shawkānī, *Nayl al-Awṭār* vol.5, p. 156.

[14] Ibid., vol. 5, p. 186.

[15] Ibid., vol. 5, p.158.

[16] Ibid., vol. 5, p.155.

[17] Ibid., vol. 5, p.156.

[18] Ibid,. vol. 5, p. 156.

14. Bay' al-Kāli' bi al-Kāli':[19]

This means exchange of credit for credit. What is prohibited by this contract is the purchase by a man of a commodity on credit for a fixed period, and when the period of payment comes and he finds himself unable to pay the debt, he says, "Sell it to me on credit for further period, for something additional. Whereupon he sells it to him. The Prophet (s.a.w.s) has prohibited such a sale.[20]

15. Bay' wa Salaf (Selling and lending):[21]

The explanation of this practice is that one man says to other "I shall take your goods for such and such if you lend me such and such. In a tradition the Holy Prophet (s.a.w.s) asked 'Attab Ibn Asīd, his representative to the people of Makkah, to stop the people of Makkah from making a selling and lending contract concurrently.[22]

16. Sale of Milk in the Udder of Animals:

The Prophet (s.a.w.s) is reported to have prohibited this transaction except when the milk was measured after milking.[23]

17. Sale of food before possession:

The Holy Prophet (s.a.w.s) has prohibited the resale of food before possession. From Ibn 'Umar, may Allah be pleased with them both who said, "I bought oil in the market and was about to take it when I met a man who offered me a good profit. I decided to strike a bargain with him and at that time someone took hold of my elbow from behind. I turned behind and saw that it was Zayd ibn Thābit. He said, 'Do not sell it at the spot you bought it from, not until you have moved it to you camel-pack. The Messenger of Allah (s.a.w.s) forbade the sale of goods on the spot they are bought, not until the traders move

[19] Ibid vol. 5, p. 165.

[20] 'Abd Allah 'Alwī Hājī Hassan, *Sale and Contracts, in Early Islamic Commercial Law*, Islamabad: Islamic Research Institute, 1994, p.65.

[21] Ibid., p.66.

[22] Shawkānī, *Nayl al-Awṭār*, vol. 5, p. 190.

[23] Ibid., vol. 5, p. 158.

them to their camel-packs".[24] The purpose of this *ḥadīth* is to emphasize the principle of liability, which means that food bought, should not be sold unless it has moved into the liability of buyer. This is·realized either through delivery of possession or identification of a particular lot of food sold.

It also aims at discouraging over-trading and middlemanship. An example is when a person purchases grain lying in an agricultural farm and without removing it from the farm sells it to another person for a higher price than the price at which he had purchased it. This new middleman sells it further at a relatively higher price than his purchase price. This process continues and everybody keeps on earning thousands of rupees without investing anything while the commodity remains where it was at the first place during its first transaction, only its price keeps on increasing and till it actually reaches the market in front of real consumer its price is increased many times. Hence, this *ḥadīth* represents an indirect order to end the profession of middlemanship.[25]

Kinds of Sale Transactions

Following are important kinds of sale in Islamic Law.

1. *Muqāyaḍah:* The sale of goods for goods, or barter trade.

2. *Bay' Muṭlaq:* The sale of goods for money.

3. *Ṣarf:* The sale of money for money or money changing.

4. *Salam:* This is a sale in which the price is paid in advance and the articles are delivered on a future date.

5. *Istiṣnā':* A Contract of manufacturing.

6. *Murābahah:* In such a transaction the vendor sells an article for the cost price in addition to a certain stated profit.

7. *Bay' al-mu'ajjal:* Credit sale or sale on deferred payment basis.

---

[24] **Ibid., vol. 5, p. 167.**

[25] See Ghulām Murtazā, *Socio-Economic System of Islam*, pp. 38-39.

I. Muqāyaḍah:

Barter trade is permissible. If the commodities to be bartered belong to the class of *ribā* commodities, then the requirement of the lawgiver is as follows:

  a). If both the commodities are of the same genus, then immediate delivery and equality has to be observed.

  b). If they differ in kind, then they should be exchanged in the same session of contract.

  c). In case of exchange of homogeneous commodities, the quality has to be ignored. The Prophet (s.a.w.s) had, reportedly rejected the transaction in which Bilāl (r.a.t.a) had exchanged two measures of inferior dates for one measure of superior ones.[26]

II. Bay' Muṭlaq:

This is sale of goods for money. Although barters trade is permitted with some qualifications, use of cash money is preferred and encouraged by Islam. This preference of cash money comes almost close the requirement when barter of the same commodity is involved. The purpose is to avoid any occurrence of *ribā*. The Prophet (s.a.w.s) had instructed Bilāl (r.a.t.a) to sale two measures of inferior dates for money and then purchase superior ones with that money. This shows the importance of money as an instrument of just and equitable exchange. The *ḥadīth* in question is indicative not only of the importance attached to money but also of the consideration of current market rates with regard to the exchange of produced goods. Needless to stress that money provides a standard for real and just exchange of value of various commodities.

III.' Ṣarf:

Sale of absolute price for absolute price is known as *ṣarf* contract. The main conditions of *ṣarf* contract are as follows:

  1. The condition that is specific to the contract of *ṣarf* and distinguishes it from all other contracts is that the counter

---

[26]Bukhārī, *Ṣaḥīḥ as quoted in Nayl al-Awṭār*, vol.5, p. 207.

values must be delivered and taken possession of within the session of the contract. In other words, a condition for delay cannot be stipulated.

2. No option can be stipulated in this contract. The reason is that an option delays the transfer of ownership and this violates the first condition of spot delivery and possession.

3. Equality or sameness in weight is must if gold is exchanged for gold, but if gold is exchanged for silver, then equality is not the requirement of the *Sharī'ah*. In this case the counter-values must be exchanged simultaneously.

4. Good and bad quality of exchanged counter-values is not relevant in this contract.

The rules of *Sarf* contract have been mentioned in a large number of *aḥādīth* The best known of these *aḥādīth* are the two that have been narrated by 'Ubādah ibn al-Ṣāmit and Abū Sa'īd al-Khudrī:

i) From 'Ubādah Ibn al-Ṣāmit, who said, The Messenger of Allah (s.a.w.s) said: "Gold for gold, silver for silver, wheat for wheat, barley for barley, dates for dates, salt for salt, like for like in equal weights, from hand to hand. If the species differ, then sell as you like, as long as it is from hand to hand".[27]

ii) From Abū Sa'īd al-Khudrī, who said: "The Messenger of Allah (s.a.w.s) said, "Do not sell gold for gold, except when it is like for like, and do not misappropriate one through the other, and do not sell silver for silver except like for like and do not misappropriate one through the other, and do not sell things absent for those that are present".[28]

The rules mentioned earlier are not specific with gold and silver or *dīnār* and *dirham* alone, but are applicable to every commodity or thing that performs the functions of money namely; a medium of exchange, unit of value, and standard of deferred payment.

---

[27] Shawkānī, *Nayl al-Awṭār*, vol. 5, p.201.

[28] Ibid.

It is worth mentioning that gold and silver are considered as species of price in Islamic Law. It makes no difference whether gold and silver is sold in the shape of coins or ornaments or otherwise. They are treated always as price because it is the very nature of these metals. When gold is sold for silver or vice versa, there is no requirement of equality in bargain but the delivery of both articles is a must. Thus, two parties exchanging dollars with rupees must have to exchange them in the same session of contract without any delay.

Some modern Scholars claim that gold and silver are real money whereas paper currency is merely a token money. They infer from this that the rules involving the exchange of gold and silver and other fungible goods cannot be strictly applied to paper currency.

In the following lines we will discuss the position of paper currency according to the *Sharī'ah*. The discussion on the legal position of paper currency in Islamic Law requires to define first what is money and what functions it performs in the economy of our time.

Definition of Money

Money has been defined as a "thing that serves as a commonly accepted medium of exchange or means of payment"[29]. Another famous and comprehensive definition of money is that "Money is any generally acceptable means of payment in exchange for goods and services and in settling debts".[30] Money performs four main functions. It is (i) a medium of exchange or means of payment, (ii) a measure of value or a unit of account, (iii) a standard of deferred payment, and (iv) a store of value.

Money is classified under two categories: (1) commodity money and (2) token money. The former functions as a medium of exchange and is bought and sold as ordinary goods. Token money, however, is considered to be a means of payments whose value or purchasing power as money exceeds the cost of its production and its value in alternative uses. Modern monies are accepted because the law requires

[29] Paul A. Samuelson and William Nordhaus *Economics*, New York: McGraw Hill Book Company, 1993 p. 226.

[30] Fischer, Dornbusch and Schmalensee, *Economics*, Singapore: McGraw Hill Book Company, 1993, p. 623.

them to be accepted. These are fiat monies or legal tender. Legal tender is the money that a government has declared acceptable in exchange and as a lawful way of paying debts.[31]

Historically, many commodities including precious metals have performed these functions, but only those metals were picked up for this purpose that were scarce and had a worldwide demand. The principal forms of money are now coinage, notes and credit instruments. But since coins are now very rarely made of precious metals, they perform the token function, being almost worthless in content when compared with its face value.[32] At the present, paper money is the most widely used form of money and is a pure token because its intrinsic price has no relevance to its face value.

The Position of Gold and Silver in the Sharī'ah

A study of *Fiqh* literature on the issue reveals that Muslim Jurists treated *dinār* and *dirham* as money, not because they were made of gold and silver, but because they possessed the characteristics of money; that is, they served as a unit of account, a medium of exchange and measure of value. To them the *'illah* (underlying cause) in gold and silver in the context of the contract of *ṣarf* is currency-value or price-worthiness (*thamaniyyah*).[33]

Gold and silver have been *thaman* or money since early ages because they were capable of effectively functioning as a medium of exchange and a common measure of value.

The Legal Position of Paper Money

Were we to consider the matter carefully it will be evident that there is no essential difference between the old metallic money and the paper money of our time since both serve as a measure to determine the value of other commodities. Paper money, therefore, is real money for all the practical purposes. This fact has been established and

---

[31] Ibid., pp. 626-27.

[32] Ziauddīn Ahmad,*Currency Notes and Indexation,*

Islamic Studies,28.1(1980) p.52.

[33] Kāsānī, *Badā'i' Ṣanā'i'*, vol.5, p.183.

emphasized in the writings of several eminent Muslim Scholars Yūsuf al-Qardāwī, for instance writes:

> We pay price of goods, wages to workers, dower to wives, *diyat in qatl al-khaṭā* in this paper money. If someone steals it, he is subjected to the punishment of theft in all codes of criminal law. Then why should we deny it the status of legal money?[34]

Keeping all these facts in view the Fiqh Academy of Makkah in its meeting held in October, 1986 maintained that paper money has all the characteristics of gold and silver. It is *thaman* from the point of view of the Sharī'ah and consequently it is subject to all the rules of the Sharī'ah pertaining to *ribā*, *zakāt*, *salam*, and other contracts which are applicable to gold and silver.[35]

The workshop held under the auspices of the Islamic Development Bank in Jeddah in April, 1987 on indexation also concluded that: "Paper money assumes the functions of gold and silver money from the point of view of the applicability of the rules of *ribā* and *zakāt* as well as being the principle of *salam* contracts, a capital of *muḍārabah* or investment in a partnership.[36]

IV. Salam Contract:

In Arabic, the word *salam* means to advance. This is a contract whereby the purchaser pays the price in advance and the delivery of subject matter is postponed to a specified time in future.

Thus, *bay' salam* is a sale in which advance payment is made to the seller for deferred supply of goods. *Salam* was also prevalent even before the advent of the Holy Prophet (s.a.w.s) perhaps with a different nomenclature. When the Holy Prophet (s.a.w.s) migrated to

---

[34]Atiq al-Zafar,*Ribā aur Bank Kā Sūd* translation of Yūsuf Qardāwī's, *Fawā'id al-Bunūk hiya al-Ribā al-Muḥaram* pp. 40,41..

[35] Rābiṭah al-'Ālam al-Islāmī, *Qarārāt Majlis al-Majma', al-Fiqh al Islāmī*, pp. 96,97.

[36] Recommendations of the Workshop on Shariah position on Indexation. (25-26 April 1987) organized by Islamic Development Bank, Jeddah.

Madinah, his Madinan Companions brought this mode of sale to his notice for seeking his guidance. He termed it as *salam* and allowed it to them with some conditions.

As a matter of principle the sale of a commodity, which is not in possession of the seller, is unlawful. This is what the Holy Prophet (s.a.w.s) is stated to have laid down as a general rule. Thus the practice of *bay' salam* is legalized as an exception. According to some jurists the legality of *bay' salam* is derivable from the Quranic verse 2:282:

> "O ye who believe; when ye contract a debt for a fixed term, record it in writing...."[37]

The reason why the Holy Prophet (s.a.w.s) permitted it with some conditions is necessity faced by growers and traders. It is stated that the practice as qualified by Holy Prophet (s.a.w.s) continued during his lifetime and the following period. The later jurists unanimously treated it to be a permissible mode of business. The jurists have not confined the application of this mode of sale to those agricultural products, which as the *ḥadīth* suggests, could be weighed or measured. But have expanded the list of salamable items to all the commodities that could be precisely determined in terms of quality and quantity.

Difference between Salam Sale and Ordinary Sale

All the basic conditions of a contract of ordinary sale remain the same in *bay' salam*. Yet there are some points of difference between the two. For example:

a) In *salam* sale it is necessary to fix a period for the delivery of goods, in ordinary sale it is not necessary.

b) In *salam* sale commodity not in possession of the seller can be sold; in ordinary sale, it cannot be.

c) In *salam* sale only those commodities, which can be precisely determined in terms of quality and quantity, can be sold; in ordinary sale every thing that can be owned is saleable, unless the Qur'ān or the *ḥadīth* prohibits it.

---

[37] Qur'ān: 2, 282.

d) A *salam* sale cannot take place between identical goods, for example; wheat for wheat or potato for potato; in ordinary sale it is permissible to sell identical goods.

e) In the *salam* sale, payment must be made at the time of contract; in ordinary sale payment may be deferred or may be made at the time of the delivery of goods.

The conditions of a valid salam

A valid contract of *salam* sale requires the fulfillment of the following conditions, which are over and above the conditions of an ordinary sale:

1. It is necessary that the buyer pay the price of the object in full to the seller in advance. If the price is not paid at the time of the contract, it will amount to sale of a debt for debt, which has been prohibited by the Holy Prophet (s.a.w.s).[38]

2. An outstanding loan due on the seller cannot be fully or partially fixed as price nor a loan outstanding on a third party can be transferred to the seller in future adjustment towards price.

3. A single amount for payment of different commodities or of the same commodity in different periods or at different places is not approved because in the former case it may lead to a dispute on pricing in the event of the seller's failure in delivery of some of the contracted items and in the latter case price fluctuation over the period may become a point of dispute if the seller fails to supply the item on some fixed period. It is, therefore, necessary that the amount for each item and for each period of delivery be separately fixed.

4. The object of *salam* should be defined by description. It requires a precise and minute description of the commodity, which does away with all vagueness and uncertainty. Identification of object should include genus,

---

[38] Shawkānī, *Nayl al-Awṭār*, vol. 5, p.165

species, colour, and country of origin and any other feature, which has an effect on the price.

5. *Salamable* articles include fungible things, i.e., weighable, measurable, and accountable by number. Non-fungible things such as precious stone cannot be sold on the basis of *salam* because every piece is normally different from the other rendering their exact specification impossible. To some jurists any article determinable by description, can be the object of *salam* contract. Thus, domestic animals are valid object of *salam* subject to identification.

6. The commodity should be well defined but not particularised to a particular unit of farm, tree or garden, because there is possibility that crop of that farm is destroyed before delivery.

7. The object of *salam* should be in existence from the time of contract until the time of delivery. This is the Ḥanafi viewpoint. Other jurists hold that it should be habitually available at the time of delivery.

8. A *salam* contract cannot be affected on things which must be delivered on spot. So, gold cannot be sold for gold by way of *salam*. Similarly wheat cannot be sold for barley because they cannot be exchanged with delay. It is necessary that the exchange of gold for gold or wheat for barley should take place simultaneously in the same session of contract.

9. About the minimum period of delivery, the jurists have the following opinions:

a). Ḥanafī jurists fix this period at one month. To some Ḥanafī Jurists minimum delay should be three days. But, if vendor dies before the delay has elapsed, the *salam* reaches maturity.

b) According to the Shāfi'ī jurists *salam* can be immediate and delayed.

c) According to the Malikī jurists, delay should not be less than 15-days.

10. The time of the subject-matter of *salam* should be fixed at the time of the contract.

11. As regards delivery before time the opinion of the majority of Muslim jurists, is that seller can discharge his obligation before the agreed term and the purchaser will be forced to accept the delivery if an early delivery does not harm him. But if he apprehends that he will suffer damage by early delivery i.e. fruits, which may be consumed or need storing, then he will not be forced to accept early delivery. Mālikī jurists, on the other hand, maintain that he is entitled to refuse it even if it does not harm him.

12. Fixing the place of delivery is requisite if it entails extra expenses, or the place of contract is not a suitable place for delivery.

13. It is not permitted to exchange goods other than those specified while the contract of *salam* still exists because it results in the sale of awaited goods before they have been received. Besides, this falls under the prohibition of selling foods before possession. The Holy Prophet (s.a.w.s) said, "Whoever buys foodstuff should not sell it before he receives "or possesses it".[39]

14. The buyer is not allowed to take back any thing in *salam* except the sum of money or goods themselves.

15. In order to ensure that the seller honours his commitment given to the buyer to supply the agreed quantity of the specified goods on the due date or at the agreed time, the buyer has a right to claim surety or pledge or both. This is generally agreed to by the jurists.

16. The buyer is not allowed to enjoy ownership rights over the purchased goods before taking them into his possession.

---

[39] Ibid., vol. 5, p. 167.

> Thus, he cannot sell them or make them a partnership capital, unless he takes over the goods [40]

Revocation of the Contract

As stated above a seller is bound to deliver the goods as stipulated. There may, however, be situations when it is not possible for him to honour his commitment; the examples are death, or damage to the goods while lying with the supplier for delivery. In the event of death of the seller the contract of *bay' salam* will be deemed to be rescinded and the buyer will claim the return of his money from the heirs.

In the event of the death of the buyer, however, the contract will remain operative. Damage to the goods will nullify the contract only when it exceeds the normal extent of damage. In the event of revocation of the contract, the buyer will receive back his advance. Ordinarily the buyer has no right to change the conditions of the contract in respect of the quality or quantity or the period of delivery of the contracted goods after payment is made to the seller. Both parties, however, have the right to rescind the contract in full or in part. The buyer will thus have a right to receive back the amount advanced by him, but not more or less than it.

Modern Applications of the Salam Contract

> Islamic banks and financial institutions use *salam* as a mode of financing. They finance the needs of farmers who need money to grow their crops. They enter into an agreement with them for advance purchase of agriculture produce, specifying complete details of the commodity, its quality, price and time of delivery; and make payment of the amount at the time of entering into the agreement. When the commodity is produced and supplied to the bank on the appointed date, they sell it at profit in the market.

---

[40] See for detailed explanation of these conditions. Zuhaylī, *al-Fiqh al-Islāmī wa Adillatuhū*, vol. 4, pp. 599-624, and Ḥasanuz Zaman, *Bay' Salam, Principles and their applications : by* paper presented in the seminar on Islamic Financing Techniques, Islamabad Dec. 1984.

The banks sometimes sell the commodity through a parallel contract of *salam.* The period in the second contract is shorter while the price is fixed a little higher than the price of first transaction. Thus, they earn profit by the difference between two prices. There may be another way of benefiting from *salam.* The bank may obtain a promise to purchase from a third party. This promise should be unilateral from the prospective buyer. Being merely a promise, and not an actual sale, the buyer will not have to pay the price in advance. Therefore, a higher price may be fixed and as soon as the commodity is received by the institution: it will be sold to the third party at a pre-greed price according to the terms of the promise.[41]

While resorting to parallel *salam* contract, two conditions must be observed by the banks:

1. In an arrangement of *salam*, the bank enters into two different contracts. In one of them the bank is the buyer and in the second one the bank is the seller. Each one of these contracts must be independent of the other. For example if A has purchased from B 1000 bags of wheat by way of salam to be delivered on 31st December, A can contract a parallel *salam* with C to deliver to him 1000 bags of wheat on 31st December. But while contracting parallel *salam* with C, the delivery of wheat to C cannot be conditioned with taking delivery from B. Therefore, even if B did not deliver wheat on 31st December, A is duty bound to deliver 1000 bags of wheat to C. Similarly, if B has delivered defective goods which do not conform with the agreed specifications, A is still obligated to deliver the goods to C according to the specifications agreed with him.

2. Parallel *salam* is allowed with a third party only. The seller in the first contract cannot be made the purchaser in a parallel contract of *salam*, because it will be a buy-back contract, which is not permissible in the *Sharī'ah.*.[42]

---

[41] Taqī 'Usmānī, *An Introduction to Islamic Finance*, p. 194.

[42] Ibid., *p.* 195.

V. Istiṣnā':

Istiṣnā' consists in ordering an artisan or manufacturer to make certain goods answering a given description. By *istiṣnā'* one may engage for example, a cobbler to make a pair of shoes for a fixed price or ask a tailor to make a suit to be delivered later.[43]

According to Imām Kāsānī the material of object must be from the manufacturer. If it is provided by the customer, and the manufacturer has used his labour and skill only, it will not be a contract of *istiṣnā'*, instead it would be a contract of *ijārah*, i.e., a contract to hire services of a person to undertake a specific work. Thus, if a person gives a piece of iron to an ironsmith to make a specific vessel for a known consideration, it is permissible but it will not be *istiṣnā'*, rather it will be called a contract of hiring.[44]

The legality of this from of contract is based on a custom, which prevailed from the time of the Holy Prophet (s.a.w.s) and is also justified having regard to the need of people.

Difference between Istiṣnā'and other Allied Contracts

The contract of *istiṣnā'* resembles the contract of *salam* and *ijārah*. It has also similarity with the "promise to sell". Here we will highlight some differences between *istiṣnā'* and the above-mentioned contracts for a better understanding of the contract of *istiṣnā'*.

Difference between Istiṣnā'and the "Promise to Sell"

istiṣnā' resembles "promise to sell" in that it constitutes a promise on part of manufacturer to make an object, which is non-existent at the time of contract

Ḥākim al-Shahīd from amongst the Hanafī Jurists is of the view that *istiṣnā'* is a promise to sell. The majority of Aḥnāf, on the other hand, hold the opinion that it is a sale not a promise to sell. Their opinion is based on the following arguments.

1. All the Jurists are unanimous on the point that legality of *istiṣnā'* is established by *istiḥsān* (juristic preference) and

---

[43] *Badā'i 'Ṣanā'i'*, vol. 5, p. 3.

[44] Ibid.

there is no denying the fact that this principle is invoked in the contracts not in the promises.

2. The Jurists allow option of inspection (*khiyār al-ru'yah*) in *istiṣnā'*, which is an evidence of the fact that it is a sale because options are valid in contracts only.

3. In *istiṣnā'* the parties have right to resort to court in case of dispute arising from some default or breach of contract. This is a proof of its being a contract because litigation is permissible in contracts which are binding on parties not in simple promises.[45]

Difference between Istiṣnā' and Contract of Personal Services

Istiṣnā' is similar to *ijārah* of professional services, because services of a manufacturer are hired to manufacture a thing as in the case of *ijārah*. But the difference between the two is that the subject matter in the former case is the object, which is required to be made while the subject matter in latter case is the work to be done, or the performance to be made by the manufacturer. So, if A, a customer asks B, a cobbler, to make a shoe out of the material provided to him by A, then the subject matter in such case would be the act of making shoe, not the shoe itself and the contract would be that of *ijārah* But if A, a customer asks B, a manufacturer to make a shoe from his own material, then the subject matter in such case is the shoe.

What strengthens this conclusion is the fact that if the manufacturer provided the object, which he had made before the contract and the customer accepted it, the contract would be valid. This shows that the subject-matter of the contract is the object itself not the work. On the other hand, contract for work or service requires that it should be done after the contract is concluded. The contract of *istiṣnā'*, however, resembles the contract of personal services in the following two points.

a) It lapses on death of one of the parties just like a contract of personal services.

---

[45] See Zayla'ī, *Tabyīn al-Ḥaqā'iq* vol. 4, p.124.

b) The man who has ordered the goods is entitled to refuse or accept it if he finds that they are not according to order.[46]

Difference between Istiṣnā' and Salam

Following are some points of difference between *istiṣnā'* and *Salam*.

1. The commodity in *salam* rests on responsibility (dimmah). It is considered a debt *(dayn)*. It is normally a weighable, measurable or countable thing, while the commodity in *istiṣnā'* is treated as determinate thing *('ayn)* such as furniture or shoe or tailoring cloths.

2. The subject matter of *istiṣnā'* is always a thing, which needs manufacturing while *salam* can be affected on every thing whether it needs manufacturing, or not.

3. The price in *salam* is paid in advance, while in *istiṣnā'* contract the price can be paid any time during the contract.

4. The time of delivery in *salam* is specified; whereas it is not requirement in *istiṣnā'* that the time of delivery be fixed. According to Imām Abū Ḥanīfah if time is fixed in *istiṣnā'*, the contract will be a *salam* contract, and will no longer be an *istiṣnā'* contract.

5. *Salam* is a binding and Irrevocable contract while the *istiṣnā'* can be revoked unilaterally. [47]

Conditions of Istiṣnā

Ḥanafī Jurists acknowledge three conditions for a valid contract of *istiṣnā'*, they are:

1. The subject of *istiṣnā'*, should be precisely mentioned in terms of its kind, quality and quantity.

2. There should be some work or performance involved in the commodity.

---

[46] See Kāsanī, *Badā'i' al-Ṣanā'i'*, vol. 5, p.4.

[47] See: Aḥmd Yūsuf, *'Uqud al-Mu'malāt' al-Maliyyah*, p. 216.

3. The time of the completion of work and delivery should not be fixed. This is the view of Imām Abū Ḥanīfa. His two disciples disagree with his teacher and hold that time should be fixed.

4. The price or consideration should also be specified.[48]

Status of the Contract of Istiṣnā'

There is a consensus of opinions among Ḥanafī Jurists that the contract of *istiṣnā'* is non-binding and terminable before the commencement of work.[49]Imām Abū Yūsuf acknowledges the option of inspection (*khiyār al-Ru'yah*) for the purchaser. To him purchaser can revoke the contract on sight even though the commodity is according to the description.[50]

Majallat al-Aḥkām al-'Adliyyah, the civil code of the Ottoman Empire, has not accepted the viewpoint of the Ḥanafī Jurists regarding the non-binding status of *istiṣnā'*. Article 392 of the *Majallah* provides that if the manufacturer brought the goods according to specification, the purchaser will be forced to accept them. It also states that once the contract of *istiṣnā'* is concluded, it becomes binding on manufacturer to manufacture the object.[51]

Termination of Istiṣnā'

The contract of *istiṣnā'* is terminated in the following circumstance:

1. By completion of work and handing over the object to the purchaser.

2. By the death of manufacturer.

---

[48] See Kāsib 'Abd al Karīm, *'Aqd al-Istiṣnā' fī al-Fiqh al-Islāmī,* pp. 133,134.

[49] See *Badā'i' al-Ṣanā'i'*, vol. 5, p. 3, *Radd al-Muḥtār* vol. 4, p. 223. *al-Mabsūṭ,* vol. 13, p.139.

[50] *Al- Mabsūṭ,*, vol. 12, p. 139; *Badā'ī' al-Ṣanā'i'*, vol. 5, p. 3.

[51] *Mujallah,* Article 392

It is pertinent to note that death causes termination of contract only when the contract is for specific performance and the heirs of deceased manufacturer do not have ability to carry out the work in required manner.

Modern applications of Istiṣnā'

Islamic Banks and Financial Institutions use *istiṣnā'* as a mode of financing. They finance the construction of houses factories on a piece of land belonging to client. The house or factory is constructed either by the financier himself or by a construction company. In this latter case, the bank enters a sub-contract with that construction company. But if the contract concluded between the bank, i.e, the financier, and the client provides specifically that the work will be carried out by the financier himself, then the sub-contract is not valid. In such a case, it is necessary that the bank should have its own construction company and expert contractors to discharge the task.

The financier in the contract of *istiṣnā'* for the purpose of construction is under obligation to construct house in conformity with the specifications detailed in the agreement. Some agreements provide that the financier will be liable for any defect in construction and destruction of the building during the period specified in the contract. In case the financier assigns the task of construction to a third party, it is necessary that it should supervise construction work in a regular manner. The price of construction may be paid by the client at the time of agreement and may be postponed till the time of delivery or any other time agreed upon between the parties. The payment may be in lump sum or in installments. In order to secure the payment of installments, the title deeds of the house or land may be kept by the bank as security till the last installment is paid by the client.

The mode of *istiṣnā'* is used also for digging wells and water canals. Islamic banks finance the agricultural sector through this mode and play their effective role in activating this important sector of the economy.

VI. Murābaḥah:

Murābaḥah is a sale of goods at a price covering the purchase price plus profit margin agreed upon between the contracting parties. In *murābaḥah*, the seller discloses the cost of the sold commodity. He tells the purchaser that he has purchased commodity, say, for hundred rupees and that he will charge ten rupees as profit over and above the original price. It is also permissible to fix the profit in percentage i.e. 5% 10% of the cost.

Murābaḥah is basically a trust sale (*bay' al-amānah*) in which the buyer depends and relies upon the integrity of the purchaser as regards the cost he mentions to buyer. Thus, it is the moral and legal obligation of the seller to be honest and truthful in stating the price at which he purchased the goods, and if he succeeded in obtaining a discount or rebate, it should also be acknowledged and accounted for the benefit of the purchaser. In Islamic Law, the contract of sale with regard to the cost of the sale's object to the seller, is divided into three kinds:

i) *Tawliyah:* resale at the stated original cost with no profit or loss to the seller.

ii) *Wadī'ah:* resale at a discount from the original cost.

iii) *Murābaḥah*, the resale at fixed surcharge or rate of profit on the stated original cost.

The main purpose of these sales is to "protect the innocent general consumer lacking expertise in the various items of trade from the wiles and stratagems of sharp traders"[52]

Commenting on the economic function of trust sales (*wadī'ah, tawliyah, murābaḥah*) Abraham Udouitch writes:

> The chief concern is to avoid any fraud on the part of the seller by setting out detailed guidelines regarding the considerations that are to enter into determining the cost of any item. Foremost among these is the price paid by the seller for the goods in question. In addition, a variety of expenses connected with the maintenance, improvement and transport of the goods may be included in the cost, which forms the basis of the *murābaḥah* sale. The custom of the merchants served as the criterion for determining exactly which expenses were to be included. The general rule emerging from the numerous cases discussed is that

[52] Marghīnānī, *al-Hidāyah*, vol. 3, p. 56.

money expended directly on the goods or on services indispensable to their sale (e.g., brokerage fee) may be included, whereas the personal expenses of the merchant and other expenses not directly involved with the goods are not to be figured into the stated original cost. As an additional protection to the consumer, the seller should avoid any misleading statement.[53]

Remedies for Swindled Purchaser

In the event of *murābaḥah* purchaser discovering that the price he has paid to the vendor, was unduly inflated Islamic Law provides relief to the deceived purchaser. The remedies suggested by different schools of law are as follows:

Opinion of the Ḥanafī Jurists

In such a case the purchaser would have to make up his mind either to accept the sale at the stated price or rescind it and take his money. But if the subject matter is destroyed in the hands of purchaser or he consumes it, he would lose his right to revoke contract. According to Imām Abū Yūsuf the *murābaḥah* purchaser has no choice except to devalue undue increase.[54]

Opinion of the Malikī Jurists

The purchaser would have right either to keep the *murābaḥah* object in consideration of its real or to relinquish the object of the transaction unless the *murābaḥah* vendor forces him to keep it at the real price.[55]

Opinion of the Shāfi'ī School

Two opinions are attributed to Imām Shāfi'ī:

i) He has the option either to revoke contract or to take undue increase and keep the object.

ii) He has no option other than to keep it at real price after devaluation of undue increase. [56]

---

[53] Udovitch, the *Partnership and Profit in Medieval Islam*, p. 220.

[54] Sarakhsī *al-Mabsūṭ*, vol. 13, p. 86.

[55] Ibn Rushd, *Bidāyat al-Mujtahid*, vol. 2, p.162.

Conditions of Murābaḥah

Following are conditions of *murābaḥah* contract are as follows:[57]

1. Disclosure of original price:

It is necessary for the validity of the *murābaḥah* transaction that the second purchaser (*murābaḥah* purchaser) should have knowledge of the original price. This means that the seller should disclose price of the commodity. If the price is not disclosed in the session of contract, and contracting parties leave the *majlis*, the contract will be invalid.

2. Fixation of Profit:

The profit should be fixed and added to the cost price and be mentioned in the contract.

3. Ascertainment of price:

Murābaḥah is valid only where the exact cost price can be ascertained. If the exact cost is not known, the commodity cannot be sold on *murābaḥah*. Instead it will be sold without reference to the cost. This is applicable to cases where a person has purchased two or more things in a single transaction, and he does not know the price of each object separately.

4. Validity of first contract:

The first contract should be a valid contract. But if the first contract is *fāsid*, i.e., irregular, then the second sale is not permitted on the basis of *murābaḥah* because the *murābaḥah* is resale of a thing for similar to its first price with the addition of profit, and the irregular sale is not allowed with the stated price. It is allowed only with the legal value, i.e., the market price.

---

[56] Ibid.

[57] See Zuhaylī, *al-Fiqh al-Islāmī*, vol. 4, pp. 704-706.

Expenses in relation to Murābaḥah

The opinion of Muslim jurists is divided as to what expenses can be added to the price and constitutes a basis for the calculation of profit.[58]

The Mālikī School

Expenses that can be added to the price are those that have affected the commodity such as dying or tailoring. The expenses incurred on services such as the fare for the transporting or storing the commodities in a warehouse rented for this purpose can be added to the price but cannot be considered for the purpose of calculating profit.[59]

The Ḥanafī School

All the expenses which are accepted normally by commercial practice can be added to the cost price whether such expenses have affected the commodity itself (e.g. dyeing or tailoring) or were incurred on account of such commodity (e.g. transporting goods or paying commission to a middleman).[60]

The Ḥanbalī and Shāfiʿī Schools

All actual expenses incurred as regards the commodity can be added to capital provided that the *murābaḥah* purchaser is made aware of the amount of these expenses and their origin.[61]

Modern applications of Murābaḥah

The Islamic Banks use this technique to finance projects. They buy commodities for cash and then sell them to a potential client on cost plus profit principle on deferred payment basis. In Islamic Banks *murābaḥah* is practiced in the following way:

[58]Nabīl Ṣāliḥ, *Unlawful Gain and Legitimate Profit in Islamic Law,*

p 118.

[59] Ibn Rushd, *Bidāyat al-Mujtahid*, vol. 2, p. 161.

[60] Kāsānī, *Badāʾiʿ al-Ṣanāʾiʿ*, vol. 5, p. 223.

[61] Ibn Rushd, *Bidāyat al-Mujtahid,* vol. 2, p. 161.

i) The client approaches the bank with the request to purchase for him certain goods. He also provides the description of the required goods.

ii) In case the bank agrees to his request, it asks the client to give an undertaking to purchase the goods with a stated profit margin. The banks can enter into an actual sale agreement with the client if the commodity is owned by the bank.

iii) After signing the "undertaking for purchase", the bank makes purchase of required goods.

iv) After the bank has purchased goods and taken possession of them, it enters into a *murābaḥah* contract with its client. The contract includes mark-up over the cost of goods and the schedule of payment. The bank hands over goods to the client in lieu of cheques bearing future dates according to the payment schedule.

v) In order to secure the payment of price, the bank may ask the buyer to furnish a security in the form of a mortgage.

vi) In case of defect in the commodity discovered later on, the buyer can return it to the bank and claim re-imbursement of what he has paid.[62] In order to avoid any *ribā* element, the bank provides that the agreement of the bank and the actual execution of buying do not contribute any legal obligation on the partner to buy. Hence the risk is still that of the bank. Until the partner fulfills his original promise of re-buying the commodity, the risk remains with the bank, which justifies the profit.

Status of promise in Islamic Law

Here a question arises as to whether such undertaking or promise to purchase is binding on the client. Muslim jurists have provided different answers to this question:

---

[62] Shanqīṭī, *'Uqūd Mustaḥdathah* Madinah: Maṭba'ah al-'Ulum wa al-Ḥikam, 1992 ,p.381.

1. Shāfi'ī and Hanbalī jurists are of the view that promises are not mandatory. They represent just a moral obligation on un promisor to fulfill his promise.

2. The Mālikī jurists regard promises as binding. This view is attributed to Ibn al-'Arabī and Ibn Shubramah.

3. The Hanafī jurists acknowledge the validity of *bay' al-wafā'* which establishes the fact that the Hanafīs also favour the concept of the binding nature of promises. In *bay 'al-wafā'* the purchaser of an immovable property undertakes that he will return it to the seller if he (the seller) returns price to him. Such a promise is binding on the purchaser[63].

The Islamic Fiqh Academy has made the promises in commercial dealings binding on the promisor with the following conditions:

a) It should be one-sided promise.

b) The promise must have caused the promisee to incur some liabilities.

c) If the promise is to purchase something, the actual sale must take place at the appointed time by the exchange of offer and acceptance. Mere promise itself should not be taken as the concluded sale.

d) If the promisor backs out of his promise, the court may force him either to purchase the commodity or pay actual damages.[64]

Islamic banks deal with this issue in two different ways. In Dār al-Māl al-Islāmī the customer requests the bank to purchase the goods and submits intent to buy same on arrival; this promise is binding. In the Kuwait Finance House the customer gives a non-

---

[63] Ibn Juzy, *al-Qawānīn al-Fiqhiyyah*, p. 258, Ibn Qudāmah, *al-Mughnī*, vol. 4, pp. 17-195.

[64] Resolution No.2 and 3, Islamic Fiqh Academy. See Academy's Journal No.5, vol. 2, p. 1509.

binding promise to buy the commodities that were purchased by the Kuwait Finance House.

Murābaḥah Practices in Pakistan

In Pakistan *murābaḥah* is used as credit vehicle. It enables a buyer to finance his purchase with deferred payment as against accepting a mark-up on the market price of the commodity. The Muslim Scholars look at *murābaḥah* as practiced in Pakistan with suspicion. They see in it the element of *ribā* since the bank does not purchase commodity for the client, it only provides finance for the purchase of needed commodity against pre-determined profit. It also does not bear any risk while according to Islamic Law it is the element of risk, which makes the financial institution entitled to the profit.

Modes of Murābaḥah

Following are some forms of *murābaḥah* practiced by commercial banks in Pakistan.

First Mode: Purchase of goods by Banks and their sale to clients at appropriate mark-up in price on deferred payment basis:

This technique of mark-up is applied for financing the requirements of trade, commerce and industry. Under the technique of mark-up, a sale transaction is arranged at price mutually agreed upon between the buyer and seller. The sale price consists of the cost of goods plus margin of profit and the same is payable by the buyer on deferred basis either in lump sum or in installments.

While sanctioning the amount of finance, the bank takes into consideration the credit worthiness, dealings and cash flow of the customer. It also studies the marketability of the commodities or goods manufactured and securities offered to ensure that finances made available to him are properly utilized and finance is received back by the bank on due date as per stipulations of the sanction.

The mark-up is calculated for the period from the date of first debit to the date of expiry of the limit plus 210-days. The mark-up amount as calculated above when added to the amount of finance becomes the marked up amount, i.e., sale price at which the goods have been sold by the bank to the client.

Sharī'ah appraisal

The mode mentioned above is, infact, .combination of *bay' al-murābaḥah* and *bay' al-mu'ajjal*, because the bank charges an increase over and above the original price which is payable in future. It is *murābaḥah* because the buyer relying on the words of seller gives increase over and above the cost to the seller. It is *bay' al-mu'ajjal* also because the payment is made on specified dates in future. It is permissible for seller in *Sharī'ah* to charge increase in price over the spot market rate. Modern *murābaḥah* transactions normally take place on the basis of order supply in which the order supplier is not required to disclose his purchase price.

The Muslim scholars in Pakistan entertain some doubts about the validity and legitimacy of mark-up financing. The objections raised by the scholars are as follows:

1. The bank does not purchase the commodity needed by the client. It only provides him finance for its purchase. This fact is confirmed by the state bank's gazette of Jan. 1981, which states that: "the bank will not provide the customer rice, but will give him its market price and it will be presumed that the bank has itself purchased required quantity of rice from the market and sold it with profit margin to the customers, after 90-days from the date of purchase". Besides, the banks use the words of "amount of finance" for purchase price in their agreements, which refer to loan provided by the bank to the client. All this confirms that it is not a sale, instead, it is mark-up financing.

2. The Bank charges a predetermined increase over the amount of finance, which makes *murābaḥah* similar to charging increase over and above the amount of loan.

3. It does not bear any risk.

4. Unlike other Islamic Banks where two agreements are made with the client and where an actual sale contract is concluded only when the commodity is purchased by the bank and taken possession of, the Pakistani banks make one agreement which contains the provisions of amount of finance, i.e., purchase price, added profit margin, sale price

and rnode of payment. Thus, the bank is not concerned with the purchase of commodity.

5. *Murābaḥah* financing represents sale of a thing, which is not owned by the seller and that, is prohibited in Islam.

Second Mode: Purchase of movable and immovable property by the banks from their clients with buy-back agreement or otherwise:

Under the system of mark-up based financing with buy-back arrangement, simultaneous transactions of purchase and re-purchase of movable and immovable, property are made between the bank and client at a mutually agreed price for a specified period. The bank purchases an asset, movable or immovable at an agreed price, which the party agrees to re-purchase at a marked-up price payable on deferred basis either in lump sum or in installment.

The technique of bnuy-back arrangement is applicable where tangible security in the shape of movable/immovable property is offered by the client for obtaining finance from the bank. The banks use this mode to meet working capital requirements of factories. They also provide finances to pay for salaries, energy bills and overhead costs. The mode for obtaining finances for the above mentioned purpose is that the client sells some of his durable goods to the bank at certain price and receives required finances and then immediately purchases them from the bank at a higher price to be paid on a specified date in future. This mode is also employed for the purchase and construction of property.

I. Purchase of Property:

The Following steps are taken for the purchase of property:

    i) The customer negotiates the purchase of property from its owner, i.e., the seller for a price known as "property cost".

    ii) The customer sells the said property for a known sum paid immediately on registration of its conveyance from the seller to the customer.

    iii) The customer simultaneously buys back the same from the bank for a sum greater than the sum at which he sold to the bank. The amount is paid in monthly installments commencing one month after the date of registration of the conveyance from the seller to the customer and thereafter at the end of each succeeding month.

iv) The customer declares that he has examined the said property and assures the bank that the property cost is fair and reasonable and the said property is free from any structural or other defects and that the title thereto is clear and unencumbered.

v) The customer obtains possession of the said property from the seller on or before registration of conveyance.

II. Construction of Property:

The procedure for obtaining finance for he purpose of construction of property is as follows:

i) The customer desirous of constructing a house approaches the bank. He submits a building plan approved by the authorities concerned.

ii) The parties fix the property cost, i.e., the cost of a completed house that includes cost of land and building.

iii) The bank buys from the customer all building materials, fixtures and fittings required for constructing the said property for a certain amount known as the bank's investment.

iv) Bank's Investment ranges between 30% to 60% of the value of the said property erected by use of the building materials as is certified by an architect nominated or approved by the bank.

v) The customer is deemed to have immediately bought back the building materials for the sum that is higher than the price at which bank has purchased building material from the customer. This amount, which is the buy-back price for the customer, is paid in monthly installments commencing one month after the date of completion of construction.

Calculation of Mark-up

The mark-up is calculated for the period from the date of first debit to the date of expiry of the limit plus 210-days (cushion period). The mark-up amount as calculated above when added to the amount of finance becomes the marked up amount, i.e., at which the security offered has been sold by the bank to the client.

The sale price (marked-up price) payable by the client to bank comprises the following:

    i) amount of finance,

    ii) mark-up for the period of finance,and

    iii) mark-up for 210-days.

The amount of installment payable is calculated as under:

    i) amount of finance,

    ii) plus mark-up (on reducing balance method), for the period of financing,and

    iii)these are divided by total number of installments.

Sharī'ah Appraisal

The buy-bank practice has been a target of grave criticism by religious scholars. They consider it a subterfuge to circumvent the prohibition of *ribā*. In buy-back arrangement no real sale takes place. Instead the parties deal in usurious loan transaction. It is a fictitious deal that ensures a predetermined profit to the bank without actually dealing in goods, or sharing any real risk. The present practice of buy-back is infact a form of prohibited sale called *bay' al-'īnah* in Islamic Law.

Bay' al-'īnah means to sell commodity on cash and then buy it back at a higher price to be paid on some specified time in future. It is called *'inah* because the *'ayn* (substance) sold by the seller returns to him. Mālik and Aḥmad ibn Ḥanbal prohibited this transaction because it is a legal device for dealing in *ribā*[65]. They argue on the basis of the tradition of 'Ā'ishah (God be pleased with her) when Umm Muḥibbah informed her that she had a slave-girl whom she sold to Zayd ibn

---

[65] *Al-Murābaḥah fī Bank Dubai al-Islāmī* p. 15.

Arqam for eight hundred dirhams till he could pay. He then decided to sell her. So, she bought her back for six hundred. 'Ā'ishah said, "It was bad what you sold and bad what you bought. Make it known to Zayd that his *jihād* alongside the Messenger of Allah (s.a.w.s) has been nullified, unless he repents". She said to her, "What if I should just take my capital from him"? She replied, "Those who after receiving direction from their Lord, desist, shall be pardoned for the past".[66] *Bay' al-'īnah* is prohibited because it is subterfuge for usurious loan. All the Muslim jurists are unanimous on the point that the intention of the contracting party by making a contract should be in harmony with the intention of the Lawgiver. If the intention of the contracting party is inconsistent with the intention of the Lawgiver, his contract will be invalid. Ibn al-Qayyim says, "The proofs and rules of the *Sharī'ah* reveal that intentions are taken into account in a contract and that affect validity and invalidity, and lawfulness and unlawfulness of the contract. A contract become sometimes becomes lawful and sometimes unlawful with the variation of intention and object, as it becomes valid sometimes and some times invalid with its variatior.".[67]

VII. Bay' al-Mu'ajjal (credit Sale):

There is no disagreement among the jurists that *bay' al-mu'ajjal* is valid in the *Sharī'ah*, firstly because it includes in the generality of trade which is permissible in the *Sharī'ah* and secondly because there is a proof from the Sunnah that Holy Prophet (s.a.w.s.) purchased a quantity of grain from a Jew on the basis of deferred payment and he pledged his armour by way of security. But there is no agreement or consensus of opinion among the jurists on the point whether a seller can increase a price of a commodity for deferred payment as compared to its spot price or not. A group of Muslim Jurists regards such increase permissible because it is against the commodity and not against money. An increase against late payment is *ribā* only where the subject matter is money on the both sides. They, therefore allow a seller to fix two prices of a commodity that is cash price and credit

---

[66] Qurṭubī, *al-Jāmi' li Aḥkām al-Qur'ān* vol. 3, pp. 359-61.

[67] Ibn Qayyim, *I'lām al-Muwaqqi'īn*, vol.3, p.96.

price and give an option to a buyer to buy a commodity at any of the two prices. Thus, it is permissible in their view to say to a prospective buyer that I sell you this item for Rs. 100/- cash in hand, and Rs. 150/- on the credit of one year. A group of modern scholars entertain some doubts regarding the validity of this transaction. They put forth following arguments to prove that such transactions are not recommended by the *Sharī'ah*.

1. There is no authority from the Qur'ān and the Sunnah to prove the permissibility of increase in price for deferred payment.

2. If a transaction on deferred payment of price is valid in *Sharī'ah* it does not mean that charging of high price than the prevalent market price of goods is also permitted.

3. In Islamic Law the basis to be considered in the contracts is the meaning and underlying objective of the contract, not its form or words. It is for this reason that Islamic Law does not regard *bay' al-wafā* as real sale. It is infact a pledge. In credit sale the objective of the seller is to make profit from the time given to the purchaser. Thus, it is substantially not different from *ribā* transaction.

4. The agreement of the purchaser to pay a price higher than the spot market rate cannot justify the transaction, because he agreed to this price owing to his inability to pay cash. Thus, such agreement does not represent a real consent of buyer. Besides, it amounts to exploitation of the need of a the buyer.

5. The profit charged by a vendor should not be exorbitant; otherwise it would fall under *ghabn fāḥish*, which renders a contract invalid. The price charged by a seller in a credit sale is higher than that prevalent in the market. Therefore, it should be treated as a case of *ghabn fāḥish*, which is a cause of the invalidity of contract. It has been mentioned earlier that *ghabn fāḥish* refers to a loss, which cannot be estimated by the experts. It also refers to a situation where a seller charges an exorbitant profit from the buyer.

6. The cash price fixed by a seller already contains a profit margin for the seller. Now the further increase in the price for deferred payment is only against time. If, for example a seller says to a buyer that the cash price of goods is Rs. 100 and credit price is Rs. 150/-, it is clear that the increase of Rs. 50/- is against nothing but the time.

In the *sharī'ah* the intentions and the objectives underlying a transaction occupy a significant place. They are a real touchstone to determine whether or not a transaction is Islamically acceptable. Charging a higher price for deferred payment may not be in technical sense an act of *ribā*, but keeping in view the objective and underlying intention, there remains hardly any doubt that it is similar to *ribā*. Such practice promotes usurious mentality and opens a back door for *ribā*. *Bay' al-mu'ajjal* is infact a method to provide relief to a purchaser who does not have enough resources to make immediate payment. It is in no way a means to exploit the hardship of buyer and earn profit. The *Sunnah* of the Holy Prophet (s.a.w.s.) permits credit sale but there is no proof in the *Sunnah* that charging a price higher than prevailing market is also permitted.

Therefore, the accurate legal position is that the price of commodity in a deal on deferred payment should be the same as being charged by the seller for cash sales. In other words it should be according to prevailing market price.

Conclusion

1. Sale is an exchange of a useful and desirable thing for a similar thing by mutual consent for the alienation of property.

2. In Islamic Law property is divided into movable and immovable, fungible and non-fungible, and finally into determinate and indeterminate property.

3. Islamic Law has prohibited all sale contracts, which contain the element of *gharar* (uncertainty) such as *mukhāḍarah, muḥāqalah,* and *mulāmasah.*

4. Important kinds of sale are:

    i) *Salam*

ii) Ṣarf

iii) Murabaḥah

iv) Bay' mu'ajjal

v) Istiṣnā'

5. Salam is a sale in which the price is paid in advance and articles are delivered on future date. It is affected on the commodities, which can be precisely determined in terms of quality and quantity.

6. *Ṣarf* refers to sale of money for money. The counter values in this contract must be delivered and taken possession of in the session of contract.

7. Islamic Law treats todays paper currency as real money for all the practical purposes.

8. *Istiṣnā'* consists in ordering an artisan or manufacturer to make certain goods answering a given description.

9. *Murābaḥah* is a transaction in which a vendor sells an article for the cost price in addition to a certain stated profit.

10. *Murābaḥah* is a trust sale in which the buyer depends and relies upon the integrity of the purchaser as regards the cost he mentions to the buyer.

11. Buy-Back agreements as practised in Pakistan do not conform to the teachings of the *Sharī'ah*.

CHAPTER-15

CONTRACT OF IJĀRAH (LEASING)

The word *ijārah* literally means to give something on rent. In the language of Law it means lending of some object to somebody in return for some rental against a specified period. It can also be described as sale of usufruct for consideration. It includes letting things moveable and immovable for hire and rendering services such as custody of property and professional services.

The word *ijārah* is used for two different situations. In the first place, it means to employ the services of a person on wages given to him as consideration for his hired services. The employer is called *musta'jir* while the employee is called *ajīr*. The second type of *ijārah* relates to the usufructs of asset and properties, and not to services of human beings. *ijārah* in this sense means to transfer the usufruct of a particular property to another person in exchange for a rent claimed from him. In this case, the term *ijārah* is analogous to the English term leasing. Here the lessor is called *mu'jir;* the lessee is called *musta'jir* and the rent payable to the lessor is called *ujrah* [1]

The jurists have formulated various definitions of *ijārah* having regard to its principle features

The definition of *ijārah* in different schools is as follows:

---

[1] Taqī 'Usmānī. *An Introduction to Islamic Finance*, pp. 156.157.

Ḥanafī School

It is contract on usufructs for a known consideration.[2]

Shāfi'ī School

It is a contract on a known and permissible benefit in exchange of a known return.[3]

Mālikī School

It is an alienation of lawful usufructs for a fixed charge for a fix period. For the Mālikī Ibn Rushd says; *ijārah* resembles a sale contract whereby price and use are exchanged.[4]

Ḥanbalī School

Ijārah is contract for the lawful and defined use of a lawful and determined corporeal object for a specific period of time. It is also defined as providing a defined work for a fixed price.[5]

Features of Ijārah

1.The preceding definitions set the following features of *ijārah*. The purpose of *ijārah* contract is alienation of usufructs unlike contract of sale, which aims at alienation of property.

2. The benefits to be derived should be known and specified.

3. The benefits, which are the subject matter of contact, should be permissible in the *Shrī'ah*. Thus, the hiring of a house for

---

[2] Kāsānī, *badā'i' al-Ṣanā'i'*, vol. 4, p.174; Zayla'ī, *Tabyīn al-Ḥaqā'iq* vol. 5, p.105.

[3] Shirbīnī, *Mughnī al-Muḥtāj*, vol. 2, p.332.

[4] Ibn Qudāmah, *al-Sharḥ al-Kabīr*, vol.4, p.2; Ibn Qudāmah, *al-Mughnī* vol. 5, p. 398. Ibn Rushd, *Bidāyat al-Mujtahid*, vol. 2, pp.219-220.

[5] Baḥutī *al-Rawḍ al-Murbi'*, p. 214.

manufacturing wine is not permissible. Similarly, hiring a woman for the purpose of singing would also be against Islamic Law.

4. The rent or compensation should be specifically fixed.

5. The period of contract should also be specified in the contract.

Legitimacy of Ijārah

The legality of *'Ijarah* is established by the Qur'ān, the Sunnah and ijmā'.

Qur'ān

i. Allah says: "And if they suckle your (offspring) give them their recompense'.[6]

ii. "Said one of the (damsels): "O my father: engage him on wages. Truly the best of men for thee to employ is the man who is strong and trusty".[7]

Sunnah

i. Said the Holy Prophet (s.a.w.s). "Give wages of the person hired before his sweat dries up".[8]

ii. "If some one hires a person, let him inform him about the wages he is to receive".[9]

iii. Haḍrat Sa'd ibn Abī Waqqās reported that in the age of the Holy Prophet (s.a.w.s) the owners of the land used to let their lands on rent.[10]

---

[6] Qur'ān,65: 6.

[7] Qur'ān,28: 26.

[8] Ṣan'ānī, *al-Salām,* vol. 3. p. 81.

[9] Shawkānī, *Nayl al-Awṭār,* vol. 5, p. 292.

[10] Nasā'ī, *Sunan* (Urdu) Karachi: Our'ān Mahal, n.d. vol.3, p.60.

Ijmā'

All the Companions of the Holy Prophet (s.a.w.s) unanimously held that *ijārah* is a lawful contract. They themselves practiced all lawful forms of this contract. In the *Sharī'ah* permissibility of *ijārah* has been constructed on *istiḥsān*, which is a departure from a rule of precedent. According to a general rule of Islamic Law of contract, an object, which does not exist at the time of contract, may not be sold. However, *ijārah* is valid despite its being sale of the usufructs, which are non-existent at the time of contract. Analogy would thus invalidate *ijārah*, but *istiḥsān* exceptionally validates it on the authority of the Sunnah and ijmā'.

Imām Sarakhsī stating the lawfulness of this contract writes:

The contract and dealings practiced before Islam are valid practices for us also in the absence of any text disapproving them. The Holy Prophet (s.a.w.s) was sent as Prophet and he saw the people practising *ijārah* and he approved that practice.[11]

Kinds of ijārah

There are two main kinds of *ijārah*, namely *ijārat al-ashyā' and ijārat al- ashkhāṣ.*.

1. *Ijārat al-ashyā'* refers to hiring of things such as houses, shops, lands, animals and beasts etc. This is also known as *ijārat al-'ayn*.

2. *Ijārat al-ashkhāṣ* refers to hiring of services, such as to hire a painter to paint a house. This kind is also called *ijārat al-dhimmah.*[12]

The person hired for rendering services is called *ajīr* who is either *ajīr khāṣ*, the employee or *ajīr mushtarak*, i.e., independent contractor. *ajīr khāṣ* renders service for one person for a fixed period while *ajīr*

---

[1] Al-Sarakhsī, *al-Mabsūṭ* vol. 15, p. 74.

[2] Al-Jazīrī, *Kitāb al-Fiqh 'alā al-Madhāhib al-Arba'ah*,

Beriut: vol. 3, p. 110.

mushtrak works for a large number of people like tailor, laundryman, and Ironsmith.

Conditions of ijārat al-ashyā'

1. The subject of *ijārah* must have a valuable use. Therefore, things having no usufruct at all cannot be leased.

2. It is necessary for a valid contract of lease that the corpus of the leased property remains in the ownership of the seller, and only its usufruct is transferred to the lessee. Therefore, the lease cannot be affected in respect of money, eatables, fuel and ammunition, because their use is not possible unless they are consumed. If anything of this nature is leased out, it will be deemed to be a loan and all the rules concerning the transaction of loan shall accordingly apply. Any rent charged on lease shall be treated as an interest charged on a loan.[13]

3. As the corpus of the leased property remains in the ownership of the lessor, all the liabilities emerging from the ownership shall be borne by the lessor, but the liabilities referable to the use of the property shall be borne by the lessee.

Example

A has leased his house to B. The taxes referable to the property shall be borne by A, while electricity bills and all expenses referable to the use of the house shall be borne by B, the lessee.[14]

4. The subject-matter of *ijārah*, namely, the usufruct should be known, and identified. There should not be any uncertainty and vagueness about the usufructs, which may lead to discord and dispute among the parties. The lessor should specifically mention the subject-matter. It is not permissible to lease an unspecified thing. Thus if a person says: "I rented you one of these two houses", the contract

---

[13] Taqī 'Usmānī, *an Introduction to Islamic Finance*, p. 157.

[14] Ibid.

would be invalid because the subject-matter in this case is unknown and unidentified.[15]

5. The leasing period should be fixed, whether, it is long or short. It is the viewpoint of the majority of the Fuqahā'. Imām Mālik, on the other hand maintains that a long period for the use of usufructs is not advisable, because it may cause dispute and tussle.[16] As regards property of orphans and waqf, the Ḥanafī jurists hold that long period of lease of these properties is not permissible so that the lessee may not claim his ownership over them because of long possession. They propose that it should not be hired out for more than three years.[17]

6. The subject-matter should be something that can be actually delivered. Thus, the renting out of a stray animal is not permitted.

7. The object and purpose of the contract should be lawful. Thus, it is not permissible to hire a house for the purpose of gambling or manufacturing wine.

8. The article to be hired should be physically fit for hire.

9. In the contract of hiring a land, the use of land should be specified whether it is for cultivation or construction of building.

10. If a beast of burden is hired for carrying a burden, the quantity and quality of burden, the destination and the period for which it is required should be stated. If the lessee loads with the burden more than the specified, he will be called to compensate. Similarly, if he uses the animal in an unusual manner, which causes its death, he will be regarded *ghāṣib* (usurper) and called for indemnification.[18]

---

[15] kāsānī, *Badā'i' al-Ṣanā'i'*, vol. 4, p. 180.

[16] See Shirbīnī, *Mughnī al-Muḥtāj* vol. 2, p. 349; Ibn Qudāmah,

al-Mughnī, vol. 5, p. 401.

[17] Ibn 'Ābidīn, *Radd al-Muḥtār*, vol. 5, p. 2-3

[18] Zaylaʻī, *Tabyīn al-Ḥaqā'iq*, vol. 5, p. 113.

11. The lessee cannot use the leased asset for any purpose other than the purpose specified in the lease agreement. If no such purpose is specified in the agreement, the lessee can use it for whatever purpose it is used in the normal course. However, if he wishes to use if for an abnormal purpose, he cannot do so unless the lessor allows him in express terms.

12. The lessee is liable to compensate the lessor for every harm to the leased asset caused by any misuse or negligence on the part of the lessee.

13. The leased asset shall remain in the risk of the lessor throughout the lease period in the sense that any harm or loss caused by the factors beyond the control of the lessee shall be borne by the lessor.

14. A property jointly owned by two or more persons can be leased out, and the rental shall be distributed between or among all the joint owners according to the proportion of their respective shares in the property.

15. A joint-owner of a property can lease his proportionate share to his co-sharer only and not to any other person.

16. Rent to be paid should be a lawful thing and known.

17. Rent should not be paid in the same genus or specifies. Thus, a house cannot be rented in exchange of house. This condition is peculiar to the Hanafi School.[19]

Conditions of ijārat al-ashkhāṣ

1. In the contract of hiring services, the work required to be performed should be specifically fixed such as the carriage of goods, or building house etc.

2. Performance or work should not be prohibited in the *Sharī'ah*. Thus, it is not permitted to hire a magician to teach magic, or a

---

[19] Kāsānī. *Badā'i' al-Ṣanā'i'*, vol. 4, p. 194.

singer for the purpose of singing. Similarly, it is not permissible to hire the services of a person to kill another person or torture him, because they are acts of sin and disobedience, hence prohibited in the *Sharī'ah*.

3. The service required to be rendered should not be a mandatory duty. It is, therefore, not allowed for a person to hire a person to pray, to perform *hajj*, to lead prayer, to teach the Qur'ān. because they are mandatory duties, so the worker is not entitled to wages if he is hired for any of them.

   As regards charging fee for teaching the Qur'ān or the principles of faith, accepted rule of the Ḥanafī School is that no one is allowed to charge any fee for teaching these subjects because it is held to be a form of worship (*ibādah*). This was the ruling of early jurists. The jurists of subsequent ages, when they saw that the people were reluctant to teach the Qur'ān gave a *fatwā* in favour of charging fee for teaching the Qur'ān. They considered it necessary in order to encourage the teaching of Islam.[20]

4. The contract of *ijārah* should not comprise any condition according to which the rent or wages might be paid from the article manufactured, or wrought upon the rental goods.

Some other rules concerning ijārah

1. The property hired is a trust in the hands of the lessee. Thus, if it is destroyed without any negligence on the part of the lessee, he will not be responsible for that loss or damage.

2. The lessee is required to exercise maximum care of property and use it properly. An improper and unusual use of the property will change his status from trustee to usurper, and in case any destruction takes place, he will be liable for compensation.

3. Rent of hired property becomes due:

---

[20] Zayla'ī. *Tabyīn al-Ḥaqā'iq,* vol. 5, p. 124.

i) on the attainment of usufruct of the hired property or goods;and

ii) ability of the lessee to use the usufruct of hired goods.

4. Ijārah is a binding and irrevocable contract. Thus, it cannot be revoked unilaterally.

5. Unlike the sale the contract, *ijārah* can be enforced from some specified future date. Thus, it is permissible to say that this contract will be effective from Jan. 1, 2000

6. Ajīr mushtarak (Independent Contractor) such as tailor or shoemaker will be held accountable for the loss of goods in his custody regardless of whether they are destroyed by his fault or without his fault. This ruling has been given by the *Fuqahā'* on the grounds of public interest so that trustees and tradesmen exercise greater care in safeguarding people's properties.[21]

Modern Applications of ijārah

There are two main types of *ijārah* (leasing) practiced by the modern banks namely finance lease and operating lease.

1. Finance Lease:

The finance lease is based on a contract between the lessor and the lessee for hire of a specific asset selected from a manufacturer or vendor of such assets by the lessee. The lessor retains the ownership of the asset and the lessee has possession and use of asset on payment of specified rentals over a period. Though the lessor is the legal owner, the lessee is given the exclusive rights to the use of the asset for the duration of the contract. The rentals during the fixed primary period are sufficient to amortize the capital outlay of the leasing company and provide an element of profit. The primary period is closely related to the estimated useful life of the asset and the lessee is normally responsible for all operating costs such as maintenance and insurance. The lessee has also the options for a secondary period of

---

[21] Kāsānī. *Badā'i' al-Ṣanā'i'*, vol. 4, p. 210, Ramlī, *Mughnī al-Muḥtāj*, vol. 2, p. 35, Ibn Qudāmah, *al-Mughnī*, vol. 5, p.487.

lease in which the rentals are reduced to nominal amount. The period of lease usually ranges from5 to 15 years depending on the useful life of the asset.[22]

Since all the risk is borne by the lessee, instead of lessor in finance lease, it makes the contract objectionable from the *Sharī'ah* point of view. In the *Sharī'ah* risks of damage, and obsolescence is exclusively borne by the lessor. Besides, the leased item or equipment cannot be returned to the lessor during the primary period of lease. The lessee cannot cancel the contract even if he finds the item unuseful during the term. The fact that the rent is related to the approximate useful life of the item and that the lessor recovers the entire cost of equipment plus some profit, make this contract doubtful from Islamic point of view.

2. Operating Lease:

This is "non-full payment" lease as rentals are insufficient to enable the lessor to recover fully the initial capital outlay. The residual value is recovered through disposal or re-leasing the equipment to other users. In this lease major consideration is given to the use of equipment. Unlike the finance lease system, the lessee can cancel the contract before it expires without paying any penalty. Under this arrangement the risk of damage and depreciation is borne by the lessor.

Ijārah in Islamic Banks

1. Ijārah wa Iqtinā' (Hire-purchase):

It is a combination of leasing movable or immovable property with granting the lessee an option of eventually acquiring the object of the lease.[23] *Ijārah wa 'Iqtinā'* is a popular mode of financing practised by Islamic financial institutions. It is used in the following manner.

---

[22] Council of Islamic Ideology, *Elimination of Ribā from the Economy and Islamic Modes of Financing*, 1991, p. 13.

[23] Nabīl A. Ṣāliḥ, *Unlawful Gain and Legitimate Profit in Islamic Law*, P.122.

The financial institution rents a movable or immovable property to one of its clients who pay an agreed sum in installments over an agreed period into a saving account held with the same institution. The lessor who is usually the *muḍārib* invests these installments in *muḍārabah* venture for the client's account. As, when the amount of deposits and accrued income on such deposits, equal the aggregate amount of the then outstanding lease payments, the lease is terminated and the lessee becomes the owner of the asset.

Thus, *ijārah wa iqtinā* is a lease agreement combined with an obligation to the lessee to purchase the asset during the lease or at the termination of the lease.

2. Direct leasing:

This is a mode whereby the Islamic banks allow the customer to use the capital assets owned by the banks for a limited period of time ranging from a few days to a few months depending upon the type of asset in question. In return the lessee pays a monthly or annual rental fee.

Conclusion

1. *Ijārah* is a contract for usufruct for a known consideration.

2. *Ijārah* includes letting things for hire and rendering services.

3. The subject-matter of *ijārah* should be permissible thing or act.

4. It should be known and identified.

5. The rent or compensation should be specified fixed.

6. The property hired is held to be a trust in the hands of lessee. Thus, if it is destroyed without any negligence on his part, he will not be held responsible for that loss or damage.

7. *Ajīr mushtarak* (Independent Contractor) is held accountable for the loss of goods in his custody regardless of whether they are destroyed by his fault or without his fault.

8. There are two main types of *ijārah* (leasing) practiced by the modern banks namely, finance lease and operating lease. Finance lease is objectionable from the *Sharī'ah* point of view because in this form of lease all the risk is borne by the lessee.

9. Hire-purchase is a combination of leasing property and granting the lessee an option of eventually acquiring the object of the lease. It is permissible in the *Sharī'ah*.

CHAPTER-16

CONTRACT OF MUSHĀRAKAH (PARTNERSHIP)

The word *sharikah* is used in the literal sense to mean mixing or mingling. *Sharikah* or Partnership implies an underlying idea of mixing shares in such a way that one of them cannot be distinguished from the other. In its technical sense, *sharikah* signifies a particular relationship that exists between two contracting parties, although there may be no actual mixing or mingling of shares.

Definition

The Muslim jurists have offered various definitions of partnerships with regard to its important features.

Mālikī definition

"It is a permission from each of the partners to the other for appropriation and disposition while retaining the right to transact personally (in such wealth). "[1]

Hanbalī definition

"*Sharikah* is the participation of two or more persons in the entitlement of a thing and disposition."[2]

Shāfi'ī definition

"*Sharikah* is an establishment of a right in a single thing held in common between two or more persons".[3]

---

[1] Ibn Qudāmah. *al-Sharh al-Kabīr* vol. 3, p.348.

[2] Ibn Qudāmah, *al-Mughnī* vol 5, p.1.

[3] Shirbīnī, *mughnī al-Muhtāj*, vol.3, p.211.

Ḥanafī definition

"*Sharikah* is a contract between two or more people for participation in capital and its profit."[4]

Of all the preceding definitions, the last one may be said to be the most comprehensive. as it encompasses all the necessary ingredients of a partnership; namely, agreement, business involving investment from the partners and sharing of expected profit.

Definition of Partnership in Law

The Pakistan Partnership Act. 1932 defines partnership as:

> "A relationship between persons who agree to share
> the profits of a business carried on by all or any of
> them acting for all"[5]

Following are the main features of modern partnership.

a) Agreement: There must be an agreement between the parties concerned. Without agreement. partnership cannot be formed. The agreement may be express or implied. It is however, preferable to reduce it to writing so that any future dispute may be settled in accordance with the provisions of the agreement.

b) Number: There should be more than one person to form a partnership. However. there is a restriction on the maximum number of the partners. In case of ordinary business, the partners must not exceed 20 partners and in case of banking contracts it must not exceed 10 partners.

c) Business The object of the formation of partnership is to carry on any type of business as long as it is lawful.

d) Profit-Sharing The basic purpose of the formation of partnership is to earn profit. The profit is to be shared as agreed between the partners. If there is no such agreement they will share profits equally

---

[4] Ibn ʿAbidīn. *radd al-Muḥtār*. vol.3. p.364.

[5] *Partnership Act 1932*, Section 34.

The contribution towards the losses will be in the same proportion as the sharing of profits unless there is contract to the contrary.[6]

e) Carried on by all or on behalf of all: The business of partnership is conducted by all the partners or any of them acting for all. But each partner is allowed to participate in the management by law.

f) Unlimited liability: Each partner is liable to the full satisfaction of the liability of partnership jointly and severally. However, one or some of the partners with the agreement of other partners may have limited liability. However, all the partners in a firm cannot be with limited liability.

g) Investment: Each partner contributes his share in the capital according to the agreement. Some persons may become partners without investing any capital to the business. They devote their time, energy, skill, judgement and ability to the business instead of capital and receive profit.

h) Transferability of share: The interest of a partner in a firm cannot be transferred, assigned to a third person without the consent of other partners.

i) Position of partners: Every partner is an agent as well as principal to the other partner. In this capacity he can bind the other partners by his acts as well as will be bound by the acts of other partners if they were carried out during the normal conduct of business by his act. In the position of an agent he can enter into a contract with another person or parties on behalf of his partner or partners.[7]

j) Duration: Partnership may be for an indefinite period of time. It may also be for a definite period. Some partnerships are formed for completion of a single venture.[8]

---

[7] *Partnership Act 1932* Section 22.

[8] *Partnership Act 1932,* Section 18 & 19.

Concept of Company in Modern Law

Definition of Company

Company is a voluntary association of different persons created by law as a separate body for specific purposes. It possesses a common capital contributed by its members, such capital being divided into transferable shares. The liability of each such member is limited to the extent of value of the shares he holds.[9]

Characteristics of a company

The following are the main characteristics of a joint-stock company.

à) Legal Entity: A company is an artificial person, which is created by law. It is a separate legal entity apart from its members. It can purchase property or transfer the title of property or sue in a court of law in its own name.

b) Perpetual existence: The company is a creation of law and it continues to exist until it is wound up by the legal procedure. The death or retirement of any member does not affect the life and existence of the company. Its life is distinct from that of its members.

c) Limited Liability: The liability of each shareholder is limited to the extent of his share. Other assets of the members cannot be taken into consideration for the liabilities of the company.

d) Constitutional Status: A company is person under the law, but it is not to be considered citizen in the eyes of law.

e) Number of Members: In case of pubic limited company, the minimum number of members is seven. There is, however, no restriction on the maximum number of members. In case of private limited company the minimum number of members is two while the maximum is fifty.

f) Transferability of Shares: The shares of a public company are transferable. This type of share may easily be purchased or sold in the stock exchange market.

---

[9] See *Company Law in Pakistan*, 1986. (p.22)

g) Management: The management of company is centralized in a Board of Directors who are elected by the general shareholder. But the shareholders, who are the actual owners of the company, are not allowed to participate directly in the management.

h) Nature of Business and Management: The nature of business is mentioned in the object clause of the Memorandum of Association, which cannot be changed except by the sanction of the court. The procedure of management, on the other hand, is laid down in the Articles of Association.[10]

Legitimacy of Sharikah

The legitimacy of *sharikah* as a valid mode of business is established by the Qur'ān, the Sunnah and *ijmā'*. Some of the relevant verses of the Holy Qur'ān and traditions of the Holy Prophet are cited in the following lines.

The Qur'ān Says:

$$\text{وَإِنَّ كَثِيرًا مِّنَ ٱلْخُلَطَآءِ لَيَبْغِى بَعْضُهُمْ عَلَىٰ بَعْضٍ}$$

$$\text{إِلَّا ٱلَّذِينَ ءَامَنُوا۟ وَعَمِلُوا۟ ٱلصَّٰلِحَٰتِ وَقَلِيلٌ مَّا هُمْ}$$

"And verily, many partners oppress one another, except those who believe and do righteous deeds, and they are few."[11]

i) The Holy Prophet (s.a.w.s.) said that Allah says:

> I am the third of the two partners as long as they do not cheat one another. But when one of them cheats
>
> the other. I leave them"[12] (i.e., they are deprived of
>
> the blessing and favour of Almighty Allah).

---

[10]Ibid, pp. 22, 23.

[11]Qur'ān, 38: 24.

[12]Abū Da'ūd, *Sunan*, Kitāb al-Buyū', Bāb al-Sharikah .

ii) The Holy Prophet (s.a.w.s) also said: "Allah Almighty is with the two partners unless they defraud each other". [13]

iii) *Sharikah* business was prevalent in the Arabian Peninsula at the advent of Islam. The Holy Prophet (s.a.w.s.) accorded his tacit approval to this practice. He himself carried on business on the basis of partnership before his declaration of prophethood.

The validity of *sharikah* is proved by the consensus of the Muslim Ummah too. The entire Muslim scholars in all ages had been in agreement in regard to the validity of *sharikah* form of business.

Kinds of Sharikah

There are two main kinds of *Sharikah*:

1. *Sharikat al-Milk* (Proprietary partnership).

2. *Sharikat al-'Aqd* (Contractual partnership). [14]

1. Sharikat al-Milk:

Sharikat al-milk is defined by the *Majallah,* as "the existence of a thing in the exclusive joint-ownership of two or more persons due to any reason of ownership, or it is the joint claim of two or more persons for a debt that is due from another individual arising from a single cause". [15]

In this type of *Sharikah* each and everyone has ownership in every smallest part of the capital. The property, which is difficult to divide and distinguish, forms the subject matter of a proprietary partnership. It is of two kinds:

a). Compulsory partnership: It is a partnership, which becomes effective without any action on the part of the partners, such as inheritance.

b). Optional partnership: It is a partnership which becomes effective through the act of parties e.g. joint-purchase or

---

[13]Ibn Qudāmah, *al-Mughnī*, vol.5, p.3.

[14]*Majallah,* Article 1045.

[15]Ibid., article 1060.

joint-acceptance of gift or a bequest, joint seizure of an article in enemy's country in the course of war or where they unite their respective properties in such a way that one is not distinguishable from the other, such as mixture of wheat with barley. [16]

Rules Relating to Sharikat al-Milk

1. Each partner is a stranger with respect to the share of the others.

2. The partners are not allowed to undertake any act of disposal with respect to the other's share except with the latter's permission.

3. Each partner can sell his own share without the other partners' consent, except in cases where share of one partner can not be distinguished from the other.

4. The share of one partner in the possession of another co-owner is governed by the rules of *wadī'ah* (deposit). If one co-owner further deposits such property with a third party without the permission of his partner, he is liable for compensation *(damān)* if the property is destroyed.

5. Right to demand the recovery of a debt belongs to each co-owner jointly and severally. A debt possessed by one partner is governed by the rules of *sharikat al-Milk*. Further, postponement of the recovery of a debt can not be granted by one co-owner without the permission of the other. [17]

2. Sharikat al-'Aqd:

It is a partnership, which comes into being as a result of agreement between two or more persons in order to share the profits. [18]

---

[16] Ibid. articles 1063, 1064.

[17] See Nyazee, Imran Ahsan. *Islamic Law of Business organization-Partnerships*. Islamabad. The International Institute of Islamic Thought and Islamic Research Institute. 1997. pp. 36-37.

[18] *Majallah*, article 1329.

Kinds of Sharikat al-'Aqd

There is a considerable difference of opinion among the various schools of thought aboutt he types of contractual partnership.

According to Mālikī and Shāfiʿī jurists, contractual partnership is of four kinds:

1. *Sharikat al-'Inān*

2. *Sharikat al-Mufāwadah*

3. *Sharikat al-A'māl*

4. *Sharikat al-Wujūh* [19]

According to the Ḥanbalīs, there are five kinds of contractual partnership:

1.*Sharikat al-'Inān*

2.*Sharikat al-Mufāwaḍah*

3.*Sharikat al-A'māl*

4.*Sharikat al-Wujūh.*

5 *Muḍārabah.* [20]

According to the Ḥanafī jurists, *Sharikah* is of three types:

1. *Sharikat al-Amwāl*

2. *Sharikat al-A'māl*

3. *Sharikat al-Wujūh*

Each of the above kinds is further divided into *'inān* (limited) or *mufāwadah* (unlimited). Thus, they are of the following six categories:

1. *Sharikat al-Amwāl* by way of *mufāwadah*

---

[19] Ibn Rushd. *Bidāyat al-Mujtahid,* vol. p.248.

[20] Ibn Qudāmah. *al- lughnī.* vol. 5, p.3.

2. *Sharikat al-Amwāl* by way of *'inān*.

3. *Sharikat al-A'māl* by way of *mufāwadah*.

4. *Sharikat al-A'māl* by way of *'inān*.

5. *Sharikat al-Wujūh* by way of *mufāwadah*.

6. *Sharikat al-Wujūh* by way of *'inān*. [21]

We will follow here the scheme of Ḥanafī School, i.e., division of *sharikah* into *amwāl, a'māl* and *wujūh*. Our emphasis in. this discussion will be on *inān* investment partnership or *amwāl* by way of *inān* and *mufāwadah* investment partnership or *amwāl* by way of *mufāwadah*

Conditions For Contractual Partnership

The following are the basic conditions common to every type of contractual partnership (*Sharikah al-'Aqd)*

Basic elements:

A contractual partnership should include all the basic elements of a valid contract, i.e.,

i) Offer and acceptance;

ii) Competence of parties: Only legally competent person capable of disposing property and conferring mandate can be a party to a contractual partnership

iii)   Subject matter: It is also necessary that the subject matter of partnership be a lawful trade. Thus, a partnership for trade in wine and other illicit things is invalid.

Agency:

Each kind of contractual partnership should contain a contract of agency. Each partner is an agent of the other partners in all dispositions made by him, in trading and in accepting work.

---

[21]Zayla'ī. *Tabyīn al-Ḥaqā'iq.* vol 3, p.313.

Division of Profit:

It should be declared in what way the profit is to be divided between the partners.

Known Portion of Profit:

Shares of profit to be divided between the shareholders must be known by division, for instance, one half (1/2) one third (1/3) or one fourth (1/4). No fixed amount or portion of the profit can be stipulated for any of the partners. The loss is to be borne in proportion to the respective capitals of the partners.

Entitlement to Profit:

According to the Ḥanafī jurists a partner in a contractual partnership becomes entitled to the profit in one of three ways.

    i)   By capital

    ii)   By work

    iii)   By the liability incurred by the partner. [22]

According to the majority of Muslim jurists, however, a partner becomes entitled to the profit by capital and labour only. According to the Ḥanafī jurists, it is lawful that the capital of each [23] partner be equal and yet the profit be shared unequally. Zufar, Shāfiʿī, and Mālik do not subscribe to this view because according to them the share in the larger portion of profit is earned without any responsibility since the responsibility is in proportion to capital which one advances. The arguments of the Ḥanafī scholars on this issue are two fold:

First: The Prophet (s.a.w.s) has said "The profit between partners should follow the agreement between them and the loss should be borne in proportion to their investments". [24] In this precept

---

[22]Kāsanī, *Badā'iʿ al-Ṣanā'iʿ*, vol.6, p.62; Ibn al-Hamām, *Fatḥ al-Qadīr*, vol.5, p.21.

[23]Ibn Juzy, *al-Qawānīn al-Fiqhiyyah*, p.284 .

[24]Jamāl al-Dīn 'Abd Allah Zayla'ī, *Naṣb al-Rāyah*,Cairo:

Dār al-Ḥadīth, 1ˢᵗed. 1938, vol.3, p.478.

of the Holy Prophet (s a w s) no distinction is made between the equality or inequality of their properties.

Second: In the same manner as a person is entitled to profit by virtue of capital, he is also entitled to it by virtue of labour as in the case of *Muḍārabah*. It may happen sometime that one of the partners is more skillful and expert in business than the other, consequently he will not agree to the other sharing equally with him in the profit.

Now we take up the kinds of *shariat al-'aqd* (Contractual partnership) in detail.

I. Sharikat al-Amwāl (Investment Partnership)

Definition

It is an agreement between two or more persons to invest a sum of money in a business and share its profits according to agreement. The investment of this partnership consists of capital contributed by the partners. It is divided into two kinds, i e , *'inān* and *mufāwaḍah*.

Specified Conditions for Sharikat al-Amwāl

There are certain conditions of *sharikat al-amwāl* which are applicable to both *'inān sharikat al-amwāl* and *mufāwaḍah sharikat al-amwāl*.[25] These conditions are as follows

a) **Present capital:** The Ḥanafīs stipulate that the capital of the *Sharikah* must be an ascertained commodity *('ayn')* and not *dayn*, i.e , wealth that is absent. Present wealth, in their view, is wealth available for transactions, and not necessarily present physically on the spot. Hence, in the opinion of the Ḥanafī jurists, the absence of capital, at the time the contract is negotiated, does not invalidate the partnership as long as the capital is in hand, when the joint purchase is made. Kāsānī says.

> Among these conditions is the availability of the wealth in the form of an *'ayn* (ascertained commodity). It should neither be a receivable (*dayn*) nor absent wealth, otherwise, the partnership will not be permissible, either as *'inān* or as *mufāwaḍah*. The reason is that the purpose of the partnership is profit and this is achievable through transactions in the capital. Such transactions are not

---

[25] See Kāsānī ,*Badā'i' al-Sanā'i'*, vol.6, p.59.

possible in a *dayn* nor in wealth that is absent. The purpose cannot be achieved. The presence (availability of the goods). however. is stipulated at the time of the transaction and not at the time of the contract. The contract of *sharikah* is completed with the purchase transaction. The availability of the goods comes into operation then.[26]

According Imām Mālik the capital should be present at the time the contract is concluded. The jurists are also unanimous that *mufāwaḍah* or *'inān* partnership cannot be concluded on debt.[27]

b) Intermingling of capitals: The majority of Muslims do not stipulate mixing of capitals (*khalt*) prior to the conclusion of the contract. In this regard Imām Sarakhsī says

> In our view. *'inān* does not require the intermingling of investment. However. according to Zufar and Shāfi'ī. mingling is pre-requisite for a valid partnership. In the Shāfi'īs view. proprietary partnership (*Sharikat al-milk*) is the underlying principle of all partnerships and that contractual partnership must be based on it.[28]

Shāfi'ī holds that the meaning of the word *sharikah* is intermingling and that this is realized only through ownership. If the two investments are mingled in a manner that makes them indistinguishable from each other. then the partnership becomes effective through ownership and a contractual partnership can be built upon it. If one of the investments is lost before they are intermingled. the loss is borne exclusively by its owner and any projected contractual partnership cannot become effective because the capital did not undergo the process of intermingling.[29]

The condition of intermingling in Shāfi'ī Law requires that the capital advanced by the parties be uniform. i.e.. the currency should be of the same denomination and quality.

---

[26]Ibid. vol. 6. p.60

[27]Ibn Rushd. *Bidāyat al-Mujtahid* vol.2. p.250 .

[28]Sarakhsī. *al-Mabsūt*, vol.11. p.177 .

[29]Nawawī. *Minhāj*. vol.2. p.213 .

c. Absolute Currency:

It is also a condition for a valid *sharikat al-amwāl* that its investment is in the form of money. Assets in the form of merchandise are unsuitable for partnership investment. According to the majority of legal scholars, a partnership in which the investment consists of goods is invalid. Imām Mālik holds that capital in the form of currency is not a pre-requisite and that partnership in goods is permissible if their value is determined on the day the contract is concluded.

According to the majority, agency is the necessary attribute of partnership and agency is unrealisable in goods as investment. Kāsānī says:

> It is not permissible for one person to say to another: Sell your goods so that we may share its price. And since agency, which is one of the indispensable features of partnership, is not permissible, partnership also is not permissible. It is, however, permissible for one to say to another: "Buy goods with the hundred *dirhams* belonging to you on the condition that what you buy be shared between us.[30]

He further writes

> Partnership in goods is not permissible because it leads to ignorance regarding the profit at the time of division. For the amount of the investment will consist of the value that will not be known except with conjecture and estimation. The amount of profit will, therefore, be unknown and this will lead to dispute at the time of division.[31]

Kinds of Sharikat al-Amwāl

As mentioned earlier, *Shariakt al-amwal* is divided into two kinds, i.e., *'inan sharikat al-amwal* or *sharikah al-amwāl* by way of *'inan* and *Mufāwaḍah amwal* partnership or *sharikat al-amwāl* by way of *Mufāwaḍah*. Following is detailed description of both these kinds.

---

[30] Kāsānī, *Badā'i' al-Sanā'i'*, vol. 6, p.59.

[31] Ibid.

A) 'INĀN SHARIKAT AL-AMWĀL

Meaning of 'Inān

It is derived from the word *inan*, i.e., reins of riding animal. The rider holds the reins with one hand, while doing something with the other. Similarly, each one of the partners in this partnership hands over the reins (right) of transaction in some wealth to the other and not in the rest. Further, the animal has two reins, one longer and the other one shorter. Similarly this partnership is permissible both with equal and unequal capital and labour.

The Definition of 'Inān

It is a contract between two or more persons to work in any particular trade with determined capital and to share profit and loss with determined rates. All the Muslim jurists are unanimous on its validity.

Types of Sharikat al-'Inān

The *'inān* partnership on the basis of its scope is divided into two general categories:

      1. General *'inān* or ordinary *'inān* partnership.

      2. Specific *'inān* or restricted *'inān* partnership.

General 'Inān

It is a partnership formed for the purpose of general trade with no restrictions with respect to the commodities that could be dealt with or the transactions that could be negotiated. Any legitimate trading activity designated to bring the profit comes within its purview.

Specific 'Inān

In this type of partnership, partners are confined to the trade with a certain category of goods defined in the partnership agreement. This agreement could be continuing one, spread over a considerable period of time and involving numerous transactions, or it could be limited to a single venture, i.e., the purchase of the desired merchandise and its subsequent sale. The mutual agency of the associates in the specific *'inān* extends only to the commodities or areas of trade agreed upon and no further.

General Rules Regarding the 'Inān Partnership

Following are the general rules regarding the *'inān* partnership:[32]

a) Management: It is lawful that the partnership is carried out by both the partners or either of them.

b) Mutual agency and not surety: Each partner in *sharikat al-'inān* is the agent of the other partner, so he possesses all the rights of the agent. He is not required to be surety for the other.

c) Equal or unequal capital: The *'inān* does not require equality, so the capital of one of the partners may be more than that of the other.

d) Equal or unequal distribution of profits: Profits may be divided equally or unequally. Thus, it is lawful that capital of each partner be equal and yet the profits be unequally distributed. It is permissible according to the Ḥanāfīs that profit be distributed unequally with the equality of capital provided the partner getting larger share of profit contributes extra labour for the extra amount because according to them the person is entitled to profit by capital labour and responsibility (*ḍamān*) and in the present case labour is causing profit. Thus, if one of them stipulates for himself a share in the profit proportionally larger than that of his colleague, this is permissible. Imām Zufar from amongst the Ḥanāfīs does not agree with this opinion. Ḥanbalī and Zaidī jurists favour Ḥanafī viewpoint that profit follows the agreement, while the loss is according to the capital. According to Mālikī, Shāfiʿī and Zāhirī jurists and Zufar both profit and loss should be strictly in accordance with the capital as the profit is an increase in the capital and loss in the decrease so both should be governed by the capital.

Rights of Partners in *'inān* Partnership

The rights, duties and obligations of the *inān* partners pertain only to that portion of their respective property invested in the joint undertaking. In all matters that are not of their partnership, each of them is a stranger in relation to his other partner. Following are some important rights of partners in an *'inān* partnership:[33]

---

[32] Zuhaylī, *al-Fiqh al-'Islāmī wa Addillatuhū*, vol.4, pp.415-416

[33] Ibid. vol.4, pp.415-416.

a) Right to sell goods for cash and credit: Each partner has the right to sell the goods of the *sharikah* for cash as well as for credit. Likewise, he has right to purchase for cash or for credit. He enjoys this right without any restriction and limitation on him. The right is conferred upon him by virtue of the contract and he does not need special permission from the other partners for doing so.

He cannot, however, purchase on credit, in excess of the capital of the *sharikah*. This would amount to *istidānāh* for which special permission is required from the other partners. If other partners expressly authorize him he may incur debts in excess of the amount of partnership fund. *Istidānāh* means to purchase on credit for the partnership in excess of the capital. It is in fact a mode of enhancing financial liability of the investors.

b) Right to Ibdā': *Ibdā'* means to hand over the property and capital of partnership to a merchant, who is not partner in partnership business, to trade with it without receiving any remuneration or commission and to return it with profit to the partnership. The *'inān* partner has right to enter into an *ibdā'* even if the partner does not expressly permit him to do so, because it is the practice among the businessmen. The reason for its permission is that he has a right to employ a person for the business in which he has to pay wages, while in *ibdā'* he is not required to pay remuneration to the merchant, so it is more beneficial for business than to hire services of somebody for remuneration.

c) Right to Muḍārabah: Each partner is also at liberty to give his capital in the way of *muḍārabah*, because the partnership is designed for profit and *muḍārabah* is a mode of earning profit.

d) Right to appoint agent: A partner in the *sharikat al-'inān* is at liberty to appoint a person as his agent for the business transactions. The businessmen cannot undertake all the business activities themselves so they often appoint others as their agents. This being requirement of business is permissible in *'inān* as well.

e) Right to Mortgage or pledge: A partner in this *sharikah* can pledge or mortgage the assets of the partnership and also accept such pledges but only with the permission of the partners.

f) Right to deposit: The partner has the right to deposit goods belonging to the partnership; for depositing is one of the customary practices of merchants.

g) Contractual obligations of a partner: According to the Hanafīs all the obligations and rights arising from a contract made by a partner will revert to him. Thus if one of them has purchased something, or hired services, he alone will be sued with respect to claims arising from such transactions. Likewise, it is he who has right to sue third parties for all claims connected with the contract he concluded, and his other partners will be considered strangers as for as these claims are concerned.

h) Right to travel: According to majority of the Muslim Jurists, a partner can also travel to another place with the *sharikah* property if there is no specification of place in the agreement, but according to Abū Yūsuf and Shāfi'ī the partner has no such right except by the explicit permission of his other partners.

i) Right to extend gift and qard: A partner does not have right to gift the property of the partnership. Similarly he does not have right to grant loan from the common funds.

Liability of Partners in the 'Inān Partnership

An *'inān* partnership comprehends mutual agency but not mutual surety. By virtue of this mutual agency but no mutual surety, each of them does not become liable for that which is owed by his colleague. Thus, liability towards third party is several but not joint.

Formation of the 'Inān Partnership

Partnership in an *'inān* partnership is open to any person meeting the minimum standards of legal competence. There are no restrictions with respect to personal status, which is peculiar to *mufāwaḍah*. Any person of either sex who is of age and of sound mind may legitimately contract an *'inān* partnership.

Similarly, a difference in personal status between prospective partners does not constitute a barrier to the formation of a valid *'inān* partnership. An *'inān* partnership negotiated between two minors with the explicit approval of their guardians is valid, as is a partnership between Muslim and *dhimmī*.

Dissolution of the 'Inān Partnership

The circumstances affecting the termination of all contractual partnerships including 'inān partnership are as follows:

a)   Recession of the contract by either party:

Partnership can be terminated by the unilateral recession of one of its members. In this case the dissolution of partnership does not become effective until the other partners become aware of their partner's action. According to Section 43 of the Partnership Act 1932 in case of partnership at will any partner may dissolve the firm, by serving notice in writing to all the existing partners of his intention to dissolve the firm.

b)   Death of one party:

The death of one of the partners results in the immediate termination of the partnership because the underlying contract of *wakālah* becomes void (*bāṭil*) upon death and the *sharikah* is structured upon *wakālah*. As each of them is also the agent of the other and the death automatically discharges the agent. whether the latter knows about it or not any transaction conducted by the surviving partner after his colleague's demise and ignorance of the fact, will be strictly on his own account. Heirs of the deceased partner have no claim to the profits Nor they are liable for any obligation. which might arise from such transaction. There is no provision in Islamic Law by means of which a partnership can remain intact after the death of one of its members. If the heirs wish to continue the association with the surviving partner. they must negotiate completely a new agreement.

c) Apostasy and emigration to enemy lands:

If both the partners are Muslim the apostasy of one of them and his emigration to non-Muslim territory (*dār al-ḥarb*) results in the termination of partnership.

d) Insanity of one of the partners:

The loss of mental competenc‹ by one of the partners also results in, the termination of partnership. provided the insanity is continuous. The Muslim jurists disagree about the period of insanity. According to Abū Yūsuf. the period is one month. but according to Muhammad it is a full year. Thus *sharikah* will not stand dissolved before the expiry of this period.

e) Expiration of Period:

If the *sharikah* was established for a limited period it will stand terminated by the expiration of that period. The same position has been taken by the law, as explained in Section 40 of the Partnership Act 1932.

f) Completion of Venture:

When the undertaking or venture is completed the partnership may be dissolved. Section-42 (b) of the Partnership Act 1932 also confirms this position.

g) Mutual Consent:

The partnership can also be terminated by the mutual consent of the whole capital or of the stock of each partner.

h) Loss of capital:

i. Before purchase: If the whole partnership capital or the capital of either partner perishes before any purchase is made, the contract of partnership is annulled.

ii. Loss of capital before intermingling: Where capital perishes after the mixture, the loss falls upon the partnership, because property of each is no longer distinguishable from other. So the loss must be borne by both parties.

iii. Loss of capital after purchase by one partner: A purchase made by one partner where the capital of the other perishes afterwards is also shared by the both.

iv. Loss of one capital before purchase of the other partner: If one partner makes a purchase with his own capital and the capital of the other afterwards perishes before he has made any purchase the purchased goods will be considered joint property of the parties and will be shared by them according to agreement.

B) MUFĀWAḌHAH SHARIKAT AL-AMWĀL

Mufāwaḍah literally means the participation in each thing with equality, but technically it has a narrower meaning, because it applies to equality in real estate and goods"[34]

The author of *Hidāyah* defines it in the following words:

"It is a contract of participation between two or more persons, with the condition of complete equality with respect to capital, profit and status, for working with their own wealth, or with their labour in another's wealth, or on the basis of their credit-worthiness, so that each partner is a surety for the other.[35] This shows that in this partnership each partner enjoys complete equality in the areas of capital, management and right of disposition.

According to the Hanafīs *Mufāwaḍah* contains the following elements.

> i) Equality in wealth (capital), profit and loss and participation in the affairs of the partnership.

> ii) Equality in contractual capacity and religion.
> iii) Each partner is an agent of other partners.
> iv) Each partner is also responsible on behalf of other partners of their acts and deeds. i.e., he is surety for his partner.

Mufāwaḍah in Mālikī Law:

According to Mālikī the term *Mufāwaḍah* is applied to an arrangement in which each party confers upon his colleague full authority to dispose of their joint capital in any manner intended to benefit their association. For them it denotes a general type of partnership in which capital and profits are distributed in indefinite shares. The Mālikī jurists lay emphasis on the *tafwīḍ* and not on equality as is the case in Hanafī law. To them *tafwīḍ* means the delegation of discretionary authority to conduct the trade with each other's capital. Each partner is his colleague's agents and can act in all commercial matters with respect of his own and his colleague's property without the latter's approval. The liability of the *mufāwaḍah* is joint, thus any obligation incurred on behalf of the partnership towards other parties, by one of the associates can be claimed in full.

---

[34] Ibn 'Ābidīn, *Radd al-Muḥtār*, vol.4, p.402.

[35] Marghīnānī, *al-Hidāyah*, vol.3, p.3 .

from any of the other partners. There is no requirement of equality in the personal and financial status of the prospective partners.[36]

Legitimacy of Mufāwaḍah:

According to the Ḥanafī and the Mālikī jurists it is valid for the following reasons:[37]

i) *Istiḥsān*: This type of partnership is permitted on the basis of *istiḥsān*. The basis of *istiḥsān* is the saying of the Holy Prophet (s a w.s). "Engage in *mufāwaḍah* for it is full of blessings".[38]

ii) Further. the people used to practice it without its denial by the Holy Prophet (s a.w.s). For this reason the rule of analogy was given up. Moreover. the *jahālah* (uncertainty) involved in it is not different from that in *muḍārabah*.

Mufāwaḍah partnership is not permitted by the Shāfi'ī, Zahirī and Imāmī jurists. They argue that the tradition quoted by the Hanafīs is not available in the authentic books of Hadīth. Moreover, the *jahālah*. (uncertainty) contained in it is of large degree. It is also impracticable because equality cannot be maintained among the partners from the beginning of partnership till the end.

Imām Shāfi'ī, while rejecting *Mufāwadah* partnership says in *al-Umm*: "*Sharikat al- mufāwaḍah* is *bāṭil* and I do not know of anything else in this world that can be declared void if it is not the *mufāwaḍah* partnership".[39]

Conditions of the *Mufāwaḍah* Partnership:

All the conditions relating to capital, contractual capacity, dispositions of partners in the '*inān* partnership are also applicable to *mufāwaḍah*, because *mufāwaḍah* like '*inān* is a kind of *Sharikat al-amwāl*. There are, however, certain. conditions, which are peculiar to the *mufāwaḍah* partnership. These are:

---

[36]Ibn Rushd. *al-Qawānīn al-Fiqhiyyah*. p.283.

[37]Ibn Juzy.'*Bidāyat al-Mujtahid*, vol.2. p.191.192 .

[38]Zayla'ī. *Naṣb al-Rāyah* vol.3. p.457

[39] Shāfi'ī. *al-Umm* vol.3. p.3. p.369.

a) Mutual agency and surety: Each partner in *mufāwaḍah* must have the capacity of being agent and surety for the other. A valid *mufāwaḍah* partnership can be contracted only between two adults and sane people. As *mufāwaḍah* is based on the idea of mutual surety in which each of the partners provides surety for his colleague, hence minors are not of that category of person who can provide surety, and for this reason any *mufāwaḍah* partnership between them is not permissible.

b) Equality in capital: The equality in the capital of the partners is the basic essence of *mufāwaḍah* partnership. Any deviation from the equality immediately renders the *mufāwaḍah* invalid.

c) Inclusion of cash capital in joint investment: *Mufāwaḍah* also requires the inclusion of all cash capital in joint investment. Hence, if one of the partners retains for himself the ownership of some capital, which is eligible for partnership, it will not constitute *mufāwaḍah* partnership. However, if the capital retained by one of the partners is in the form of goods, or is a debt owed to him by another person, then the partnership between them is not valid. This is because goods and debts are not suitable form of partnership investment. The equality is not also required in family belongings. Inequality in personal and household property is not barrier to a valid *mufāwaḍah* partnership.

d) Equality in profit and loss: Where the partners invest equal amount of capital but agree on an unequal distribution of the profits, or conversely, they invest unequal amount of capital and agree on equal distribution of the profits, the partnership is not considered to be *mufāwaḍah*.

e) Equality in religion: The demand for equality between the partners in *mufāwaḍah* extends to religious affiliation as well. According to Abū Ḥanīfah and Muḥammad it can only take place between two Muslim only. It cannot be held between Muslim and a Christian or a Jew because a non-Muslim may handle such goods, which are prohibited for Muslim such as wine and pig. But according to Abū Yūsuf, a non-Muslim can be a partner in *mufāwaḍah* with a Muslim because the basic essence of partnership according to him is mutual agency and mutual surety and the non-Muslims are qualified for both these purposes.

f) The use of the term Mufāwaḍah: According to the Ḥanafī jurists, the *mufāwaḍah* partnership cannot be contracted except with the term *mufāwaḍah* or any other word having the meaning of *mufāwaḍah*. It is necessary because most of the people are not aware of the rules governing the *mufāwaḍah* partnership. Therefore, the consent of the parties relating to its rules cannot be effective until they know them. The express use of the word *mufāwaḍah* is only the substitute to remove this difficulty.

Rights and duties of Partners in Mufāwaḍah partnership

The relationship that exists between partners in a contract of *mufāwaḍah* is based on the agency (*wakālah*) as well as on the contract of surety (*kafālah*). By virtue of the contract of surety, each partner is fully liable for the actions and commitments of the other in all commercial matters. The claims of third parties are actionable against either partner; and conversely, either partner can press a claim against a third party, regardless of whether or not he was actually involved in the transaction. In all partnerships except the *mufāwaḍah*, the liability towards third parties is several but not joint. In *mufāwaḍah* liability towards third parties is several and joint.[40]

The following are some rights and duties of the partner in *mufāwaḍah* Partnership:

a) Admission of debts:

A creditor can claim his debt from either of the partners, from one due to his admission and from the other for being the surety.

b) Debts in Mufāwaḍah:

Money indebted by one of the partners during the course of business can be collected from any one of them because a commitment made by one is binding on the other. Thus, liability is joint and several.

c) Suretyship for a stranger:

A partner can become surety for a third party. Such guarantee will be binding on all partners. Imām Abū Ḥanīfah justifies such guarantee by

---

[40]See Udovitch Abraham L., *Profit and Partnership in Medieval Islām*.p.100.U.S.A Princeton University Press. 1970.

saying that although it is a gratuitous contract in the beginning but at the end it becomes a commutative contract, and the guarantor has the right to claim reimbursement of what he has paid on the demand of debtor The two pupils of Imām Abū Ḥanīfah, however, do not approve to this suretyship.

d) Investment with third parties:

The *mufāwaḍah* partner, without prior permission of his colleague, may invest cash or goods in *muḍārabah* or accept capital from outside parties for *muḍārabah*.

e) Pledging by the partner:

Each partner may give a pledge as guarantee of payment of debt or take a pledge as a security

f) Demands relating to transactions:

Either of the partners can be demanded for the price or performance of transactions relating to the business although it is contracted by other partner. Also, any one from amongst the parties can take the possession of the thing although contracted by the other. Misappropriation affecting third parties in the course of business make the other partner liable. The aggrieved party can sue any of them. The claims of third party are thus, actionable against any partner.[41]

g) Exclusion from mutual liability:

A *mufāwaḍah* partner is not liable for any obligation of his partner arising from the following categories of activities

    i)   Criminal acts

    ii)   Wrongful appropriation of someone else's property

    iii)   Marriage and divorce

    iv)   Surety provided by a partner for the commercial activities of third parties.

Following dispositions are not permissible for the partners.

    a) *Qarḍ and ʿārah*.

See Zuhaylī, *al-Fiqh al-Islāmī*, vol.4, pp. 821-823.

Qarḍ and *i'ārah* are not allowed for the partners because both are acts of charity and donation. and donation is not permissible from partnership funds.

> b) *Hibah* and *Ṣadaqah* are not also allowed for the same reasons.

> c) Torts and crimes: It is not allowed for a partner to be surety for the other in torts and crimes that are not related to business.

> d) Expenses of partners:

All expenses connected with the pursuit of trade are to be covered from partnership fund. But the expenditures incurred on the purchase of food. cloths. transport and house for partners' families will be paid by the partners from their private funds.

Dissolution of a Sharikat al-Mufāwaḍah:

Following are circumstances. which affect termination of *mufāwaḍah*:

> i) Death of one of the contracting parties.

> ii) Apostasy of one of the partners. and his emigration to non-Muslim territory.

> iii) Unilateral abrogation by one of the partners.

> iv) Lack of equality: The lack of equality can be three-fold by which *mufāwaḍah* can be terminated.

> a) Lack of equality in the capital.

> b) Discontinuance of equality during the course of business.

> c) Increase in the exchange value of the capital of one partner before the transaction is performed.

Thus. *mufāwadah* is terminated when the equality of capital is disturbed. The balance of equality can be upset in a number of ways. If during the operation of the partnership one of the partners collects a debt owed to him prior to the contracting of the partnership. and if the payment is in a form of cash then the equality is breached and the *mufāwaḍah* is invalidated.[42]

II. Sharikat Al-a`māl: Work Partnership

Definition

It is a partnership in which the partners contribute investment in the form of labour and skill. It is also called *Sharikat al-abdān* because the partners perform manual labour, like tailors, butchers and so on. It is also known as *Sharikat al-ṣanā'i'* because the capital of the partners is their skill.

Through this *mushārakah* the artisans, technician and others skilled and unskilled labour join together in one or different places, without any capital to produce some commodity or perform some work, on the condition that they will divide between them the profits arising from it. The type of labour envisaged is usually a skill in some kind of manufacture such as tailoring, dyeing, or weaving.

The work partnership can take the form of limited partnership or unlimited partnership namely;

i) *'Inān* Work Partnership

ii) *Mufāwaḍah* Work Partnership

'Inān Work Partnership

Inān work partnership is based on the concept of agency and not on suretyship. Thus, each partner is liable only for the obligation personally incurred by himself.

Condition for Acceptance and Performance of Work

a) Right of accepting work and performing it.

Each partner has the right to accept work and then to perform it himself on behalf of the *Sharikah*. It is also permitted that one of them accepts work, while the other performs it. In a business that requires mixed labour, the work may be accepted by one and then

---

[42]See Uduvitch, Profit and Partnership in Medieval Islām, pp.117,118.

performed jointly by both. For example, in the tailoring business, it is permitted that one person accepts work, cuts the cloth and then hands it over to his partner for stitching and completion.

b. Right to delegate the work accepted:

No partner can be forced for personal performance of the work that he accepted. He is at liberty to do the work personally or to delegate it to another. If the customer stipulates performance of the work by a particular partner, in that case the partner has to perform it.

c. Performance of work is liability of each Partner:

The general rule in the contracts of personal services is that performance can be demanded from the person making the contract alone. As such, the Partner accepting the work should be sued for its performance. This rule, however, is given up in *'inān* work partnership on the basis of *istiḥsān*. Thus, either of the partners may be required to perform the work, which is accepted by his other partner. Similarly each partner has right to demand remuneration from the customer.

> The *Majallah* has explained this point in some detail:.

> Each Partner is the agent of the other in the acceptance of work. For the work that is accepted by one of them, performance is binding upon him as well as his partner. *'Inān* by way of *sharikat al-A'māl* has the same *hukm* as *mufāwaḍah* with respect to *ḍamān al-'amal* (liability of work). Thus, the work accepted by one of the partners may be demanded by the customer from any partner he chooses. Each partner is (legally) bound for the performance of such work. He does not have the right to say: "This work was accepted by my partner and I have nothing to do with it."[43]

Section 1388 of the Majallah states that: *'Inān* by way of *Sharikat al-A'māl* takes the *hukm* of *mufāwaḍah*, in the demand for compensation from the customer and for full satisfaction of the claim for wages. The customer is absolved of this liability by paying to one of them

---

[43] *Majallah*, Article. 1387. See also Nyazee, *Islamic Law of Business Organization:Parnterships*, pp. 150, 151.

Division of Profit

The profit in *'inān* work partnership is divided according to liability of work. It is not linked with the actual work undertaken by either of partners. The loss is also divided in proportion to liability borne. For example, if a partner becomes liable for one-third of the whole work accepted by the partnership, he would be entitled to 1/3 of the total profit earned by the partnership. In regard to the division of profit in *'inān* work partnership Imām Sarakhsī expounds his opinion in the following words:

> In the case of partners in work, if one of them is absent or is ill, or does not work, while the other is working, the profit is still to be shared by them according to what they have agreed upon. This is due to the tradition from the Messenger of Allah (s.a.w.s) that a person came to him and said: "I work in the market and I have a partner who prays in the mosque." The Messenger of Allah said: "Perhaps your work is blessed because of him". The meaning here is that claim to reward derives from acceptance of work and not necessarily from its direct execution. The acceptance is (presumed to be) from both, even if one of them works. [44]

The ratio fixed for the liability for performance is what will determine the ratio for sharing profits. It is obvious that if such a ratio for *ḍimān al-amal* is not fixed, it will be presumed to be equal. [45]

Mufāwaḍah work partnership

This partnership requires equal share of liability undertaken by each partner, and equal share of profit and loss. The compensation received for the work is shared equally by all the partners, irrespective of the fact that the work is done in the partnership or outside the business. In the *'inān* partnership wages for work done by a partner outside the business belong to the partner alone.

---

[44]Sarakhasī. *al-Mabsūṭ* vol. 11, pp. 152-158.

[45]Ibid., vol. 11, p.154 .

Mālikī work partnership

Mālikī work partnership resembles the Ḥanafī work partnership closely, but in some aspects it is more restrictive than Ḥanafī partnership. For example it requires that all its members should follow the same trade or profession.

The Following are some distinct features of the Mālikī work partnership:

1-Similarity of trade and uniformity of place:

The partners should follow the same trade or profession like partnership between two tailors. The Mālikī jurists also prefer that both the partners should work in the same place, i.e., in the same stall.

2-Actual participation in work:

All the partners should participate in actual work. A partnership in which all the work is assigned to one partner while the other provides some equipment but not work is invalid partnership. The non-working party would be entitled to some equitable rental fee for use of equipment. It is also not permissible that one accepts the work and the other undertakes the work.

3-Division of profit according to work:

The division of profit and loss in this partnership follows each partner's work, which he contributes. No premium is placed on the quality of each partner's labour. [46]

III. Sharikat al-Wujūh (Credit Partnership):

According to Sarakhsī it is a partnership of two people without capital upon the condition that they will buy on credit and sell for cash. It has been called by this name on the grounds that they employ their credit-worthiness, because credit is extended only to those who have good reputation among the people (traders).[47] *Sharikat*

---

[46] For Mālikī work partnership see Ibn Rushd, *Bidāyat al-Mujtahid*,

vol. 2, p.192.

[47] Sarakhsī, *al-Mabsūṭ*, vol.II, pp.152-158.

al-wujūh or credit partnership can be of two types according to the Ḥanafīs:

    i)`*Inān* credit partnership

   ·ii) *Mufāwaḍah* credit partnership.

Condition for sharing profit and loss in the 'inān credit partnership

According to the Ḥanafī jurists the conditions for sharing of profit and loss in this type of partnership are as follows:

1-Specified share in the goods purchased:

The primary condition for this type of partnership is that the share of the partners in the goods purchased must be specified. The remaining stipulations are based on this condition.

2-Entitlement to profit based upon liability:

The type of liability mentioned in the *'Anān* work partnership was called *ḍamān al-a'māl*. The type of liability involved here is the liability for the price of the purchased goods, and is based upon the share of ownership in the property purchased. Once something is purchased, it becomes the asset of the partnership and its value is based upon its price. The ratio in which this asset is owed by the partners is the basis and not the ratio of the debt owned. Thus, if the share of a partner is one-half in the purchased goods, he is liable for half the price owned for these goods. He is, therefore, entitled to half the profits. This shows that the profit in this partnership must correspond with the liability.

3-Unequal ownership in the purchased goods:

Equality of ownership in the purchased goods is not a requirement. The partners may agree on any ratio of ownership they want, and the profit between them has to be distributed according to that ratio.

4-Stipulation of profits contrary to ownership:

The stipulation of profits contrary to ownership is of no consequence. If an additional profit is stipulated for any partner, it means that the ratio of ownership is violated. The condition will, therefore, be ignored, if the liability for the price is equal. The reason appears to be that the skills, reputation and good work of one partner are already linked with the amount of credit a partner can raise. The ratio of ownership in the price has already taken all those things into account

5-Excess work:

Excess work in this partnership is of no consequence for entitlement to profit. Sarakhsī says:

In this contract a stipulation of profits in excess (over the ratio of ownership) is not valid when there is equality of ownership in the thing purchased. The reason is that this excess is not linked either to the share of the partner in wealth or to his work or to *damān*. Stipulating such a part of the profits will amount to something that is not supported by liability to bear loss. If an excess of the profits is desired, it is necessary to stipulate corresponding excess in ownership of the purchased goods (and thus in the liability to bear loss). This way, it may be, that one third is for one partner and two-third for the other, and thereafter the other profits may be shared in proportion to the ownership.[48]

Conditions for mufāwaḍah credit partnership according to the Ḥanafī jurists

The conditions of *mufāwaḍah* credit partnership differ from those of *'inān* in the following respects:

1. It is not necessary in this partnership to specify the share of a partner in the goods purchased on credit, because the contract of *mufāwaḍah* requires equality, and all the shares are equal. This makes equality of shares in goods

---

[48]Nyazee, *Islamic Law of Busines Organization: Partnerships.* p.155.156.

purchased. a condition for this partnership. In *'inān*, the shares have to be specified.

2. Any partner may be sued for the price of the goods purchased. because he is an agent as well as surety for his partner(s). In *'inān*. the *ḥuqūq* (rights of performance) revert to the dealing partner. and the other partner cannot be sued.

3. Each thing purchased on credit by a partner for business purposes is bought for the joint business. This stipulation does not apply to goods purchased on cash for his personal business as the business transactions are entirely on a cash basis and should not be a part of the credit *Sharikah*, because business on credit-worthiness is based upon credit purchased alone. The employment of cash payments would convert it to a *mufāwaḍah* based on *mal* (*sharikat al-amwāl* by way of *mufāwaḍah*).[19]

Modern Forms of Partnership

The Islamic financial institutions frequently use *mushārakah* as a mode of financing which is considered also a real alternative to interest under an Islamic economic system. Following are some forms of *mushārakah* financing.

1. Project financing:

Islamic Banks provide project finance on the basis of *mushārakah* One or two or more entrepreneurs approach the bank for finance and the bank along with other partners provides complete finance All the partners. including the bank. have the right to participate in the management of the project. Any one or all of them also have right to waive this right. The profits are distributed according to agreed ratios. which need not be the same as capital proportion but loss has to be shared exactly in the same proportion in which different partners provided finance

Since the finance in the above mentioned case is provided completely by the bank and its partners, they jointly assume the role of

---

[19] Ibid.. p.173.

arbāb al-māl (financers) and the entrepreneurs. the *Mudāribūn* Thus. it is a type of *mudārabah* partnership. But if the investment is provided by both the parties, i.e., the bank and entrepreneurs or the businessmen then it is a *mushārakah* arrangement. The bank before financing any project gets it evaluated by its experts. If it is found feasible and is expected to be profitable. and there is satisfaction on the part of bank that the entrepreneurs have sufficient experience to handle the project. then the partnership is negotiated. Profits are allocated according to an agreed proportion, allowing for managerial skills to be remunerated This type of *mushārakah* terminates with the project's completion

2. Financing of a single transaction:

Islamic banks also provide finances in order to meet day to- day needs of small traders. The traders approach the bank requesting it to finance purchase of certain goods. Now if the bank considers transaction profitable. it finances purchase of required goods on the basis of *mushārakah*. Then the goods are sold in the market and both the parties share profit in proportion to their investment.

This instrument can also be employed for financing of imports and exports. If the letter of credit has been opened without any margin. the form of *murabahah* is adopted, and if the L/C is opened with some margin. the form of *mushārakah*.is observed. After the import goods are cleared from the port. their sale proceeds are shared by the importer and the financer according to a pre-agreed ratio In this case the ownership of the imported goods remains with the financer. to the extent of the ratio of his investment.

3. Redeemable Mushārakah:

In this category. the bank participates in the capital of a company. or a business venture or agricultural project on the condition that it will recapture its initial investment along with its agreed share in the profit. The other partner or partners also promise at the time of contract that they will purchase the share of bank in the investment and will gradually become the sole owners of that project. Suppose A. a client. owns a piece of land worth 100,000/- rupees. He does not have money to construct house. So he approaches B. a bank for finances B agrees to provide required finance on the condition that it will share the rent of that house and will also get back its initial investment of Rs

100000. They also agree that on the return of B's capital, A, the client will become the sole owner of that house. On the completion of house, rent is fixed, say, at Rs. 1000/- per month, which is to be shared by the parties in proportion to their share in the investment. It is also agreed between the parties that A, the client will pay to the bank after every six month a sum of Rs. 20000 worth capital of bank B The client A pays first instalment of the capital to A on stipulated date. This payment increases the share of A in the investment from Rs. 100000 to Rs. 120000 i.e. from 50% to 60%, and consequently his share in the rent is also increased from Rs. 500 to Rs. 600. After the payment of second instalment share of A in investment goes up to Rs. 140000 raising his ratio of capital also to 70% while the share of B, the bank is reduced to Rs. 60000/- and consequently its share in rent is also reduced to that proportion. This process goes on until after the payment of all instalments in a period of two years and half, the client becomes the sole owner of that house.[50]

Conclusion

1. *Mushārakah* is a relationship between persons to share profit of a business.

2. *Mushārakah* is based on the principle of agency.

3 There are two main kinds of *mushārakah*. i.e., proprietary partnership and contractual partnership.

4 Contractual partnership is further divided into three kinds:

    i) *Sharikat al-amwāl* (investment partnership.

    ii) *Sharikat al-a'māl* (work partnership).

    iii) *Sharikat al-wujūh* (credit partnership)

5. According to Ḥanbalī jurists *muḍārabah* is also a kind of contractual partnership.

6. In *sharikat al-amwāl* and *muḍārabah* it is necessary that the capital should be in the form of money, present at the time of contract. In case of *muḍārabah* the additional

---

[50] See Taqī 'Usmānī, *Introduction to Islamic Finance*, p.61.

requirement is that it should be handed over to the *mu*ḍ*ārabah*

7. Entitlement to profit: A partner is entitled to profit in a contractual partnership by capital, work and liability.

8   *Sharikat al-amwāl* may be concluded either in the form of *'inān* or *mufāwaḍah*. In case of *'Anān* partnership, the partners may contribute amounts and may share profits at different rate while in *mufāwaḍah* they contribute equal capital and get equal share of profit.

9. In *mufāwaḍah* each partner provides surety for the other partner because it is based on the idea of mutual surety.

10. In all partnerships, the liability towards third party is several but not joint, while in *mufāwaḍah* liability towards third parties is several and joint.

11. *Sharikat al-a'māl* (work partnership) is a partnership on work and labour as the capital of partnership. According to the Mālikī jurists the partners must belong to the same trade, and they should work in one place. Besides, all he partners should participate in actual work and should get profit according to their work.

12. In *sharikat al-wujūh* (credit partnership) profit flows from the responsibility undertaken to provide capital from loans raised by the partners on account of their goodwill or influence.

CHAPTER-17

CONTRACT OF MUDĀRABAH

Muḍārabah, *qirāḍ*, and *muqāraḍah*' are different terms used to express special type of the business arrangement in which the capital is from one side while the labour or work is from the other side.

The word *muḍārabah*' is derived from the phrase *"al-ḍarb fīl arḍ"* which means to make journey. It is called so because the worker strives and toils in course of business. Likewise, the words *qirāḍ* and *muqāraḍah* are derived from the word *qaraḍa'* that means to cut off. It is so called because the investor cuts off the disposition of his sum of money from himself and transfers its disposition to the agent.

Various Definitions of Muḍārabah

The following are the definitions of *muḍārabah* in different schools of law.

Ḥanafī School

"It is a partnership *(sharikah)* for participation in profit in which capital is from one side, whereas labour or skill *(ʿamal)* is from the other side."[1]

Mālikī School

"*Qirāḍ* is an agency for trading in delivered cash for a part of profits if their extent is known"[2]

Shāfiʿī School

It is an agreement whereby an owner hands over the capital to a worker who trades with it and the profit is shared by the parties.[3]

---

[1] Ibn ʿĀbidīn, *Radd al-Muḥtār*, 5: 645.

[2] *Kharshī* 6:2

Ḥanbalī School

It is where a person gives his capital to another person for business in order to share the profit according to stipulation.[4]

Modern Definitions of Muḍārabah

A renowned scholar ʿAlī al-Khafīf has defined *muḍārbah* as "contract for sharing the profit of a business in which one party contributes with capital and other with his labour."[5]

Dr. Rashād Khalīl, another scholar, has defined that it is a contract whereby a legally competent person hands over a known and defined capital to a person possessed with reason and discretion to trade with it for a part of profit defined in proportion.[6]

It is important to note here that Islamic Law, unlike English Law does not differentiate between a company and partnership firm. Therefore, *muḍārabah* can be a partnership firm as well as a company. This difference has given rise to a controversy between State Bank of Pakistan (SBP). Corporate Law Authority (CLA), and the Finance Ministry as to which category of business organization a *muḍārabah* will be referred to, and what rules of taxation, tariffs and revenue will be activated against it. The stance of CLA is that it is a financial institution like House Building Finance Corporation (HBFC), whereas SBP is arguing that it is a bank.

Legitimacy of Muḍārabah

The legitimacy of *muḍārbah* is established by the Qurʾān. the *Sunnah* and *ʿijmāʿ*.

---

[3] Shirbīnī. *Mughnī al-Muḥtāj*. vol. 2 p. 309.

[4] Ibn Qudāmah,. *al-Mughnī*, vol. 15, p. 134.

[5] Alī al-Khafīf. *al-Sharikāt fī al-Fiqh al-Islāmī*, Cairo: 1941, p.65.

[6] Rashād Khalīl. *al-Sharikāt fī al-Fiqh al-Islāmī*, Maktabah Tawfīqiyyah. Cario: 1399/1979. p.154.

Qur'ān

The Qur'ān says, "And others who journey through the earth seeking the bounty".[7] Abū Bakr Jaṣṣaṣ explains that they seek bounty of Allah through trade and disposition.[8]

Sunnah

1. The Holy Prophet (s.a.w.s.) is reported to have said: "There is great blessing in three things: The credit sale, the *muḍārabah* and mixing wheat and barley for domestic consumption, not for sale".

2. The Holy Prophet (s.a.w.s) gave his tacit approval to the conditions imposed by Ibn 'Abbās (r.a.t.a.) who used to give money on the basis of *muḍārabah*.

3. The aforesaid tacit approval has also been reported in the case of Ibn Ḥizām (r.a.t.a).

4. The Holy Prophet (s.a.w.s.) himself acted as *muḍārib* (agent/manager) for Khadījah (r.a.t.a.) prior to his marriage.

Ijmā'

Many instances have been cited to prove that *Muḍārabah* was a lawful business and was frequently employed by companions of Holy Prophet (s.a.w.s.). Some of the examples are the following:

Abū Mūsā, the Governor of Kūfā wanted to remit public money to the *Bayt-al-māl*. He gave the amount to Abd Allah (r.a.t.a.) and 'Ubayd Allah (r.a.t.a.) sons of caliph 'Umar (r.a.t.a.) They traded with it. The Caliph's assembly that comprised of many companions of the Holy Prophet (s.a.w.s.) treated it to be an ex-post facto *muḍārabah* and took half of the profits earned by two brothers, in addition to the public money.[9]

---

[7] Qur'ān 73:20..

[8] Jaṣṣaṣ. *Aḥkām al-Qur'ān* 3:45.

[9] Shawkānī. *Nayl al-Awṭār* 5:236; Kāsānī, *Badā'i'* vol.6, p.79, Mālik ibn Anas. *al-Muwaṭṭa*. vol.2, p.987.

It is also reported that Caliph 'Umar (r.a.t.a.) used to invest orphan s property on the basis of *mudārabah*'.

Qiyās

As for as analogy is concerned, diverse views of scholars are found This diversity is because some say that *mudārabah* defies analogy while others allow analogy.

According to Imām Sarakhsī *mudārabah* is proved by way of juristic preference (*istihsān)* and not by analogy. He writes: Analogy is not permissible, because it is hiring for unknown wages, in fact for non-existent wages. The work too is unknown. It is permissible on the basis of *istihsān*.

He adds:

> It is also allowed because people have a need for this contract. The owner of capital may not find his way to profitable trading activity, and the person who can find his way to such activity, may not have the capital. And profit cannot be attained except by means of both of these, that is capital and trading. By permitting this, the goal of both parties is attained.[10]

Elements of Muḍarabah

According to the Ḥanafīs, *mudārabah* consists of only one element, i.e forms (offer and acceptance). This is provided in *Majallah*, in the following words:

> The essence of a *mudārabah* is an offer and acceptance. For example: If the owner of capital says to the person who provides the labour "Take this capital and do the work and labour in return, on the terms that the profits are to be divided between us, half and half, or, as two to one." or if he says anything else which represents the meaning of a *mudarabah* like, "Take this money and make it capital and let the profit be in common between us in this proportion," and the *mudārib* (working partner) accepts, a contract of *mudārabah* is concluded.[11]

Sarakhsi, *al-Mabsūt*, vol.22, p.19

Majallah, Article 1405

Shāfiʿīs acknowledge five elements for a *muḍārabah* contract namely:

a) Parties to *muḍārabah* contract *(ʿāqidān)*

b) Work/labour. *(ʿamal)*

c) Profit

d) Capital

e) The form (offer and acceptance)

In the opinion of the majority or *jamhūr*, *muḍārabah* has three elements:

a) Parties to *muḍārabah* contract. *(ʿĀqidān)*

b) Subject matter (*maʿqūd ʿalayh)*

c) The form (offer and acceptance)[12]

Conditions Of Muḍārabah

Conditions relating to *muḍārabah* are of three kinds:

a) Conditions Concerning Partners:

The partners must have legal capacity to enter into a contract of *muḍārabah* This legal capacity includes competence to develop a ʿPrincipalʾ-ʿAgentʾ relationship. This requires that none of the parties should be insane or minor or placed under interdiction because of insolvency or weakness of intellect *(safah)*. The competency of a partner is codified in the *Majallah* as under.

> It is a condition that the owner of property should be competent to appoint an agent. and that the *muḍārib* should be competent to be his agent.[13]

---

[12] See Kāsānī. *Badāʾiʿ al-Sanāʾiʿ*. vol. 6. p.87; *Ḥāshiyat*

al-Dusūqī vol.3. p.517.

[13] *Majallah* Article 1408.

b) Conditions relating to capital:

The capital used in *mudārabah* must fulfill the following conditions:

1. Capital must be in absolute currency. It must be in absolute currency or in financial form or must contain money properties (as economists call it). Merchandised form' or goods are prohibited. However, Ḥanafīs and Ḥanbalīs allow it in the case, financing partner first sells them out and then gives money for business to his working partner. Some details about it are given in the *Majallah* which are as follows: "It is a condition that the capital be some kind of silver or gold money."[14] "Brass coins which pass current are by custom considered to be like silver or gold".[15]

Goods and commodities are not regarded eligible capital in *mudārabah* partnership, because they render the amount of profit uncertain which may lead to dispute and litigation among the parties. Kāsānī Says:

> The *mudārabah* in goods leads to uncertainty concerning the amount of the profit at the time of division. This is so because the value of the goods is known only by estimation, chance and conjecture and will differ with the difference of those who do the estimating. An uncertainty in turn leads to dispute and, consequently, to discord.[16]

They may also lead to inequitable advantage and undue enrichment for one of the parties and converse disadvantage to the other, because of the fluctuation of price of goods between the date they are remitted to the agent-manager and the date of their conversion into ready money. Writes Sarakhsī:

> Since the profit in *mudārabah* emerges only after the investment has been returned, in fact to the investor, any marked rise in the market value of goods serving as the basis for the *mudārabah* would cancel out any profit for the agent.

---

[14] Ibid., Article 1338

[15] Ibid., Article 1339.

[16] Kāsānī, *Badā'i' al-Sanā'i'*, vol.,6,p.82.

Any drop in the market value would put the investor at a disadvantage and provide the agent with unjustified and, in a sense, unearned profit.[17]

2. It should be known and defined in terms of quality and quantity. An uncertainty and indeterminacy concerning the amount of capital renders the contract invalid.

3. It should be ready cash, and not absent money in the form of debt, or money usurped by someone. But it is permissible to authorise a person to collect the debt and make it a capital of *mudārabah*. It is also lawful to the majority of jurists to start *mudārabah* with a capital lying as deposit with the agent *(mudārib)* or someone else. The investor in this case may instruct the agent to collect the money from the depositor and use it as capital of *mudārabah*, or he may directly arrange with the depositee to change the status of his capital from that of a deposit to that of *mudārabah* investment.[18]

The Mālikī jurists do not permit the shifting of capital in the form of debt into *mudārabah* capital. Udovitch explains the position of Maliki Law on this point in the following words:

> For a creditor to ask the debtor to use the amount of money owed as a *mudārabah* investment is not permissible because a *mudārabah'* cannot be formed with liable money, i.e., money for which the agent has some liability. Undoubtedly another reason for excluding this type of arrangement, although not stated in the sources, is the easy abuse to which it could be put in concealing a usurious loan.[19]

4. It should be handed over to the agent. All the Muslim jurists are unanimous on the point that the transfer of control over the money to the agent is pre-requisite for the validity of

---

[17] Sarakhsī. *al-Mabsūt.* Vol. 22 P. 23.

[18] Ibid. ; Shirbīnī. *Mughni al-Muhtāj* 2:31: Dusūqī. *Hāshiyat al-Dusūqi* 3:518. Ibn Qudāmah. *al-Mughnī* 5:68

[19] Uduvitch. *Partnership and profit in Medieval Islam,* p.187.

Muḍārabah. This is necessary so that agent is able to trade with it.

c) Conditions relating to profit:

The conditions of profit are as follows

1. Both the parties should know it. It is not valid to leave profit unsettled at the time of agreement.

2. Division of profit should be on proportional basis such as one-half, one-third, one-fourth. It is, therefore, not permissible to fix a specific amount as profit for one of the contracting parties. In case all the profit is stipulated for *muḍārib*, then it is no longer a contract of *muḍārabah* instead; it is a contract of loan. This is the viewpoint of the Ḥanafi and Ḥanbalī jurists.[20] According to the Shāfi'ī *fuqahā* the contract of *muḍārabah* will become invalid because *muḍārabah* requires proportional division of profit, which is non-existent in this case. It cannot be called loan contract also, because the contract was not concluded for that purpose.[21] If all the profit is stipulated for investor, then the contract is no longer a contract of *muḍārabah*, rather it will become an *ibḍā'* activity[22] It is necessary that profit should not be stipulated for one party, as also it is necessary that it should be proportional. Any violation of proportional division rule renders the *muḍārabah* invalid and in such case it is treated as a regular hire *('ijārah)* with the agent entitled to an equitable remuneration *(ajr mithl)* for his work, but thereby disqualified from any share in the profit. On the other hand, in case of loss, the agent is free of responsibility because in this matter he is a trusted person.[23]

---

[20] Kāsānī. *Badā'i' al-Ṣanā'i'*. Vol. 6. P 86.. Ibn Qudīmah. *al-Sharḥ al-Kabīr* vol.5,p.131.

[21] Shirbīnī. *Mughnī al-Muḥtāj*, vol. 2.p.313.

[22] Kāsānī. *Badā'i' al-Ṣanā'i'*. Vol. 6. P 86

[23] Udovitch. *Partnership and profit in Medieval Islam*. p.191.

Types of Muḍārabah

Muḍārabah is of two types: absolute or unrestricted *muḍārabah* and restricted *muḍārabah* The absolute type is the one in which the capital is handed over without determination of the type of work that is to be done, the location, the time, the quality of work and the person with whom the *muḍārib* has to trade.

Unrestricted Muḍārabah

It is also called unlimited mandate or perpetual or absolute *muḍārabah* The *Majallah* defines it in the following words

> Unrestricted *muḍārabah* is a *muḍārabah*, which is not restricted in terms of time, place, kind of trade, or person from whom he is to buy and to whom he is to sell. But if it is restricted with one of these, it is a restricted *muḍārabah*. For example: If one says, "Buy and sell at such a time or in such a place, or sell such a kind of property, 'or, trade with such person or with the inhabitants of such a town." It is a restricted *muḍārabah*.[21]

The above mentioned definition imparts that if a *muḍārabah* is free from restrictions regarding time, place, trade policy, and person with whom business is to be done, it is called absolute or unrestricted *muḍārabah* The working partner in all such cases is left exclusively on his own prudence and discretion. His authority may extend from very minor issue to major issues in investing the capital money for earning profit. Thus, the working partner has every right to use money in the manner he deems fit. In such case he is permitted to undertake all such transactions, which are allowed in commercial usage.

Permissible Dispositions in absolute Muḍarabah

The Following are transactions and dispositions, which are allowed for *muḍārib*.

1. To buy and sell all types of merchandise as he sees fit.

2. To buy and sell for cash and credit.

---

[21] *Majallah*, Article 1407.

3. To give goods as *bi ḍā 'ah*.

4. To keep them as deposit or pledge.

5. To hire helpers as needed

6. To rent or buy animals and equipments.

7. To travel with the capital.

8. To mingle it with his own resources

9. To give it as *muḍārabah* to a third party.

10. To invest it in a partnership with a third party.[25]

Summarizing the permissible dispositions of *muḍārabah* Sarakhsī Writes:

> If the investor says to the agent. "act with it as you see fit". then he may practice all of these things except the loan. For the investor has consigned the control of his capital to the agent's discretion in a comprehensive way: and we know that his intention is the inclusion of all that is the customary practice of merchants. The agent. thereby. has the right to engage in *muḍārabah*, a partnership and to mingle the capital with his own capital because this is a practice of the merchants.[26]

From this we may conclude that the validity of agent's action will be determined by comparing his questioned action with the customary practice of the merchants. If such action conforms to the practice. then it is legitimate and binding upon the investor. He, however, is not allowed to commit *muḍārabah* partnership to any sum greater than the capital in hand without the investor's specific authorization. Similarly, he is not permitted to borrow money on behalf of *muḍārabah* unless he is specifically authorized to do so

Restricted Muḍārabah

Muḍārabah is restricted when the liberty of action of agent *(muḍārib)* is restricted in terms of kind of trade. time, and place. The restrictions

---

[25] Uduvitch. *Partnership and profit in Medieval Islam*. p.204.

[26] Sarakhsī. *al-Mabsūt* vol.22.p.39.

allowed to be imposed by the investor are not a matter of agreement among the jurists. For, example, the restriction to purchase from a particular person is permissible to Ḥanfīs and Ḥanbalīs but not permissible to according to Shāfiʿīs and Mālikīs.[27]

The restriction to purchase goods from a particular place is valid according to the Ḥanafī, Ḥanbalī jurists but not valid to Malikis and Shāfiʿīs. The condition to trade in particular merchandise such as books, gold and silver is valid to all the jurists. The Mālikī and Shāfiʿī jurists, however, suggest additional condition that such merchandise should be habitually available in the market.[28] As regards restricting *mudārabah* with a predetermined duration, the Mālikīs and Shāfiʿīs refuse to recognize the validity of such condition whereas Ḥanbalīs and Ḥanafis regard it to be valid.

It is worth noting that when a *mudārabah* is of predetermined duration, this does not mean that the investor and the agent-manager are precluded from making use of their basic right, that of withdrawing from *mudārabah* at will. It only means that the agent-manager is not entitled, after the elapse of the pre-agreed duration to continue performing act of commerce on behalf of *mudārabah*, if we accept the liquidation.[29]

From preceding discussion we may conclude that imposing restriction on the activity of agent is permissible, provided these do not grossly hamper and frustrate the purpose of *mudārabah*, which is to get profit.

Sarakhsī. *al-Mabsūt* vol. 22. P. 42; Ibn Qudāma. *al-Muhgnī*

   Vol.5. P 69. Ibn Rushd. *Bidāyah al-Mujtahid*. Vol. .2 P.213.

   Shīrāzī. *al-Muhadhdab* Vol.1 P 392.

[28] Dusūqī. *Hāshiyat al-Dusūqī* Vol.3 P 53. Shirbīnī. *Mughnī*

   al-Muhtāj, Vol. 2. P 311.

[29] Nabīl Salih. *Unlawful gain and Legitimate Profit in Islamic Law*.

   pp. 140-141

Dissolution of Muḍarabah

The *mudārabah* contract is dissolved under the following circumstances:

1. **Unilateral termination:**

   Since the contract of *mudārabah* is a non-binding contract, any partner can terminate it unilaterally provided the other partner is made known of this decision and the capital is in the cash form. However, if the capital is in the form of goods, the termination of contract and the disengagement of agent by investor is not allowed. In such case the agent has right to sell the goods in order to reconvert them to cash.

2. **By expiry of fixed time:**

   If the *mudārabah* was for a fixed time, it will be terminated on the expiry of that period. This is provided in *Majallah* in the following words: "When the owner of the capital has fixed the duration of *mudārabah*, the *mudārabah* is dissolved when the prescribed time elapses".[30]

3. **By death of any of the partners:**

   If any of the partners in a *mudārabah* dies, *mudārabah* comes to an end. *Majalla* puts it in the following words: "If the owner of the capital, or the *mudārib* (working partner) dies, the *mudārabah* is dissolved".[31]

4. **By Insanity of any of the partners:**

   In case any of the partners becomes insane the *mudārabah* will come to an end.

   "If the owner of the capital, or the *mudārib*, dies, or becomes continuously mad the *mudārabah* is dissolved".[32]

---

[30] *Majallah*, Article 1423.

[31] Ibid., Article 1429.

[32] *Majallah*, Article 1429.

5. **By disregard of express direction:**

The working partner is under the obligation to abide by direction of financing partner in a restricted *muḍārabah* Thus, if he does not comply with these instructions the *muḍārabah* will be dissolved by virtue of the breach of trust on which *muḍārabah* stands.[33]

Majallah explains this point in the following words "If the *muḍārib* (working partner) goes beyond what he is permitted, or acts contrary to the condition, he becomes a wrongdoer (*ghāṣib*). In case he has done so, the profit and loss from the trading falls on him, and if property of the partnership is lost, he is responsible" [34]

6. **By destruction of capital:**

The *muḍārabah* is also dissolved by the destruction of capital before initial purchase has taken place. The agent will not be held liable for this destruction if he exercised maximum care. But if it is destroyed due to his negligence or by some action on his part, then he is responsible However, the *muḍārabah* in all such cases will stand dissolved.

Conclusion

1. *Muḍārabah* is a partnership in which capital is from one side whereas labour or skill is from the other side.

2. The capital in this partnership must be in absolute currency, it should be ready cash not in the form of debt and should be handed over to the *muḍārib*

3. The division of profit should be on proportional basis such as one-half, one third etc.

4. *Muḍārabah* is of two types i e restricted and unrestricted

---

[33] Ibid., Article 1422.

[34] Ibid., Article 1421.

5. *Muḍārabah* is dissolved by unilateral termination, expiry of fixed time, death and insanity of a partner and the destruction of capital.

CHAPTER-18

CONTRACT OF KAFĀLAH (SURETYSHIP OR GUARANTEE)

Definition

Literally the word *kafālah* means joining and merging. Technically it is defined as merging of one liability with another in respect of demand for performance of an obligation.[1] Thus, the liability of principal obligor is merged with that of the surety for the discharge of a pecuniary obligation or debt or the delivery of property. According to this definition the claim or demand may be addressed to both the surety and principal debtor. The creditor or obligee can call upon either the original debtor or the surety to perform the obligation. As regards debt the principal debtor remains primarily liable for his debt.

Elements of Kafālah

According to majority viewpoint, contract of *kafālah* has five elements:

i) *Kafīl* or *ḍāmin (surety)*

ii) *Makfūl bihī* or *maḍmūn* (subject matter of *Kafālah)*

iii) *Makfūl 'anhu* or *maḍmūn 'anhu* (obligor)

iv) *Ṣīghah*, i.e., offer and acceptance (form of contract)

v) *Makfūl lahū* (obligee or creditor)

Legitimacy of Kafālah

Kafālah is established by the Qur'ān, the Sunnah and *ijmā'* (consensus of opinion).

---

1 Marghinānī, *al-Hidāyah*, pp. 317,318.

Qur'ān

In *Surah Yūsuf*, the prophet Yūsuf (s.a.w s) guaranteed to give a camel-load to the one who would restore the missing drinking cup of the king. The Qur'ān says " He who restores it. shall have a camel-load. and I guarantee it."[2]

Sunnah

i. Holy Prophet (s.a.w s) said "The guarantor is responsible".[3]

ii. It is narrated in Ṣaḥīḥ Bukhārī that the Holy Prophet (s a w s) once refused to lead the funeral prayer of a person because he had not paid off his debts. On that Abū Qatādah. a companion of the Holy Prophet (s.a.w.s) undertook to pay his debt. so the Prophet (s.a.w.s) accepted his guarantee and led the prayer.[4]

Ijmā'

Besides, there is a consensus of opinion among all Muslim jurists that *kafālah* is a valid contract because it serves the need of the people. It secures the right of the creditor and repels harm from the debtor.

Kinds of Suretyship

Suretyship is of two kinds

1. *Kafālah bi al-nafs*. i.e.. suretyship for the person.

2. *Kafālah bi al-māl*. i.e.. suretyship for the property or the surety for the discharge of claim.

1. Kafālah bi al-Nafs:

This is a contract whereby the surety undertakes to produce the person. This is generally required when a person becomes surety to produce an accused person before the court of law. The *kafālah* for person is lawful in the opinion of all jurists except Imam Shāfi'ī who is of the

---

[2] Qur'ān 12:72.

[3] Ibid , vol. 5. p. 314.

[4] Shawkānī. *Nayl al-Awṭār*. vol. 5. p. 251.

view that surety for the production of person cannot exercise authority over the accused person and as such it is not valid.

2. Kafālah bi al-Māl:

It is the suretyship for the satisfaction of claim whereby the surety may be called upon to perform the obligation of the principal debtor if he makes default in the payment of his debt. *Kafālah bi al-Māl* is further divided into following kinds

i) *Kafalah bi al-dayn* (suretyship for debt) It means to guarantee the payment of debt to the creditor owed by the principal debtor.

ii) *Kafālah bi al-Taslīm* (Suretyship for possession) It is to be surety to deliver property to its owner such as to be surety on behalf of a lessee to transfer possession of leased property to the lessor or his agent on expiry of the lease period.

iii) *Kafālah bi al-dark* *Kafālah bi al -dark* is a guarantee by a seller that he will return the price of object if it is taken over by somebody else in exercise of his better right. It is also defined as a "guarantee in favour of seller that if the title of the seller is defective, the surety will make good the loss suffered by the purchaser on that account".

Contract of Guarantee in English Law:

Contract Act 1872 describes a contract of guarantee and its related terms in the following words:

> A Contract of guarantee is a contract to perform the promise. or discharge the liability of a third person in case of his default. The person who gives the guarantee is called "surety". the person in respect of whose default the guarantee is given is called the "principal debtor" and the

---

Shirbīnī. *Mughnī al-Muhtāj*. vol. 2. p. 203: Shīrāzī. *al-Muhadhdhab*. vol. 1. p. 342.

person to whom the guarantee is given is called the creditor.[6]

This definition suggests that a surety can undertake to perform the promise, i.e., to discharge the liability on behalf of the principal. The Pakistani Law relating to guarantee provides the following three types of guarantee

1. General Guarantee: It is a guarantee, which is given for all acts and obligations of a person(s). It is usually without any condition and restriction.

2. Specific Guarantee: When a guarantee is given for a specific transaction only, it is called specific guarantee.

3. Continuing Guarantee: It is provided in Sec-129 in the following words: "A guarantee, which extends to a series of transactions is called continuing guarantee".[7].

Rules of Kafālah

Following are some important rules of the contract of *kafālah*. They relate to *makfūl 'anhu* (Principal debtor or obligor), *kafīl* (surety) *makfūl lahū* (creditor or obligee) and *makfūl bihī* (subject-matter)

Kafālah for principal debtor who dies insolvent

According to Imam Abū-Ḥanīfah a suretyship for a principal debtor who dies in a state of insolvency is not valid, because he is unable to perform his obligation. It is a debt, which stands discharged after his death. But if a person dies solvent, he will be considered capable of performing his obligation. Imām Abū Ḥanīfah interprets the suretyship of Abū Qatādah as an acknowledgement of an old suretyship concluded between him and the deceased (principal debtor) during his lifetime. In opposition to this view, Imām Abū Yūsuf and Muḥammad hold that *Kafālah* for an insolvent deceased is valid, because death does not discharge the liability of an insolvent debtor. Commenting on the *ḥadīth* of Abū Qatādah they say that the Holy Prophet (s.a.w.s) had urged his Companions to become surety for the debt of deceased

---

[6] *Contract Act*, 1872. Art 126.

Contract Act, 1872. Art 129

person. He had asked them to undertake the payment of debt at the time of funeral prayer. The undertaking and suretyship of Abū Qatādah was in response to that appeal. It was not an old suretyship concluded during lifetime of debtor, as understood by the other jurists. This is an evidence of the fact that the debt existed and was not annulled by the death of the principal debtor.[8]

Another proof of the existence of debt is that if a person accepts the payment of debt voluntarily on behalf of deceased, it is lawful for creditor to demand from him. This also proves that the deceased is not released from his liability in any manner.

The possibility of there being an old suretyship in the *ḥadīth* of Abū Qatādah has been ruled out by the majority. They say that another *ḥadīth* makes manifest that it was creation of new suretyship. *Ḥadīth* discloses that Abū Qatādah voluntarily became surety for the undischarged liability of the deceased debtor.[9]

The stand point of Imām Abū Ḥanīfah has been explained by the author of "*I'lā al-Sunan*" in the following words: "If the purpose of *kafālah* of deceased is to safeguard and secure creditor's right and to provide him a right to claim his debt from surety, then such *kafālah* is invalid because obligation of *kafālah* is to share the responsibility of the principal debtor regarding the repayment of debt while in case of the death of the principal debtor, his liabilities die with him. But if *kafālah* of deceased means to discharge principal debtor from the accountability in the hereinafter without acknowledgement of right of creditor to claim his debt, then such *kafālah* is lawful.[10]

Ibn Qudāmah, a Ḥanbalī jurist has concluded from the *ḥadīth* of Abū Qatādah that *kafālah* is valid for everyone who is under some obligation regardless of whether he is alive or dead, solvent or

---

[8] Kāsānī *Badā'i' al-Sanā'i'*, vol.6 p.6; Ibn Rushd, *Bidāyat al-Mujathid*, vol.2.p.294.

[9] Shawkānī. *Nayl al-Awṭār*, vol. 5, p. 251.

[10] Zafar Aḥmad 'Usmānī, *I'lā al-Sunan*, Karachi: Idārah al-'Ulūm al-Islāmiyyah. vol.14. p. 496.

insolvent because *ḥadīth* is absolute and does not make any distinction between solvent debtor and insolvent debtor.[11]

The conclusion of this discussion is that in the opinion of Imām Abū Ḥanīfah *kafālah* for insolvent deceased is not valid while according to majority it is valid for every debtor. In former case surety cannot claim its reimbursement of what he paid, and in the latter case he is entitled to claim.

Imām ibn Ḥazm is of the view that if the debtor dies insolvent, there is no need for *kafālah* on his behalf and he will not be accountable in hereinafter because he was not able to discharge obligation during his life time. So far as the rights of creditors are concerned, their debts are payable from *zakāt* property as the payment of debt from *zakāt* property is also permissible.[12]

Rules Relating to Surety

Since the contract of suretyship creates a liability for surety, it is necessary that he should be legally competent to enter a contract. Legal competence in the context of suretyship is defined as sanity, puberty and capacity to wisely handle financial matters. Following persons are considered to be incompetent for the purpose of suretyship.

1. *A Minor insane, idiot and all other persons suffering from any legal disability:* A minor insane, idiot and all other persons suffering from any legal disability with regard to incurring of financial obligation cannot become sureties for any person. A suretyship by a minor is invalid regardless of whether he is authorized for business by his guardian. He cannot undertake any guarantee even with the permission of his guardian because the guardian is not authorized to approve of any action of the minor that involves any financial loss to him. Such suretyship would be invalid even if the surety on attaining puberty acknowledges the existence of suretyship because such suretyship does not exist in the eyes of law. But if a guardian borrowed something for providing necessities of life to an orphan and asked that orphan to be surety for this debt, this is lawful.

---

[11]   Ibn Qudāmah, *al-Mughnī*, vol. 4, p. 593.

[12]   Ibn Ḥazm, *al-Muḥallā*, vol. 5, p. 164.

Likewise if a father purchased something on credit for his minor child who also owns property and instructed him to undertake the payment of debt as his surety, it is valid because he has undertaken a liability which existed even before this suretyship on account of being owner of some property and the guardian or father was entitled to recover what he spent on him from his property.

2 *A person on deathbed:* A person on deathbed can be a surety but such suretyship is enforceable only to the extent of one third of the property. If such a person declared that he had undertaken this liability while legally competent, then the suretyship can extend to whole of his property.

3. *A person placed under interdiction:* According to Imām Aḥmad ibn Ḥanbal a person who is suffering from a legal disability on account of being spendthrift is not competent to be surety because by this contract he undertakes a financial liability, which is harmful to him. On the other hand an insolvent person can be a surety, because insolvency by itself is no bar to the contract of suretyship. He can be pursued after the removal of insolvency.[13]

Rules Related to the Makfūl Lahū (Creditor)

1. The obligee or creditor should be known to the *kafīl*, because without this the objective of suretyship i.e. the security of right cannot be realized. This purpose can be attained only when the person whose right is secured through the contract of suretyship is known to *kafīl*.

2. According to Imām Abū Ḥanīfah and Imām Muḥammad *makfūl lahū* should be present in the session of contract. In this respect they hold that if creditor is not present in the session there must be someone to approve the contract on his behalf. The reason is that *kafālah* involves a contract, which entitles creditor to claim his debt from the surety. This necessitates offer from the surety and acceptance from the creditor. But according to Imam Abū Yūsuf *kafālah* does not require acceptance by the creditor. *Kafālah* only conveys the meaning of junction, which is realisable by the unilateral declaration of *Kafīl*. Therefore, his offer alone is valid

---

[13] Ibn Qudāmah, *al-Mughnī*, vol. 5, p. 598.

for the completion of suretyship and the presence of the creditor is not necessary.[14]

Rules Related to Makfūl Bihī (Subject-matter)

Kafālah or suretyship is permissible in respect of all pecuniary claims related to the enforceable rights of the creditors such as the amount of loan, price of a commodity in credit sale, rent of leased property, commodity in *bay' salam*, amount of dower, blood-money, value of usurped property, remuneration or wages of a worker.

2. Suretyship for the property held by somebody in a fiduciary capacity is not permissible such as:

   1. deposits;

   2. capital of *muḍārbah* and partnership;

   3. loan for use or commodate loans;

   4. hired property; and

   5. property of the seller taken by a person with an intention to purchase it before the price is mentioned to him.

3. *Kafālah bi al-Taslīm* (Suretyship for possession) Suretyship for giving possession is valid, and the surety will be bound to ensure the delivery of possession. In the case of surety for the production of a person, the surety is released from his responsibility by the death of the person. In the same way, the suretyship for possession comes to an end when the reversionary claim expires.

4. It should be an established debt. A debt, which has not been established, yet in the *dhimmah* of a person, cannot be the subject matter of suretyship. Therefore, suretyship for maintenance of wife before it is fixed by the court or mutual agreement is not valid because it becomes an established debt only when it is decided by court or by mutual agreement between husband and wife. On the other hand suretyship for dower (*mahr*), price of sold property, debt of *salam* is valid as these are the established debts and there is genuine need to secure them.

---

[14] Ibn Humām, *Fath al-Qadīr*, vol. 5, p. 390.

5.It is not a condition that the extent of debt be known to the surety. The suretyship is lawful for an unascertained amount. The reason is that suretyship rests upon a broad foundation and a small degree of uncertainty does not vitiate it.

The author of *Badā'i' al-Sanā'i'* constructs his arguments in favour of suretyship for unknown and undefined property on the saying of God: "He who restores it shall have a camel load". Here God has permitted *kafālah* for camel load, which is unspecified. He also takes its validity from a *hadīth* of the Holy Prophet (s.a.w.s) in which he declared "He who died and left any debt unpaid, I am responsible for its payment". Here the Holy Prophet (s.a.w.s) guaranteed payment of an unascertained debt.[15]

6 Suretyship in crimes is not valid. The suretyship for any right, the fulfillment of which is impracticable by means of suretyship, is not valid, as in cases of *hadd* punishments or retaliation because substitution and proxies are not admitted in case of corporeal punishment. But guarantee for the production of persons of criminals under the sentence of such punishment is lawful.

The *Majallah* explains this point in the following words:

> In punishment a substitute is not allowed. Therefore, to become surety for carrying out a death penalty or punishment for personal correction is not valid. But it is lawful to become surety for the payment of money as penalty imposed on the culprit in case of murder and injuries.[16]

The prohibition of *kafālah* in *hadd* punishments is founded on the following grounds:

1.It does not stand to reason that a person who is not criminal should substitute a criminal for imposition of punishment.

2.Holy Prophet (s a.w.s) said: "No *kafālah* in *hadd* punishment"

---

[15] Kāsānī. *Badā'i' al-Sanā'i'*. vol.6, p.6.

[16] *Majallah*. Article 632.

3. In case of *ḥadd* punishments the *Sharī'ah* stresses the annulment of *ḥadd* for doubts and not the imposition of punishment while the suretyship requires performance of obligation.

Suretyship for production of person in case of retaliation, (*qiṣāṣ*) and slander (*qadhf*) can be exacted according to Imām Shāfi'ī.[17] Imām Abū Ḥanīfah on the other hand, holds the view that if such criminal gives in voluntary manner bail of himself, it is admissible but judge cannot compel him to exact it. It is allowed in cases of retaliation and slander and theft to some jurists, because here the right of individual prevails over the right of Allah. That is why suit in such cases must be instituted by the victim. Here the stress of the *Sharī'ah* is on the imposition of punishment. This, the suretyship that criminal will be produced in the court is relevant and necessary for security of the right of aggrieved party.[18]

Legal effects of Suretyship

The effects of suretyship are as follows:

1. Right of creditor to claim his debt from surety is established. However, he is at liberty to demand payment either from principal debtor or from his surety.

2. In case of suretyship for production, the right of court of law is established to demand the production of accused person in the court.

3. In case of suretyship for possession, surety is required to give possession of property to its owner.

Contract of suretyship does not imply the release of the principal debtor from his liability. If the release of the principal debtor is stipulated in the contract, in such case the contract will become a contract of *ḥawālah*. Imām Shāfi'ī does not validate such a stipulation as it is inconsistent with the purpose of suretyship. The majority also does not favour the release of the principal debtor. This viewpoint is founded upon a tradition of the Holy Prophet (s.a.w.a.) in which he

---

[17] Shirbīnī, *Mughnī al-Muḥtāj*, vol. 2, p. 203.

[18] Zuhaylī, *al-Fiqh al-Islāmī*, vol. 5, pp. 145-146.

said. "the soul of a believer does not rest until his debts are paid"[19] From this it is established that the principal debtor is not released as a result of the contract of suretyship and the creditor can claim his debt from any of the two persons. i.e.. surety and principal debtor.

1. In the case of suretyship for production of a person. if that person dies, the surety is released from his responsibility.

2. The death of the surety also terminates the contract of *kafālah bi al- nafs*. (suretyship for production of person).

3. In the case of suretyship for property if the surety dies, the suretyship is not terminated. The debt can be collected from his property. If the creditor dies his heirs or executors may demand the discharge of the obligation.

4 The surety in the contract of suretyship for production is released by producing the accused person in the court of Law. The effect is also the same in case that person himself appears before the court.

5 In case of suretyship for property, the surety is released from his liability by the payment of the debt regardless of whether the payment is made by the principal debtor or the surety.

6 He is also released when the creditor absolves the surety or the principal debtor from the liability of payment of debt. and forgoes his claim against the debtor.

7. In case of suretyship for giving possession the surety is released from his liability by handing over the property to its owner.

Right of surety to claim reimbursement of what he paid. is established. However. claim is established only after the payment of debt. not before

Conclusion

.Islamic Law has introduced a number of contracts to safeguard the right of creditor and to ensure the safe return of his amount of capital. These contracts are:

---

[19] Abd al-Latīf Āmir. *al-Duyūn wa Turuq Tawthīquhā fī al-Fiqh al-Islāmī*. p. 212.

a-Kafālah (suretyship)

b-Ḥawālah(assignment of debt)

c-Rahn (pledge)

2. *Kafālah* means merging of one liability with another in respect of a demand for performance of an obligation.

3. *Kafālah* is of two types i.e. suretyship for production of person and suretyship for Property.

4. *Kafālah* for principal who dies insolvent is not valid in the opinion of Imām Abū Ḥanīfah. According to other jurists such *kafālah* is permissible.

5. *Kafālah* is permissible for the pecuniary obligations and debts due on the principle, not for the property held on trust.

CHAPTER-19

CONTRACT OF ḤAWĀLAH
(ASSIGNMENT OF DEBT)

Ḥawālah is an effective mode for the security of debts. The word *ḥawālah* is derived from *taḥwīl*, which conveys the meaning of shifting a thing from one place to another. In the language of law it means "the shifting or assignment of debt from the liability of the original debtor to the liability of another person".[1] It can also be defined as substitution of one obligor for another with the agreement of the creditor. The purpose of *ḥawālah* is the payment of debt through the assignment of a claim. The meaning of *ḥawālah* can be understood by the following illustrations:

i) A is indebted to B and has a claim against C. He can settle his debt by transferring his claim against C to the benefit of B.

ii) A has debt owing to him from B and owes debt to C. C, instead of realizing from A and A his debt from B, can realize it from B through the contract of *ḥawālah*. In this case debtor B is substituted for debtor A with the agreement of C. A is discharged.

The debtor who transfers debt is called *muḥīl* (debtor-assignor), the creditor *muḥāl* (creditor-assignee) and new debtor to whom transfer is made, *muḥāl 'ālayh* (transferee).

Lane provides three forms of transfer while discussing the nature and scope of *ḥawālah*. These forms are as follows:

1) The transfer of a claim of debt by shifting the liability from one person to another.

---

[1] Zayla'ī. *Tabyīn al-Ḥaqā'iq*, vol 4, p. 1717.

2) The transfer of a debt by shifting the liability of him who transfers it to whom it is transferred.

3) An order for the payment of debt or of a sum of money, given by one person, upon another, to a person [2]

Validity of Ḥawālah

Following are some traditions, which establish the validity of transfer of debt. i.e., *ḥawālah*.

It is related by Abū Hurayrah (r.a t.a.) that the Holy Prophet (s a.w s) said: "To evade and defer (payment of loan) on the part of a person who is rich, is tyranny. If loan is transferred to a rich person he (the transferee of liability) should be pursued (for its payment)".[3]

It is narrated by Ibn 'Umar (r.a.t.a): "To evade and defer (payment of loan) on the part of rich person is cruelty. And if it (liability) is transferred to a rich person, he should be followed".[4]

Several inferences can be drawn from these traditions:

1) It is lawful to transfer one's debt from one to another.

2) In case of transfer of loan from the debtor to the transferee, the latter should be asked to pay as he substitutes the debtor.

3) After the transfer is made, the original debtor may be discharged from his liability towards creditor whose interest is safeguarded by the transfer of debt.

4) The transfer of loan from the debtor to the transferee requires consent of all. i.e. debtor, creditor and transferee.

5) The creditor should accept the assignment of debt and pursue the new debtor for collection of his debt as long as the assignment is to a solvent person.

---

[2] Edward William Lane. *Arabic-English Lexicon*. S.v. "ḤAWĀLAH".

[3] Ṣan'ānī. *Subul al-Salām*. vol. 3. p.61.

[4] Shawkānī. *Nayl al-Awṭār*, vol. 5. p. 250.

The negotiability or assignability of debt in the history of Islam is as old as Islam itself. It started with the undertaking by a man of means to pay the debt of another in straitened circumstances and developed into a medium of commercial transactions. In this age also negotiability of instruments of loan is of utmost importance in all commercial-cum-banking transactions. *Hawālah* has the ingredients of guarantee. An instrument is also negotiated for the purpose of guaranteeing or securing the payment of the loan due on a promissory note, a cheque or a bill of exchange. As such, when A, a drawer, draws a bill upon B ordering him to pay C, he in fact guarantees him, i.e . C the payment of his debt due on A. Similarly when A, a holder of instrument negotiates it to B, he secures the payment of debt due on the bill An acceptor of an instrument after accepting it becomes primarily liable while a drawer's liability becomes secondary and conditional. In the same way a transferee in a contract of *hawalah* becomes primarily liable

Imām Abū Ḥanīfah's Viewpoint Regarding Ḥawālah

Imām Abū Ḥanīfah defines *hawālah* as a transfer of debt, terminating the liability of the original debtor, to a third person.[5] This definition implies that after the conclusion of *hawālah* the principal debtor will be relieved from the liability. He argues that the term *hawālah* is derived from the word *taḥwīl*, which necessitates the transfer of debt to the transferee and the exemption of the transferor. The transferor is also exempted because of the acquiescence of the transferee.

Imām Muḥammad's viewpoint

Imām Muḥammad is of the opinion that *hawālah* is the transfer of demand only while the actual burden of payment rests with the principal debtor.[6]

Imām Zufar also maintains that the transferor is not exempted because of the analogy that subsists between his case and that of bail, for both are contracts of bail. The person who is bailed is not exempted from the debt so neither should the transferor.[7]

---

[5] Kāsānī. *Badā'i' al-Sanā'i'*. vol.6. p.17.

[6] Ibn Nujaym. *Baḥr al-Rā'iq*. vol. 6. p. 344.

[7] Kāsānī. *Badā'i' al-Sanā'i'*. vol. 6. p.18; Ibn Nujaym. *al-Baḥr al-Rā'iq* vol. 6. p.344.

In fact *ḥawālah* is different from suretyship in the sense that in the contract of suretyship or bailment if the creditor releases the original debtor from his liability, the same will be applicable to his surety and as such he will automatically be released from his liability towards his principal debtor. On the other hand, in a contract of *ḥawālah* if the creditor releases the original debtor from debt, this release may not necessarily extend to the transferee. He remains under obligation to pay the debt until he is also released expressly by the creditor.

Effects of Ḥawālah

Normally the effect of *ḥawālah* is to discharge the debtor (*muhīl*) from the debts he owes to the creditor/assignee (*muḥāl lahū*) *Ḥawālah* can also occur with the condition that the debtor/assignor (*muḥīl*) shall remain liable for the debt, in such case *ḥawālah* is similar to a guarantee. Thus, the creditor/assignee has the right to claim settlement from either debtor/assignor or the substituted debtor.

According to Imām Aḥmad ibn Ḥanbal and Imām Shāfiʿī, when the new debtor is solvent, the creditor/assignee has no recourse what so ever against the creditor/assignor in the event that the debt is not settled by the substituted debtor. Thus, the discharge of the debtor/assignor is total and irrevocable unless his guarantee was obtained especially for the case of non-payment by the substituted debtor. This is substantially the opinion of the Mālik, with the difference that for Mālik the creditor/assignee has the right of recourse against the debtor/assignor in the case of misrepresentation in assignment to the new debtor who was already bankrupt before the *ḥawālah* was concluded.[8]

For the Ḥanafīs, *ḥawālah*, in principle discharges the debtor-assignor with the exception that the creditor/assignee (*muḥāl lahū*) has a right of recourse against him in the event that his claim is in danger of failing either for the reason that the new debtor is insolvent or

---

[8] Khaṭṭāb. *Mawāhib al-Jalīl.* vol.5. p.95.

because he renounces the existence of *ḥawālah* and the creditor has no proof thereof.[9]

Kinds Of Ḥawālah

Ḥawālah is either absolute *(muṭlaq)* or conditional (*muqayyad*). Absolute *ḥawālah* refers to that contract where payment is not restricted to the property of the transferor in the hands of transferee.

Ḥawālah is conditional when it contains a stipulation that the creditor's debt may be paid up from the debt of the debtor due from the transferee or anything belonging to the debtor, which is in possession as a security with the transferee. All other forms of *ḥawālah* are unrestricted and absolute.[10]

This distinction is the creation of Ḥanafī fiqh but the other three Schools do not subscribe to *ḥawālah muṭlaq* as *ḥawālah*. The effect of the two categories determine the validity of other classification i.e. *ḥawālat al-ḥaq* and *ḥawālat al-dayn* because *ḥawālat al-ḥaq* is a form of *ḥawālat muṭlaq*.

It is to be noted here that in *ḥawālat al-ḥaq*, the right of creditor in the debt due from the debtor is transferred to a new party. It is against *ḥawālat al-dayn* in which the liability is transferred to a new party. While discussing the subject our primary concern will be the *ḥawālat al-dayn*. i.e.,the assignment of liability or debt.

Rights and Duties of Parties

1. In an absolute *ḥawālah*, the transferee, after making payment to the creditor steps in the shoes of the creditor as against the original debtor.

2. In a restricted *ḥawālah* the right of the debtor to property in possession of transferee, ceases. Thus, if the transferee after accepting the liability returns the property to debtor, he will remain liable to perform his obligation towards the creditor.

---

[9] Nabīl Ṣālih. *Unlawful Gain and Legitimate Profit in Islamic Law*. p. 105.

[10] *Majallah*, Artical 678 - 679

However. after making payment to him. he can claim his money from the debtor.

3 The jurists differ among themselves regarding a *hawālah* which is with condition that creditor's debt may be paid up from the debt of the debtor due from transferee or from the property belonging to the debtor in the hands of transferee. and the debtor died before the payment. The question here is as to who has the superior right to this property: the creditor of *hawālah* or other creditors of the debtor?

Majority of the Hanafī jurists hold that all creditors are equal as far as this right is concerned Thus, if this property is distributed and the creditor gets some portion of it. he cannot demand the remaining from the transferee. as the *hawālah* was restricted with that property only [11]

On the other hand Imām Zufar is of the view that the right of creditor of *hawālah* is superior to other creditors. as the right of creditor was attached to property, and the property in question is no more his property because he isolated himself from it in his life The same situation continues to exist after his death. Moreover. the right of the creditor of *hawālah* was attached to it in the debtor's life. while the right of other creditors was attached after his death As such former's right is superior to latter's right like the right of pledgee over the pledged property [12]

4. If *hawālah* was with a condition that the transferee would make payment from the amount realised from purchaser in a credit sale. Then the subject matter is destroyed before delivery to the purchaser or it is returned by him exercising his option of inspection or defect. in such case. the *hawālah* is still valid and the transferee is liable to pay. However. after the payment he can claim it from the transferor. This means that the transferee (new debtor) is liable to honour his commitment even if the cause of his obligation ceases to exist.

---

[11] Kāsānī. *Badā' i' al-Sanā'i'*. vol. 6. p. 16.

[12] Ibid.

How is Ḥawālah concluded?

The different modes of concluding *hawālah* are as follows:

a) *Ḥawālah* with consent of all the parties By concerned parties is meant the debtor/assignor (*muḥīl*), the creditor/assignee (*muḥāl Lahu*) and the substituted debtor. This is in principle an ideal situation where all concerned parties' consent to the substitution of a new debtor for the original debtor;

b) *hawālah* by agreement of the creditor and the new debtor: The original debtor does not participate in this sort of *hawālah*, which is not of common occurrence but can still be encountered. This is lawful according to Ḥanafī jurists;

c) *hawālah* by agreement of debtor/assignor (*muḥīl*) and the creditor/assignee (*muḥāl lahū*) For the Ḥanafīs this is contingent upon the new debtor's agreement. To others his consent is not necessary, especially when he is solvent; and

d) *hawālah* by agreement of the debtor/assignor (*Muḥīl*) and the new debtor (*muḥāl alayh*) This *hawālah* is contingent upon the creditor's agreement according to Ḥanafī, Shāfiʿī and Mālikī jurists Ḥanbalī jurists hold that when the new debtor is solvent his consent is not necessary.[13]

Legal Capacity of the Parties to Ḥawālah

The Ḥanafī jurists differentiate, in terms of legal capacity, between the transferee on the one hand and the creditor/debtor on the other.

1. As for the transferee, they postulate that he should be sane and of age. A discerning minor (*sabī mumayaiz*) is not legally competent to accept the *hawālah*; because such *hawālah* may entail risk or financial loss for the minor assuming the position

---

[13] Nabīl Sālih, *Unlawful Gain and Legitimate Profit in Islam*, pp. 103, 104

of transferee. If he accepted the *ḥawālah* on the demand of the transferor then it is a gratuitous act in its beginning though he may get it back at the end. But if he undertook this liability without the acquiescence or orders of the transferor then it is by every respect (by its beginning and end) a gratuitous act quite identical to giving the gift, which is not permissible for a minor. A guardian of a minor cannot also accept *ḥawālah* on behalf of his ward, as it is a harmful act, for which he has no authority.

In a restricted *ḥawālah* where the transferee has a debt due from the transferor, the condition of puberty and sanity is not necessary to some jurists as in such *ḥawālah* the transferee is already under obligation to pay the debt or to deduct what he paid from the property of the transferor.

2. As regards the capacity of the creditor and the debtor (transferor), their ability of discretion and understanding is sufficient for the conclusion of *ḥawālah*. However it will remain suspended upon the approval of the guardian.

This is quite a logical and reasonable viewpoint because *ḥawālah* does not create any liability for them rather it benefits them. The transferor is a beneficiary because he is exempted from his liability while the creditor, as a result of such contract, ensures the recovery of his debt. However, if the creditor fails to recover this debt due to the transferee being less prosperous than the transferor, then the law gives him right to have recourse to the original debtor. Therefore a minor with discretion after he has obtained the approval of his guardian, can transfer his debt in the same manner as he can accept the transfer upon some third party if he is a creditor. In the later case the person to whom the minor has transferred must be more prosperous than the debtor. In Islamic law the guardian of the property of minors is allowed to undertake only those transactions, which are unequivocally in the minor's best interest. In disposing of their property the guardian or father is not permitted to take the risk of accepting the *ḥawālah* to a person who is less prosperous than the purchaser.

Circumstances under which absolute Hawālah is terminated

According to Imām Abū Ḥanīfah, contract of *hawālah* is terminated and debt reverts to the principal debtor in the following circumstances:

i) Where the transferee denies the existence of the contract upon oath, and the creditor cannot produce witnesses to prove it.

ii) Where the transferee dies poor and insolvent. In either case the debt is destroyed, since in neither case is it practicable for the creditor to receive payment from the transferee. [14]

View point of Abū Yūsuf and Muḥammad

Imām Muḥammad and Imām Abū Yūsuf maintain that *hawālah* is terminated under one of three circumstances. Of these, two are the same as those above cited and the third is a declaration by the court of the poverty and insolvency of the transferee during his lifetime. This third circumstance is not admitted by Abū Ḥanīfah because according to his doctrine, poverty and insolvency cannot be established by the decree of court, since property comes in the morning and goes in the evening. But according to the two disciples the decree of the court can also establish poverty. Before this declaration the creditor is not entitled to make any claim against the transferor.

Imām Shāfi'ī holds that the creditor has no right to make any claim for his due upon the transferor, although his right is destroyed. It is because in consequence of the transfer the transferor becomes exempted from the debt and this exemption is absolute and not restricted to the condition of payment from the transferee. Hence the debt cannot revert to the transferor, except on account of some new cause and no such cause is to be found in this case.

The argument of the Ḥanafī jurists is that although the exemption be absolute in the terms of the contract yet it is restricted in the sense, by the condition of right being rendered to the creditor. The contract is, therefore, cancelled in case of his right being destroyed; because the contract is capable of cancellation, and may be cancelled

---

[14] Marghinānī. *al-Hidāyah*. vol. 3. p. 99.

by the agreement of the parties. Moreover, the condition of the safe delivery of the debt to creditor is equivalent to that warranting the subject of a sale to be free from blemish. Such a warranty implicitly exists as a condition in every sale although it may not be specifically mentioned In the same manner the security of the debt exists as a condition in a contract of transfer although not specified in it.[15]

Termination of restricted Ḥawālah

1. If *ḥawālah* was with condition that payment is to be made from property of the debtor-assignor in possession of the transferee, and then a person who was the rightful owner of that property turned up and took its possession, the *ḥawālah* is void and the debt is returned to the debtor who made the *ḥawālah*. In other words. restricted *ḥawālah* is terminated when the property in the hand of transferee does not belong to the assignor and is taken possession of by its owner.

2. It is terminated, if the property held by the transferee in fiduciary capacity is destroyed without any negligence on part of transferee

3. It is not terminated in the following two cases:

   a) If the property was held in trust. and destroyed by negligence.

   b) It was a property of assignor usurped by transferee.

Comparison between Ḥawālah and Negotiable Instruments

In Islamic Law *ḥawālah* is introduced to guarantee the payment of debt on behalf of the original debtor. An instrument is also negotiated for the purpose of guaranteeing or securing the payment of loan due on a bill of exchange or promissory note.

2. In the opinion of majority the valid form of *ḥawālah* is the one in which the transferee of liability is the debtor of the original debtor In other words the *ḥawālah* must be with consideration. The same is the position in the negotiable instruments. It is presumed that every negotiable instrument when it has been

accepted. endorsed, drawn, or made was accepted, endorsed, drawn or made for consideration.[16]

3. In Hanafi Law it is not necessary that the transferee be the debtor of the original debtor. He may accept the liability voluntarily. The section relating to acceptance for honour and payment for honour with reference to promissory note and bill of exchange conveys the same sense.[17]

4. In Islamic Law a thing for which a *hawalah* is made must be a debt. Negotiable instruments are also restricted to dealing in money only.

5. The drawing of a bill or instrument by one bank on another for the benefit of a third person would be *hawalah*. According to the Hanafis and those who agree with them it is immaterial whether the drawee is a debtor of the drawer or not because for them it is not a condition that the transferee should be debtor of the transferor but the acceptance by a drawee is a condition precedent for implementation of *hawalah*. The majority of the jurists do not treat acceptance by the drawee as essential if he is indebted to the transferor or drawer in the same amount. According to this view it becomes a *hawalah* only if the person in whose name the bill of exchange is made payable, is a creditor of the drawer. In case he is not a creditor, the bill creates an agency in which the drawer shall be the principal and the payee shall be his agent. In this case it will be possible to call the instrument as a bill of exchange.

6. About the right of a third party the position of the Act is the same as that of Islamic Law. If the obligation of the drawer towards the first payee terminates or becomes void and the payee then endorses the cheque or any other negotiable instrument in favour of a holder in due course and the latter demands its payment or reimbursement from the drawer, the drawer is stopped from pleading termination of his liability as

---

[16] 'Abd al-Latīf 'Āmir. *al-Duyūn wa Tawthīquhā fī al-Fiqh al-Islāmī*. Cairo: pp. 160,161

Negotiable Instruments Act Section 108 (a)

the right of the third person has accrued in this case. Thus, if A draws a bill on C. Later on the obligation of the A towards C becomes void, and C then endorses it in favour of D. who is holder in due course. A's liability towards D is not terminated.[18]

In Islamic Law, also, the transferee of liability of the debtor is not competent to defend against the claim of the creditor by pleas with which he could defend the action of the debtor unless the debt of the debtor due against him be factually non-existent. If the creditor transfers to a third person his right against the purchaser for a sum of one thousand *dirham* and thereafter the purchaser exercises his option for defect and cancels the sale, the transfer is not terminated, because it now involves the right and interest of persons who were not party to contract.

The general rule is that contracts without consideration and those that are fictitious or forged are void. The following sections form an exception to the rule on account of the provision of negotiability, which may involve the interest of a number of third parties who in their turn may have paid consideration for it under a bonafide belief about the document being genuine and legal. The Act protects the interest of such holders in due course of the negotiable instruments. The presumption of the Law is that an innocent party should not be made to suffer.

Section 41 provides that an acceptor of a bill of exchange already endorsed is not relieved from liability, by reasons that such endorsement is forged, if he knew or had reason to believe the endorsement to be forged when he accepted the bill.[19]

Section 42 states that an acceptor of a bill of exchange drawn in a fictitious name and payable to the drawer's order is not, by reason that such name is fictitious, relieved from liability to any holder in due course claiming under an endorsement by the same

---

[18] *Negotiable Instruments Act*, Section 9.

[19] *Negotiable Instruments Act*, Section 14.

hand as the drawer's signature. and purporting to be made by the drawer.[20]

Section 43 declares that negotiable instrument made. drawn, accepted. endorsed or transferred without consideration or for a consideration. which fails. creates no obligation of payment between the parties to the transaction. But if any such party has transferred the instrument with or without endorsement to a holder for consideration. such holder. and every subsequent holder deriving title from him may recover the amount due on such instrument from the transferor for consideration or any prior party thereto.[21]

Ḥawālah and the Concept of Assignment in English Law

The concept of assignment and transfer in the legal history of Islam is as old as Islam itself. The *ḥawālah* was followed not only as a guarantee for the payment of debt tó the creditor but also as a medium of commercial transactions. *Ḥawālah* in its later form was known as *saftajah* (bill) which is infact precursor of todays negotiable instruments. A deep study of the subject reveals that from the 1st or 2nd century Hijrah it was used not only in commercial transactions but also in transfer of money from one place to another so as to avoid dangers of road a practice which is also prevalent in contemporary banking system: Ibn Zubayr used to take money from some persons in Mecca and would give them a letter addressed to Mus'ab ibn Zubayr in Iraq, instructing him to pay that money. to those persons in Iraq. Ibn Abbās and Ḥadhrat 'Alī were questioned about the legality of the transactions and they found no harm in it.

The concept of assignment remained alien for centuries for Europe It was in early eighteen century when the concept started creeping into its legal system. In the French Law the term *"Avel"* is used for a special guarantee of indemnity on negotiable instruments. whether used in favour of stranger or any person signing it. The word *"Avel"* is not therefore used in the sense of *ḥawālah*. rather the term

[20] *Negotiable Instruments Act*, Section 42.

[21] *Negotiable Instruments Act*, Section 43.

kafālah is nearer to it. Whatever be the sense of *"Avel"*, there is no doubt that the concept traveled to Europe from Islamic fiqh.

As regard the assignment or transfer of the contractual rights and liability, the basic presumption of the law was that, all such rights being personal to the parties concerned, cannot be transferred to a third person who is not party to the contract, as such act might encourage multiplying litigation or maintenance of the suit. But with the passage of time the growing needs compelled the jurists to accept some modification in the harsh rule. The first thing which was subjected to such modification, was the question of the assignment of debt from here the area of assignability was widened to cover the other rights and liabilities.

Conclusion

1. *Hawālah* means shifting or assignment of debt from the liability of original debtor to the liability of another person.

2. After the transfer of debt, the original debtor is discharged from his liability

3. In absolute *hawālah*, the transferee after making payment to the creditor can claim its reimbursement from the debtor. In restricted *hawālah* the right of debtor to property with the transferee, ceases.

4. The absolute *hawālah* is terminated when the transferee dies poor and insolvent.

5. Restricted *hawālah* is terminated when the property of transfer in the hand of transferee is taken by the one who is entitled to it, or when it was a trust in his hand and was destroyed without any fault or negligence on his part.

6. *Hawālah* resembles negotiable Instruments in that its purpose is to guarantee the payment of debt to the creditor. An instrument is also negotiated for the purpose of guaranteeing or securing the payment of loan due on a bill of exchange.

CHAPTER-20

CONTRACT OF RAHN (PLEDGE)

Definition

1. According to the Majallah *rahn* is the security that can be lawfully employed for satisfaction of a claim in respect of a debt.[1]

2. According to Lane "*Rahn* means to pledge or lodge a real or corporeal property of material value in accordance with the law, as security for a debt or pecuniary obligation".[2]

Legitimacy

The legitimacy of *rahn* is established by a number of texts from the Qur'ān and the Sunnah. Some of such texts are as follows:

Qur'ān

"If you are on journey and cannot find a person to write (your debt), then pledge in hand (shall suffice)".[3]

It is to be mentioned here that it is not necessary that a pledge may be held on security only on a journey. The fact is that pledge has been mentioned in the context of journey because such situation generally arises when a person is on journey. In such state it is likely that he may not find a scribe to write down the debt. The jurists are unanimous on the point that the principle regarding loan against security as laid down in the verse will also apply when the parties, even though at home, agree to lend and borrow money against security. This will also apply to cases where the lender does not trust borrower.

---

[1] *Majallah*, Art. 701.

[2] E.W. Lane, Arabic English Lexicon, letter, S.V. "R".

[3] Qur'ān 2: 282.

Sunnah

1. Ḥaḍrat Qatādah narrated that Anas (r.a.t.a.) went to the Prophet (s.a.w.s.) with barley bread with some dissolved fat on it and he (the Prophet s.a.w.s.) had mortgaged his armour to a Jew in Madinah and took from him barley for his family'.[4]

2. Ḥaḍrat ʿĀishah narrated that the Prophet (s.a.w.s.) bought some foodstuff on credit from a Jew for a limited period and mortgaged him armour for it.[5]

Legal status of the pledged property

According to the viewpoint of the majority of Muslim jurists the pledged property assumes the status of trust in the hands of pledgee.. Thus, if it is destroyed or lost without negligence fault or wrongful action on his part he will not be held liable. He will remain entitled to his debt due on the pledger. The Ḥanafī jurists hold the view that the pledgee after taking the possession of the property becomes responsible in case of its being destroyed in his hands. The responsibility of the pledgee extends to the amount of the debt owing to the pledgee. Thus, if a pledged property equivalent to the amount of debt is destroyed in the pledgee's hand, his claim is rendered void and he is deemed to have obtained a complete payment. If, on the contrary the value of the pledge exceeds the amount of the debt, the excess is in that case considered as a trust for which the pledgee will not be held responsible in case of its destruction. But if the value be less than the debt, the pledgee forfeits that part of his debt and the pledger will pay the remaining to the pledgee.[6]

In opposition to the above-mentioned opinion, the Shāfiʿī jurists maintain that the pledge is a trust in the hands of the pledgee. Thus, if it is destroyed in his possession, still he does not forfeit his

---

[4] Bukhārī , *Ṣaḥīḥ*, vol. 3, p.54.

[5] Ibid.

[6] Kāsānī, *Badā'i' al-Ṣanā'i'*, vol. 6, p.163.

due because it is recorded in the tradition that no pledge shall be distrained for debt and the pledger shall be liable for all risks.[7]

Conditions of pledged property

i) It should be a thing having some monetary worth and legal value.

ii) It should be a thing in which transactions are permissible in the *Sharī'ah*. Thus, it should not be prohibited by Islamic Law such as pork and wine.

iii) It should be existent at the time of contract: Thus to pledge fruits on trees when their quality is yet to be established is not valid, because the object of pledge in this case is non-existent.

iv) It should be deliverable. Thus, to pledge a stray animal is invalid, because its possession cannot be given to the pledgee.

v) It should be precisely determined with regard to its essence, quantity and value. An indefinite part of any thing cannot be the subject-matter of pledge because the pledge is taken with a view to obtaining payment of a debt. This objective cannot be realized if the pledge is an undefined part of property.

vi) An article naturally conjoined cannot be pledged separately. Thus, it is not valid to pledge fruits without trees which bear it, crops without the land, trees without ground, because the pledge in all these cases has connection with an article which is still unpledged, and the possession of which cannot be taken while the possession is a requirement of pledge.

vii) It is not permissible to pledge the usufruct of a thing; such as to allow the creditor to stay in the house of debtor for some specified period in consideration of debt, these usufructs cannot be delivered at the time of the contract. Their continuation and permanence cannot be ensured

---

Shirbīnī, *Mughnī al-Muḥtāj*, vol.2, p.137.

from the time of the contract till the time of repayment of debt.

viii) It should be handed over to the pledgee. In other words physical possession of the property should be given to the pledgee.

ix) It should be of sufficient value to cover the amount of debt.

Conditions of claim or debt for which pledge is given

1. It should be an established and enforceable debt. Thus a pledge may be given for loan, price in credit sale, commodity of *Salam*, claim after usurpation, damages in the torts against property, amount of dower, blood money and all the other binding and irrevocable claims.

2. Pledge is not permitted for the things for which, there is no liability of compensation such as deposits, commodate loans, capital of *muḍārabah* and *mushārakah* partnerships, leased property in the hands of lessee .

3. It is not permissible to give pledge for an amount, which the pledger will borrow, from the pledgee.

4. It is not permissible to give pledge for a claim or debt, which is not recognized in the *Sharī'ah*. Thus, it is not permissible to give pledge for the remuneration of a dancer or singer, because hiring a woman to dance or sing is an invalid and impermissible act, hence pledge for an obligation arising from an invalid act is also invalid.

5. The claim or debt should be known and defined. Thus, it is not permissible to give something as security for one of the two loans without specifying one of them.

Maintenance of pledged property

The Muslim Jurists are unanimous on the point that the maintenance of pledge property is primarily the responsibility of the owner, i.e., pledger in this case. He will incur the cost of maintenance because the

Holy Prophet (s.a.w.s.) has said: "To the pledger returns its profit, and he is held responsible for its loss".[8]

The Ḥanafī jurists, however, divide the expenses incurred on maintenance of pledge into two categories;

    i.   Expenses required for its subsistence, improvement, and continuation of existence; and

    ii.   Expenses incurred on its conservation and safekeeping.

In the opinion of Ḥanafī jurists the expenses of first category will be borne by the pledger. As such he is responsible for feeding the animal, the wages to be paid to the shepherd, expenses of the watering of the garden, its weeding, grafting and the cleaning of the water channels because these expenses relate to the improvement and continuation of the existence of the property.

The expenses of the second category are to be borne by the pledgee Thus, the rent of the house wherein the pledge is kept as well as the wages of the keeper will be payable by the pledgee. However, if the pledge be a living animal and require a keeper and maintenance, the expenses of these will be incurred by the pledger.[9]

The other Jurists do no accept this division. In their opinion all the expenses will be borne by the pledger.[10]

Benefiting From Pledged Property

A. By Pledger:

The majority of Muslim jurists is of the view that pledger cannot benefit from the pledged property. The Ḥanafī jurists allow the benefiting from pledged property with the permission of pledgee. Mālikī jurists regard such benefiting invalid even with the permission f pledgee. In their opinion such permission amounts to termination of

---

[8] Ṣan·ānī ,*Subul al-Salām*, vol.3, p.52.

[9] Kāsānī , *Badā'i' al-Ṣanā'i'*, vol 6, p.151.

[10] Bahutī. *Kashshāf al-Qanā'* vol.3, p. 326. Ibn Qudāmā. *al-Mughnī* vol.4, p.392.

Contract.[11] The Shāfi'ī Jurists permit all kinds of benefits provided its does not cause devaluation of property.[12]

B. By Pledgee:

According to majority view the pledgee cannot use the pledge. The permission given by *hadīth* to milk·or ride the animal will be availed only in a situation where the pledger, the owner of animal refuses to bear the expenses of its feeding. Hanbalī Jurists allowed the benefiting from pledged property if it is animal. They allow the pledgee to ride it or milk it in consideration for fodder given to it. They support their view point by a *hadīth* that, "the pledged animal can be used for riding as long as it is fed and the milk of a milch animal can be drunk according to what one spends on it. The one who rides the animal or drinks milk should provide expenditures".[13]

The contract of *rahn* is basically meant for the security of debt, and not for investment and profitable use. Any profitable use of pledged property is regarded usury in Islamic Law, because of the *hadīth* that "any loan which brings some benefit (for creditor) is a kind of *ribā*".[14] Thus, if he earns any profit out of it, he is bound to return it to its owner. Mawlānā Mawdūdī in this connection writes:

> If the pledge is productive, the creditor should keep a regular account of the produce and deduct it from the debt; otherwise any profit drawn from the pledged property would be interest. The only object in view of holding a pledge is the security of the repayment of the debt and it does not entitle the creditor in any way to make profit out of it. For instance, if a creditor lives in the houses which he holds as pledge for his debt or if he lets it to someone else, he is in fact guilty of taking interest, if he does not credit the rent of the house to the debtor, for there is no difference between taking direct interest on a debt or earning money

---

[11] Kāsānī. *Badā'i' al-Sanā'i'*, vol. 6, p.146.

[12] Shirbīnī. *al-Mughnī al-Muhtāj*, vol.2, p.131.

[13] Ibn Qudāmā. *al-Mughnī*. vol.4. p.190.

[14] San'ānī. *Subul al-Salām*. vol.3, p.53.

from it or making use for the property delivered as a pledge.[15]

C. Benefit From Pedged Property Under Bay' al-Wafā'

Bay' al-wafā' is a transaction in which a person in need of money of sells a commodity to the lender on the condition that when he wishes the lender would return it to him upon the return of price.

According to Sir 'Abd al-Rahīm this contract partakes of the attributes of a valid sale in as much as the buyer is entitled to the income of the property and of a vitiated sale as both the parties are entitled to annul it and of a pledge in as much as the buyer cannot sell or otherwise dispose of the property.[16]

But the fact is that it has the effect of pledge because the seller aims to raise commercial loan through this contract. He delivers commodities as pledge to the purchaser. He allows him to benefit from it during the period of indebtedness. In Islamic Law the basis to be considered in contract is the meaning and spirit, not the name and form. *Bay' al wafā'* is not a real sale, instead it is a contract of pledge whereby the buyer (creditor) utilizes the commodity for the period during which it stays in his possession. The Muslim Jurists disapprove this transaction because it is a legal fiction for charging interest.

Legal consequences of pledge

Some of the legal consequences of pledge are as follows:

1. The pledge has a right to keep possession until redemption of the pledge, and if the pledger has died, he has better right than the other creditors and can make full payment of the debt from the pledge.

2. The pledgee can sell the pledged property with the permission of pledger, when the debt becomes due in order to satisfy it out of the proceeds. He can also ask the court to have the pledge sold.

---

[15] Abul A'lā Mawdūdī, *Tafhīm al-Qur'ān*, Lahore: Maktabā Ta'mīr Insāniyyat, 1983, vol.1, note # 331.

[16] 'Abd al-Rahīm, *Mohammadan Jurisprudence*, p.233.

3. The pledger cannot sell pledge without consent of pledgee. But if he sells the pledged property without seeking his permission the sale will remain suspended and will come into force only after the debt is paid to the pledgee. Likewise if the pledgee consents to the sale, it will become effective and debt will remain due to the pledger.

4. It is permissible for the pledger to appoint the pledgee his attorney to sell the property when the time of payment approaches. In such case the pledger cannot dismiss him from attorneyship nor will he be dismissed by the death of either the pledger or pledgee.

5. The pledgee is not allowed to let out or give the pledge in loan because he is himself prohibited benefiting from it and consequently not authorized to confer the power of enjoyment upon others.

6. If after the discharge of the debt the pledge perishes in the hands of pledgee, he will be liable to return the money, he has received to the pledger, and the contract of mortgage is not dissolved until the property is restored to the pledger.

7. On the death of the pledger, his heirs of age will stand in his place and it will be their responsibility to free the thing pledged by paying the debt from the property of deceased person.

Conclusion

1. *Rahn* (pledge) is to make a property security in respect of a right or claim.

2. According to majority's standpoint the pledged property assumes the status of trust in the hands of the pledgee.

3. Maintenance of pledged property is primarily the responsibility of pledger.

4. The pledgee is not allowed to benefit from pledged property.

BIBLIOGRAPHY

Al-Qur'ān al-Karīm

'Abd al -Latīf 'Āmir, *al-Duyūn wa Tawthiquhā fī al-fiqh al-Islāmī.* Cairo:[n.d].

'Abd al -Karīm Zaydān, *al-Madkhal li-Dirāsah al-Islāmīyyah;* Beirut: Mu'assasah al-Risālah, 1402 H. 1982.

'Abd al -Sattār al-Jibālī, *Aḥkām 'aqd al-Bay'*,Cairo: Jāmi'ah al-Azhar, 1993.

'Abd al -Rahīm, Sir, *The Principles of Muhammadan Jurisprudence,* Lahore, All Pakistan Legal decision, 1977.

'Abd al -Razzāq al-Sanhūrī, Dr., *Maṣādir al-Ḥaqq fī al-Fiqh al-Islāmī.* Cairo: Dār al-Ma'arifah, 1967;

.... *al-Wasīt, fī Sharḥ al-Qanūn al-Madnī,* Cairo: Dār al-Nahḍa al-'Arabiyyah, 1964

'Adil Muṣṭafā Basyūnī, *al-Tashrī' wa al-Nuẓum al-Qānūniyyah al-Wadiyyah,* Cairo.

'Abdullah 'Alwī Hājjī, *Sales and contracts in Early Islāmic Commercial Law,* Islamabad: Islamic Research Institute, IIU, 1994

'Abdullah Yūsuf 'Alī, *The Holy Qur'ān: Text Translation and commentary,* al-Rajhī Company, 1983.

Abū al- A'lā Mawdūdī, Tafhīm al-Qur'ān, Lahore:Maktabā Ta'mīr Insāniyyat,1983.

Abū Dawūd al-Sijistānī. Sulaymān. *al-Sunan*. Cairo Ihyā' al-Sunnah al-Nabawiyyah. 1975 A D

Abū Zahrah. *al-Milkiyyah wa Nazariyyah al-'Aqd*. Cairo Dār al-Fikr al-'Arabī. 1939

Aḥmad ibn Ḥanbal. *Musnad*. Egypt: Dār al-Ma'ārif. 1375 H / 1956

Aḥmad Ḥassan. *Principles of Islāmic Jurisprudence*. Islamabad Islamic Research Institute. 1993.

Aḥmad Yūsuf. Dr. *'Uqūd al-Mu'āwadāt al-Māliyyah*. Cairo:

Dār al-Naṣr. Cairo University

Al-'Aṣṣāl. Aḥmad Muḥammad and Fatḥī Aḥmad. *al-Nizām al-Iqtisādī fi al-Islām*. Cairo. Maktabah Wahbah, 1977

Al-Jassās Abu Bakr. *Ahkām al-Qur'ān*. Dār al-Kitāb al-Arabī. Beirut.

Al-Jaziri. *Al-Fiqh 'alā al-Madāhib al-arba'ah*. Dar Ihyā al-urāth al-'Arabī. Beirut. 1963.

Al-Mawasū'ah al-Fiqhiyyah. (Government of Kuwait) 1986.

Ibn Juzey. *Qawānīn al-Ahkām al-Shar'iyyah*. Dar al-'Ilm lil Malāyih. Beirut. 1973

Amīr Alī. Syed. *Muhammadan Law*. Lahore Law Publishing Company. Fifth Edition. 1965.

Amīr Bādshāh, *Taysīr al-Tahrīr*. Cairo. Muṣṭafā al-Bābī al-Ḥalabī, 1351 A-H

Anwar Iqbal Quraishī. *Islām and Theory of Interest*. Lahore Sh. Muḥammad Ashraf Publishers. 1991.

Aḥmad Ibrāhīm Bik. *al-Iltizāmāt fī al-Sharḥ al-Islāmī*. Cairo: Dār al-Ansār. 1944.

Babertī *'Ināyah 'Alā al-Hidāyah*. Cairo:1389 H

Babilli. Maḥmūd Muḥammad. *al-Māl fi al-Islām*. Beirut: Dār al-Kitāb al-Lubnānī. 1975.

Bahūtī. Mansūr ibn Yūnus. *Kashshāf al-Qinā' alā Matn al-Iqnā*. Maṭba'ah Anṣār al-Sunnah-al-Muḥammadiyyah. 1366 H.

Baillie, *A Digest of Muhammadan Law*, Lahore, premier Book House, 1957.

Bank Dubai Islāmī, *al-Murābaha fī bank Dubai al-Islāmī*.

Black, William, E.A. *Law Dictionary*, U.S.A. West Publishing Company, 1979 A.D.

Bukhārī, Muhammad ibn Ismāʻīl, *al-Ṣaḥīḥ*, Beirut : Dār al-Kitāb al-ʻArabī, 1323H.

Business Law, Cavendish Publishing Limited.

Council of Islamic Idiology. *14th Report on Contract Act, 1872* Islamabad 1983.

Darīr, Muhammad Ṣiddīq, *al-Gharar fi al-ʻUqūd wa Āthāruhu fi al-Taṭbīqāt al-Muʻāsirah*, Islamic Development Bank, Jeddah, Saudi Arabia.

Dusūqī, Muhammad ibn Aḥmad, *Hāshiyah ʻalā al-Sharh al-Kabīr*, Cairo: ʻĪsa al-Bābī al-Ḥalabī, 1350 H.

Egyptian Civil Code, 1948.

Federal Shariat Court, *Suo-Moto Examination of Laws in the Contract Act*, Islamabad: 1986.

Fischer and Dornbuseh, *Economics*, Singapore McGraw-Hill Book Company, 1993

Ghazi, Dr Mahmood Ahmad, *Muḍārabah Financing: An appraisal*. Paper read at Conference on Islamic corporate Finance

based solutions Nov.21.22.1998at Karachi.

Ghulām Murtaza, Dr., *Socio-Economic System of Islam*, Lahore Malik Sons Publishers, 1990.

Haskafī, ʻAlāuddīn, *al-Durr al-Mukhtār Sharh Tanwīr al-Abṣār*, Bombay: al-Maṭbaʻah al-Haydariyyah, 1309 H.

Hassan, Dr. Hussain Hamid, , *Introduction to the Study of Islamic Law*. Islamabad : Sharīʻah Academy, 1977.

__________________,*al-MadKhal li Dirāsāt al-Fiqh al-Islāmī*,Cairo: Maktabh al-Muthannah,1979.

__________________, *al-Ḥukm al-Shar'ī 'ind al-Usūliyyīn.* Cairo, Dar al-Nahḍah al-'Arabiyyah, 1972.

Ḥassanuz Zaman, *Indexation of Financial Assets: An Islamic Evaluation,* The International Institute of Islamic Thought, Islamabad, 1993.

Ḥattāb, *Mawāhib al-Jalīl li Sharh Mukhtasar Khalil,* Tripoli, 1329.

Ibn Ābidīn, Muhammd Amin, *Radd al-Muhtār,* Maktabah Majididiyyah, Quetta, 1982 A.D.

Ibn al-qayyim al-Jawziyyah, *I'lam al-Muwaqqi'īn 'an Rabb al 'Ālamin,* Cairo, Maktab'ah al-Kulliyyah al-Azhariyyah, 1968.

Ibn Ḥazm, *Ihkām fi usul al-Ihkām,* Dar al-Āfāq al-jadidah, Beirut.1347A.H.

__________________, *al-Muhallah,* Beirut, Dar al-Afāq al-Jadīdah, 1347 A.H.

Ibn -Hummam, *Fath al-Qadir,* Dar Inyā, Beirut, 1315 H.

Ibn Majah, Mohammad Ibn Yazid Al-Qazwini, *Al-Sunan,* Dar al-Da'wah, istanbul, 19:2.

Ibn Nujaim, Zain al-din, *Al-Bahr al-Rā'iq Sharh Kanz al-Daqā'iq,* Cairo, 1893.

'Ibn Qudāmah, Muwaffāq al-Dīn, *al-Mughnī,* Beirut, Dar al-fikr, 1405/1985.

__________________, *Al-Sharh al-Kabīr,* Dar al-Fikr, Beirut, 1404/1984.

Ibn Rushd, Muhammad Ibn Ahmad, *Bidāyah al-Mujtahid,* Maktabah al-'Ilmiyyah, Lahore.

Ibn-Taymiyah, *Al-Fatāwā al-Kubrā,* Beirut, Dar ai-Kutub al-'Ilmiyyah, 1987.

__________________, *Nazriyah al-'Aqd*

__________________, *al-Qiyas fi al-Shar' al-Islāmī* , Cairo, Maktabah al-Salafiyyah, 728/ 328

Kasanī, *Badā 'i' al-Sanā 'i 'fi Tartib al-Sharā 'i '*, Cairo, Sharikah al-Matbū'āt al-'Islamiyyah.

Kāsib, Abdul Karīm, *'Aqd al-Istisnā' fi al-Fiqh al-Islamī,*

Khafīf, 'Ali, *Ahkām al-Mu 'āmlat al-Shar 'iyyah,* Cairo, 1941.

Kuwaiti Civil Code

Lane, Edward William, *Arabic-English Lexicon,* Islamic Book Centre, 1978.

Liaqat Ali Khan Niazi, Dr. *Islamic Law of Contrct,* Research Cell, Dayal Sing Trust Library, Lahore.

Majallah al-Ahkām al-'Adliyyah, (Codified Civil Law of Otoman Caliphate, Turkey) Noor Muhammad Karkhanah Tejarat-e-Kutub, Karachi, 1968.

Muslim, Muslim Ibn al-Hajjaj, *Sahīh Muslim,* Dar Ihyā al-turāth al-'Arabī, Beirut.

Marghinānī, Burhanuddin, *Al-Hidāyah Sharh Bidāyah al-Mubtadi,* Maktabah Imdadiyyah, Multan, Pakisan.

Mullah, D.F., *Muhammadan Law,* Mansoor Book House, 1989.

Mullah, D.F. *The Contract Act (IX) of 1872,* Commentary by Ahsan Suhail Anjum, Lahore, Mansoor Book House, 1987.

Mushtaq Ahmad, Dr., *Business Ethics in Islam,* International Institute of Islamic Thought, Islamabad, 1995.

Malik Ibn Anas, *Al-Mudawwanah al-Kubrā,* Beirut: Dar Sadir, n.d.

Mohammad Sidqi al-Burno, *Al-Wajīz Fī Īdāh Qawa 'id al-Fiqh al-Kulliyyah,* Beirut:Mu'assasat al-Risalah, [n.d].

Mahmamad 'Amim al-Ihsān al-Mujaddidi, *Qawā 'id al-Fiqh,* Al-Sadaf Publishers, Karachi.

Madkur, Mohammad Salam, *Al-Madkhal li al-fiqh al-Islami,* Dār al-nahdah al-'Arabiyyah, Cario, 1380/1960.

Nabil Salih, *Unlawful gain and Legitimate Profit in Islamic Law,* Graham & Trotman, 1992.

Nayla Comair Obeid, *The Law of Business Contracts in the Arab Middle East.* Kluwer Law International, 1996.

Nasā'ī, Al-Hafiz Abu 'Abdur Rehmān Ahmad Ibn Shu'āb, *Sunan Nisā'ī,* Dar al-da'wah Istanbul.

Nyazee, 'Imran, Ahsan, *Outlines of Islamic Jurisprudence, ALSI,* Islamabad.

Nawawi, *Kitāb al-Majmū',* Maktabah al-'Āsimah, Cairo, 1966.

Paul Al Samuelson and William, *Economics,* New York: McGraw Hill Book Company, 1993.

Al-Qarāfī, *Al-Furūq,* Dar al-Kutub 'al'Ilmiyyah, Beirut, 1986.

Rayner, Dr. S.E. Rayner,

    The Theory of Contracts of Islamic Law, Graham and Trotman, London, 1991.

Rabitah al-'Ālam al-Islamī, *Qarārāt Majlis al-Majma' al-Fiqh al-Islami,* 1398 A.H - 1405 A.H (Makkah:1985).

Al-Razi, Fakhruddin Mohammad Ibn 'Umar, *Al-Tafsīr al-Kabīr,* Dār al-Kutub al-'Islamiyyahm, Tehran.

Sadr al-Sharī'ah, 'Ubaidullah Ibn Mas'ud, *al-Towdīh,* al-Maktabah al-Khayriayyah, Cairo, 1322.

Shīrazi, Abu Ishāq, *Al-Muhaddab,* Cairo.Dar al Nasr [n.d].

Shah Wali Ullah al-Dehlawi, *Hujjatullah al-Bālighah,* Al-Maktabah al-Salafiyyah, Lahore.

Sarakhasi, Abu Bakr Mohammad Ibn Ahmad, *Al-Mabsūt,* Dar al-Ma'rifah, Beirut, 1398/1978.

Shanqiti, Mohammad al-Amin Mustfā, *Dirāsah Shar'iyyah le ahamme al-'Uqūd al-Maliyyah al-Mustahdathah,* Matbah al-'Ulūm Wa al-Hikam, al-Madīnah, 1992.

Sanhūri, Abdul Razzaq, *Al-Wasit.* Dar al-Nahdah, Cairo, 1964

, *Masādir al-Haqq*, Dar al-Ma'rifah, 1967.

Showkāni, *Nail al-Aowtār Sharh Muntaqa al-Akhbār*, Matba'ah Mustafa al-Halabī, Cairo, 1982.

San'anī, Muhammad Ibn Isma'īl, *Subul al-Salām*, Dar al-Fikr, Beirut, 1938.

Shirbīnī, *Mughnī al-Muhtāj*, Sharikah wa-Matba'ah Mustafa al-Bābī al-Halabī, Cairo, 1933.

Salih, Nabil, *Unlawful gain and Legitimate Profit in Islamic Law*, Graham & Trotman, 1992.

S.M. Yusuf, Dr., *Economic Justice in Islam*, Da'wah Academy, International Islamic University, Islamabad 1990.

Taftazanī, Mas'ūd Ibn 'Umar, *Al-Talwīh*, Cairo, Maktabah Wa Matba'ah Muhammad Ali.

Taqi. Usmani, Moulāna, *An Introduction to Islamic Finance, Idaratul ma'arif, Karachi, 1998.*

Uduvitch, A, *Partnership and Profit in Medieval Islam*, Princeton University Press, 1970.

Yusuf Al-Qardāwi, *Fawa'id al-Bunūk hiya al-Ribā al-Muharram*, Urdu Translation by Prof. Atiq al-Zafar, Institute of Policy Studies.

Zaydān, Abdul Karim, *Al-Madkhal li Dirasah al-Shari'ah al-Islamiyyah*, Mu'ssasah al-Risālah, Beirut, 1402/1982.

Zuhaili, Wahbah Zuhaili, *Al-Fiqh al-Islamī Wa adillahtohū*, Damascus, Dar al-Fikr, 1984.

Zain Uddin Zafar, *Bay' al-Ma'dūm; An Analysis*, Paper Presented in the International Islamic Capital Market Conference, held in Malaysia, 15-16 july 1997.

Zail'ī Fakhruddin 'Usmān Ibn Ali, *Tabyīn al-Haqa'iq*, Al-Matba'ah al-Kubrā, Bulaq, 1318 A.H.

Ziauddin Ahmad, Dr. *Currency Notes and Indexation.* Islamic Studies, Islamic Research Institute, 28-1-1980.

Zaki al-Badawi, *Nazariyyah al-Ribā al-Muharram*

al-Majlis al-'Alā le Ri'āyah al-Funūn.

Zarqa, Mustafa Ahmad, *Al-Madkhal al-Fiqhi al-'Ām*, Matba'ah
  Tarbīn, Damascus, 1387/1968.

INDEX

Siddīq al-Darīr, 95
sīghah, 25, 27,29,76, 96,131,290
single venture, 241, 253
Sir Abdur Rahim, 180
slander, 298
special accounts, 114
specific guarantee, 292
State Bank of Pakistan (SBP), 222
State Bank's Gazette, 222
subject-matter, 25, 29, 32, 33, 35, 36, 37,
39, 42, 43, 61, 64, 68, 75, 76, 80,82, 88,
89, 90, 91, 93, 95, 98, 99, 101, 102, 118,
190, 191, 202, 205, 210, 211, 215, 227, 232,
238,280,289, 293,298
succession, 180
Sūrah al-Baqarah, 121,122
Sūrah al-Rūm, 119
Sūrah al-Nisā', 120
Sūrah āle-'Imrān, 120,121
Sūrah al-Yūsuf, 290
surety, 175, 182,261,262,289, 291, 292, 293, 294,
295, 296, 297, 298, 299, 300, 301
suretyship, 62, 81, 82, 85,176, 180, 181, 182, 184,291,
293, 294, 295, 296, 297, 298, 299, 300, 301, 290
stock, 242, 243, 258
stray animal, 42
swindled purchaser, 150

tabarru', 108, 112, 113, 114,
tadlīs, 145, 151, 144
tadlīs bi al- 'ayb, 151
taflīs, 58
Taftāzānī, 12
taghrīr, 93,145
takāful, 106,107,108,109, 110, 111, 112, 113, 114
Talhah, 170
talaqqī al-rukbān, 149, 154

Glossary

'adadiyyāt : Countable things.
aḥkām: Rules of Sharī'ah.
ahliyyat al-adā: Legal capacity
   for execution.
ahliyyah :   Legal capacity.
ajīr: Rent. wages. remuneration.
ajīr khāṣ   Employee
ajīr mushtrak Independent Contractor,
   shared worker
ajr mithl: Equitable remuneration,
   reasonable wages.
al-ba'īr al-shārid   Stray animal.
al-ḍarb fīl arḍ: To make journey
al-ḥajr: Interdiction,
   authoritative prohibition.
al-māl: Property, wealth.
al-malāqīḥ   Sperm.
'al-nafs: Life.
al- ru'yah: Examination,
   inspection.
al-taslīm   Delivery.
al-waṣiyyah: Bequest.
'amal: acts.
amanah   Trust
amr Command.
'aqd muḍāf li al- mustaqbal : Contract effective
   from future date.
'aqd mu'allaq : Contingent.
'aqd munjaz ' Contract immediately enforceable.

'āqidān   Contracting parties.
'āqil   Sane.
'aql: Sanity
'arbūn   Earnest money.
'āriyah :   Commodate loan.
'asb al-faḥl: To sale services of male
      animal to cover female.
aṣl: Foundation.
aṣīl: Principal.
'atah.   Lunacy, partial insanity.
a'yān   plural of 'ayn.
'ayn: Substance. determinate property
bāligh: Person who has attained Puberty
bāṭil :   Void. invalid.
bay' al-amānah: Trust sale
bay' al-fāsid   Irregular sale
bay' al-ghā'ib   Sale of something not
      seen by the parties to a contract
bay' al-ḥaṣāt: Sale taking place through
      pebbles
bay' al-ḥaml: Sale of feotus in the womb.
bay' al-'īnah   Buy-back agreement
bay' al-juzāf: Sale of food stuff at random
bay' al-kāli' bi al-kāli'   Sale of credit for credit.
bay' al-ma'dūm   Sale of non-existent thing
bay' al-majhūl   Sale in which the object of sale .
      its price or the time of payment and delivery
      remains unknown.
bay' al-mu'ajjal   Credit sale
bay' al-muḥāqalah   Sale of wheat for wheat in
      ear of grain.
bay' al-mukhāḍarah: Sale of fruits on tree
      before their benefit it is evident
bay' al-mulāmasah   Sale that is affective
      by touching a commodity
bay' al-munābadhah :   Sale of fresh fruit in
      exchange of dry fruits
bay' al-muzābanah   Sale of fresh fruits for dry fruits

351

bay' al-salam   Sale with advance payment
    for future delivery of goods
bay' al-wafā'   Archaic sale with redemption
bay' ḥabal al-ḥablah   Sale of younglings to
    be brought later in the feotus of animal
bay' muṭlaq   Sale of commodity with money
bayt al-māl: Treasury.
bay' wa salaf: Selling and landing.
buyū' al-a'yān   Sale of Objects *in rem*
daman Compensation, liability
ḍamān al-'amal   Liability of a partner to
    complete the work accepted by either partner
ḍāmin Surety, guarantor
ḍarbat al-ghā'is   Divers dive
dayn Receivables, debt, indeterminate property
dhimmah, Liability, obligation, responsibility
diyat Blood money
fāḥish   Grave
fāsid   Irregular
fuḍūlī   Self imposed agent,
    an authorized agent.
fuqahā'   Muslim Jurists.
ghabn   Lesion, damage
ghabn fāḥish   Exorbitant loss suffered
    by a party to a contract or excessive lesion
gharar   Uncertainty, indeterminacy
ghaṣb   Usurpation.
ghāṣib   Usurper
ghayr lāzim   Non-binding.
ghayr munjaz   Minor not possessed with
    discretion
hadd   Punishment prescribed in the
    Qur'ān or Sunnah
hajr   Interdiction, authoritative
    prohibition
ḥalāl   Ritually Lawful, permissible
ḥarām   Unlawful
Ḥatt wa ta'jjal   Discounting for hastening

352

the payment of loan
haṉālah   Assignment of debt
hibah.   Gift.
ḥuqūq   Rights. rights of
    performance of Contract
iʿārah   Commodate loans
ʿibādāt   Rituals. devotional acts.
ʿiddat   Waiting period.
ījāb   Offer
ijāra   Leasing or hiring
ijārat al-ashkhās   To employee a person.
    to hire services of some body.
ijārat al-ashyāʾ   Letting things
ijārat al-ʿayn   Another name
    for ijārat al-ashyāʾ
ijārat al-dhimmah   Another name
    for ijārat al-ashkhās.
ijārah waʾiqtinā   Hire-Purchase.
ijmāʿ   Consensus of jurists.
ikrāh   Coercion
ikrāh tāmm   Perfect coercion.
ikrāh nāqiṣ   Imperfect coercion.
ʿillah   Legal effective cause.
ʿinah   Buy-Back agreement.
ʿinān   Partnership in which services
    and capital are shared on proportional basis.
iṣāʾ   Appointment of an executer to
    look after the minor and his property
ishtirāk   Participation
isqātāt   Contracts extinguishing rights.
    waiver of rights
istidānah   To purchase on credit for
    the partnership in excess of the capital
istiḥsān   Juristic Preference
istiṣnā   Contract of manufacturing
iṭlāqāt   Authorization
jahālah   Lake of knowledge
jahl   Ignorance

353

jā'iz Non-binding
jamhūr . Majority of jurists
junūn Insanty
kafālah Surety
kafālah bi al-nafs Surety for producing
  a body of person accused in the court of Law
kafālah bi al-dayn Surety for debt.
kafīl Guarantor.
khalt Mixing of shares
khatā':Mistake.
khatar al-'adam : Fear of non-existence
khayārāt . Options
khilābah Cheating
khitāb 'ibādāt: Divine communication
   relating to acts of worship.
khitāb jinā'ī Divine communication
   relating to offences.
khitāb mu'amalāt: Divine communication
   relating to transaction
khiyār Option.
khiyār al-'ayb Option of defect.
khiyār al-ru'yah Option of inspection.
khiyār al- shart Option of stipulation
khiyār al-ta'yīn Option of determination
khiyār al-wasf: Option of description.
lāzim binding
madāmīn Embryo.
madhrū'at Things, which are estimated
  by linear measurement.
madmūn Subject-Matter of surety
madmūn 'anhu Obligor
mahall Subject-Matter.
mahr mithl Customary dower
majlis Session of contract
makfūl 'anhu Another name
   for madmūn 'anhu
makfūl bihī : Subject-matter of surety.
makfūl lahū Obligee/Creditor.

354

makīlāt: Things, which are estimated
  by measurement of capacity.
māl: Property
manqūl. Moveable.
ma'qūd 'alayh: Subject-Matter.
marad al-mawt: Death illness
marīd marad al-mawt: Patient of death-
    -illness
ma'tūh: Lunatic, partially insane.
mawqūf: Suspended, held in abeyance.
mawzūnat: Things, which are estimated
    by weighing
milk: Ownership, Property
mithlī: Fungible.
mu'āmlāt: Transactions
mu'atah: By conduct
mu'āwadāt: Counter-Values.
mu'āwamah: Sale of fruits in advance for
    two or three years.
mudārabah: Partnership between financier
  and entrepreneur
mudārib: Working partner.
mudāribūn: Entrepreneurs/workers
  in mudārabah
mufāwadah: Partnership in which capital,
  work and liabilities are shared on equal basis
muflis: Bankrupt.
muhāl: Debtor.
muhāl 'ālayh: Debtor-assignee
muhāl lahū: Creditor-Assignee/Transferee.
muhīl: Debtor-Assignor.
mu'jir: Lessor.
mukrah: Coerced person
muqāradah: Another name for mudārabah
muqāyadah: Barter transaction.
murābahah: Cost plus profit.
musāqāh: Contract for watering of trees
    between worker and owner

355

musāwamah Contract without reference
  to cost price
mushārakah Partnership.
muṭlaq Absolute
muwakkil Principal
muzābanah see bay' al-muzābanah
muzāra'ah Contract for sharing crops
nāfidh Enforceable.
najāsh.False bidding to raise price
nāqis Imperfect.
qabūl : acceptance.
qadhf: Slander.
qarḍ:Loan.
qatl al-khaṭā Unintentional murder
qīmī Non-Fungible
qirāḍ Another name for Mudarabah used
  by Mālikīs
qiṣāṣ Retaliation
qiyās Analogy
rahn : Pledge/Mortgage
ribā Usury/Interest.
rushd Discernment. Prudence and
  sound judgment.
ṣabī minor.
ṣabī ghayr mumayyaz Minor not
  possessed with discretion.
sabī mumayyaz Discriminating minor.
minor possessed with discretion
ṣadaqah Charity
safah Weakness of Intellect
safīh Weak of Intellect. spendthrift
salam See bay' al-salam
sarf Sale of money for money
sharikah Partnership
sharikat al-abdān : See sharikat al-a'māl
sharikat al-a'māl Work partnership
sharikat al-amwāl Investment partnership
sharikat al-'aqd .Contractual partnership

356

sharikat al-'imān See 'inān
sharikat al-milk Proprietary partnership
sharikat al-muḍarabah See muḍarabah
sharikat al-mufāwaḍah See mufāwaḍah
sharikat al-wujūh Credit partnership
shufa'ah Pre-emption.
sīghah :Form of contract/Offer and acceptance.
tabarru' Donation
tadlīs Fraud.
tadlīs bi al-'ayb Fraud with defect.
taflīs :Bankruptcy/Insolvency.
tafwīḍh Delegation
taghrīr Misrepresentation.
talaqqī al-rukbān transaction whereby a
  city-dweller takes advantage of the
  ignorance of a Bedouin to purchase some
  commodity on cheaper price
tamlīkāt :Transferring ownership
tāmm Food - Value.
tamyīz Discretion.
tanajush See najash
taṣriyah . Leaving a female milking animal
  unmilked for some time to hoodwink the buyer
tawliyah Resale at cost price
tawthīqāt : Contracts of surety
thaman Price
thamaniyyah Currency-Value.
ujrah Rental.
'uqūd al-ḍamanāt Contracts of guarantee.
'uqūd al-ḥifz : Contracts of bailment
'uqūd al-isqaṭāt See isqaṭāt
'uqūd al-iṭlāqāt See iṭlāqāt
'uqūd al-mu'āwaḍāt. Exchange Contracts
'uqūd al-sharikāt Partnership Contracts
'uqūd al-tabarru'āt. Gratuitous Contracts
'uqūd al-taqyidat Contracts restrictive of
  the rights of others
'urbun Earnest money.

wadī'ah : Deposit. bailment.
wakālah : Agency
wakīl : agent.
waqf : Charitable trust.
  religious endowment.
waṣf : Description.
waṣiyyah : Bequest
wilāyah : Guardianship.
yaqūt : Ruby
yasīr : Light.
ziwāj : Marriage